ECONOMIC CRISIS
AND
POLITICAL DISASTER

Ratnakar Gedam

HERITAGE
HERITAGE PUBLISHERS
New Delhi (India) *1993*

ISBN 81-7026-184-8

Published by Heritage Publishers, 5, Ansari Road, New Delhi-110 002.

Laser Typesetting by APCON PLUS and printed at Efficient Offset Printer, 215 Shahzada Bagh Industrial Complex, Phase II, Delhi-110 035.

Preface

Economic stability leads to political stability and *vice versa.* Economic development is a function of political austerity. Politics, administration, government organization, trade and industry, etc. devoid of corruption, determine the case of socio-economic development and efficiency of resources utilization. Economic development and political commitment for well-being of poorest of poor are complementary to each other. It will however be paradoxical to ask whether political stability is a prerequisite for economic development or economic development is a prerequisite for political stability. The growth as a prerequisite for economic development is no more true because in case of India there was substantial economic or industrial growth but economic development was absent. In fact poor countries are lacking the real technical knowhow of managing national economy. All the politicians, thinkers, academicians, economists and bureaucrats, administrators, legislators etc. are equally responsible for the poor state of the country. The need for availability of resources for economic development is of secondary importance. Because practically nothing came from heaven, everything that we hear, use, or admire has its origin in the same earth where rich and poor nations exist or poor and rich people live.

Why economic crisis and political disaster occur is precisely not known. Had it been known, every country would have taken all precautions to avoid occurrence of the crisis. The conventional economic theories have some kind of explanation and also solution to every identified problems but these solutions are not foolproof. Every solution to domestic problems comes from foreign countries. But one thing must be borne in mind that these solutions are not like a technically manufactured machine embodied with universal scientific truth which would ensure working of machine even if it is transported from one corner of the globe to other. That is, economic systems of different countries respond differently to same economic prescription, controls, and administrative procedures because human factor is involved and all humans are not equally motivated for their integrity, honesty, working capacity and commitment to national cause. In economics there is not and unlikely to exist any law of proportionality which would explain precisely the intensity of response of an economy would be proportional to the imposed economic condition (through control of policy instruments and economic variables) and the value of proportionality constant for different countries would be calculated under different conditions.

There ought to be a process which explains the course of transition leading eventually to economic crisis and political disaster. These processes could be studied from events of India and former USSR. India has been facing economic crisis since mid-1991 and USSR no more exists on the earth since December 1991. Therefore theorising the "Stages of Economic Crisis and Political Disaster" was obvious in contrast with Rostow's "Stages of Growth" or Karl Marx's "Stages of Economic Crisis and Political Disaster". The contemporary events or events leading to crisis or disaster in India and former USSR have been critically observed and critically analyzed as a part of deductive and inductive research.

As India has opted for structural adjustment, economic reform and liberalisation, free market economy, devaluation, setting right the prices, collecting users charges, privatisation of public sector enterprises, curtailing the subsidies etc., these topics have been dealt in this book. Similarly, the controversies concerning Indian patent system and its implication in view of Trade Related Intellectual Property (TRIP) Rights and Trade Related Investment Measures (TRIMS) under GATT instead of World Intellectual Property Rights Organisation (WIPRO) or Paris Convention. The challenge of biotechnology to patent system has been another controversial topic which has been dealt with in this book.

Date : 23.6.1992 **Dr Ratnakar Gedam**

New Delhi

CONTENTS

8. SUBSIDIES IN INDIAN ECONOMY

9. IMPLICATION OF GATT WITH S & T

10. BIOTECHNOLOGY — CHALLENGE TO PATENT SYSTEM

List of Tables

1

Economic Crisis 1991

1.01 Introduction

In the history of India, 1990-91 and 1991-92 can be treated as the years of economic crisis and attempts to regain path of its economic growth through restructuring. Crisis-91 is used in this book to signify economic crisis in India in the second half of 1990-91 when the balance of payment position was very critical. The factors aggregating the economic crisis were both exogenous namely Gulf War and indigenous namely political instability in 1987-88 to 1990-91. The oil shock was solely attributed to Gulf War in the second half of 1989-90 to first half of 1990-91. The Gulf War had tremendous impact on India's balance of payment as rise in oil prices was responsible for higher import bill and reduced exports due to war. The faulty import-export policies enunciated for the years 1987-88 to 1989-90 were equally responsible for drain of foreign exchange. The political instability and civil war like situation in India prior to 1990-91, change of three governments, general elections in short span etc. were responsible for economic crisis in 1990-91. The droughts in India for consecutive years just before the Gulf War had also some impact. That is there was sufficient climate for incubation and nucleation of economic crisis during political instability in India. As explained earlier, the political instability along with other factors caused initiation of economic crisis as manifested through balance of payment and nearly the bankruptcy or collapse of the country. In fact, theoretically economic crisis could be explained through three stages viz.:

(i) Sufficient economic-political condition for incubation and nucleation of economic crisis. This is the first stage. This could also be termed as *initiation* of economic crisis.

(ii) Rapid or gradual propagation of economic crisis. That is, second stage involving propagation of economic crisis both inter and intra economy.

(iii) Third stage is final collapse of economy as manifested through inability to pay foreign debt, fall in foreign exchange reserves, & balance of payment deplorable, loss of credibility in international market and inability to pay the interest on loan of international donor agencies.

India's economic crisis-91 could be viewed from the following aspects :

(1) Decline in trade balance

(2) Decline in net invisibles

(3) Increase in deficits

(a) Budget deficits
(b) Revenue deficits
(c) Monetised deficits

(4)Decline in foreign exchange reserves

So-called measures initiated to overcome crisis are nothing but artificial manipulation of data showing decrease in imports, increase in exports, decline in trade deficits, enhanced or overestimates of invisibles etc.

1.02 Exports-Imports

In terms of percentage of GDP, exports of India had been 5 per cent of GDP for the period from 1980-81 to 1984-85. Except for the year 1982-83 and 1984-85 when export was 5.1 and 5.2 per cent of GDP respectively. India's exports in the years 1980-81, 1981-82 and 1982-83 were of the order of 4.9 per cent of GDP (See Table 1). There was decline of exports from 1985-86 to 1987-88 as compared with previous years accompanied by higher imports in these years has caused trade deficit to increase from an average of 3.4 per cent of GDP for the period from 1980-81 to 1984-85 to 3.7 per cent, 3.2 per cent and 3.6 per cent of GDP. Current account balance deficit has increased from 1.2 per cent of GDP to 2.3 per cent of GDP on an average for the period 1980-81 to 1984-85 and 1985-86 to 1989-90 respectively. The imports were of the order of 9.3 per cent of GDP in 1989-90 as compared with exports of 6.4 per cent of GDP. Net invisibles have declined from an average of 2.2 per cent for the period from 1980-81 to 1984-85 to the level of 1.0 per cent for the period from 1985-86 to 1989-90.

Table 1: Balance of Payment (as a percentage of GDP)

Year	*Exports*	*Imports*	*Net Invisibles*	*Trade Balance*	*Current Account Balance*
1980-81	4.8	9.2	3.2	—4.4	—1.2
1981-82	4.9	8.7	2.4	—3.8	—1.4
1982-83	5.1	8.4	2.0	—3.3	—1.3
1983-84	4.9	7.7	1.7	—2.8	—1.1
1984-85	5.2	8.1	1.7	—2.9	—1.2
*Avg.*80-85	5.0	8.4	2.2	—3.4	—1.2
1985-86	4.4	8.1	1.4	—3.7	—2.3
1986-87	4.5	7.7	1.2	—3.2	—2.0
1987-88	4.9	7.7	0.9	—2.8	—1.9
1988-89	5.3	8.9	0.8	—3.6	—2.8
1989-90	6.4	9.3	0.6	—2.9	—2.3
*Avg.*85-90	5.1	8.3	1.0	—3.2	—2.3
1990-91QE	6.3	9.1	0.4	—2.8	—2.4

Source : Economic Survey 1990-91, pp.52 and Economic Survey 1991-92, Part II, pp. 60 for 1990-91 QE

1.03 Gross Fiscal Deficit

The budget deficit, revenue deficit and monetised deficit has been rising every year. From an average of 6.3 per cent of GDP for the period 1980-81 to 1989-90, gross fiscal deficit has increased to 8.2 per cent of GDP on an average during 1985-86 to 1989-90. In 1990-91, the budget deficit was 2.1 per cent of GDP, revenue deficit was 3.5 per cent of GDP and monetised deficit was 2.8 per cent of GDP. That is, the gross fiscal deficit was 8.4 per cent of GDP (see Table 2).

Table 2: Budget Deficit, Revenue Deficit Monetised Deficit and Gross Fiscal Deficit of the Central Government (As per cent of GDP at Current Market prices)

		Deficit		
Year	*Budget*	*Revenue*	*Monetised*	*Gross Fiscal*
1975-76	0.5	1.1	0.3	4.1
1980-81	1.9	1.5	2.6	6.2
1981-82	0.9	0.2	2.0	5.4
1982-83	0.9	0.7	1.9	6.0
1983-84	0.7	1.2	1.9	6.3
1984-85	1.6	1.8	2.6	7.5
Avg.80-85	1.2	1.1	2.2	6.3
1985-86	2.0	2.2	2.4	8.3
1986-87	2.8	2.7	2.4	9.0
1987-88	1.7	2.7	2.0	8.1
1988-89	1.4	2.7	1.6	7.8
1989-90	2.5	2.6	3.1	7.9
Avg.85-90	2.1	2.6	2.3	8.2
1990-91RE	2.0	3.3	2.8	8.2
1990-91AN	2.1	3.5	2.8	8.4
1991-92BE	1.3	2.3	1.3	6.2

Note : *GDP at current market prices is estimated to grow at 15 per cent in 1991-92.*

(Source : Economic Survey 1991-92 Part II, p.3)

1.04 Current Account Deficit

In terms of absolute currency value, the net current account deficit has been rising form Rs 1656.6 crores in 1980-81 to Rs 10,410 crores and in US dollars, it was estimated at US $ 7188.4 million. There has been continuous rise in deficit in net current account. The balance of payment deficit has been rising from year to year (see Table 3). It has reached Rs 6308.0 crores in 1988-89 and Rs 6230.8 in 1989-90.

Table 3: Balance of Payment

Year	Current Account (Net) Rs Cr.	Current Account (Net) US $ Mil.	BOP Deficit Rs Cr.	BOP Deficit US $ Mil
1960-61	—392.4	—824.4	—315.8	—663.4
1970-71	—445.4	—593.8	—907.3	—1209.7
1980-81	—1656.6	—2094.9	—2639.5	—3337.8
1985-86	—5927.3	4844.6	—3187.7	—2605.4
1986-87	—5830.0	—4562.5	—3788.4	—2964.7
1987-88	—6292.6	—4862.5	—5410.1	—4172.6
1988-89	10410.0	—4853.2	—6308.9	—4356.5
1989-90	—9823.8	—7188.4	—6230.8	—3742.4

(Source : Row 6 and row 9 of the Table on BOP in Economic Survey 1991-92, Part II, Table S-74)

1.05 Foreign Exchange Reserves

Foreign exchange reserves at the end of the year had been steadily declining from 1980-81 from US dollar 6823 million to lowest of US $ 3962 million in 1989-90. Table 4 indicates the yearly movements in foreign exchange and net drawals of IMF. Similarly, details of drawals from International Monetary Fund are shown in Table 5.

Table 4: Movement in Foreign Exchange Reserves (In Rupees Crores and U.S. Dollars Million)

Year	Foreign Currency Assets of RBI at the end of year		Foreign exchange reserves at the end of the year		Movements in Foreign exchange Reserves		Net Drawals in I M F	
	Rs Cr	$ Mil	Rs Cr	$ Mil	Rs Cr	$ Mil	Rs Cr	$ Mil
1	2	3	4	5	6	7	8	9
1980-81	4822	5850	5544	6823	—390	—538	814	1029
1981-82	3355	3582	4024	4390	1520	—2433	637	639
1982-83	4265	4281	4782	4896	758	506	1893	1985
1983-84	5498	5099	5972	5649	1190	753	1342	1298
1984-85	6817	5482	7243	5952	1271	303	63	53
1985-86	7384	5972	7820	6520	577	568	—327	—267
1986-87	7645	5924	8151	6574	331	54	—8480	—690
1987-88	7287	5618	7687	6223	—464	—351	—1388	1123

1	2	3	4	5	6	7	8	9
1988-89	6605	4226	7040	4802	—647	—1421	—1749	—1175
1989-90	5787	3368	6251	3962	—789	—840	—1688	—1035
1990-91	4388	2236	11416	5834	5165	1872	—2043	—1183
1991-92*	9766	3774	19392	7501	7976	1667	2167	794

** Up to January end*

(Source : Economic Survey 1991-92, Part, II, p.62)

Table: 5 Drawals from International Monetary Fund 1990-92

Date	*Facility*	*SDR*	*US$*	*Rs Cr*
July-Sept. 1990	RT	490	660	1177
23. 01. 1991	FCT	552	789	1450
23. 01. 1991	CCFF	717	1025	1884
22. 07. 1991	CCFF	166	221	570
12. 09. 1991	CCFF	469	639	1654
15. 11. 1991	UCT	85	117	305
02. 01. 1992	UCT	185	265	683
Expected by March 1992	UCT	461	650	1700
Total		3125	4366	9423

Abbreviations: RT = Reserve Tranche
FCT = First Credit Tranche
CCFF= Contingency Compensatory Finance Facility

(Source : Economic Survey 1991-92, Part II, p. 15)

To summarise the crisis-91, India's economic crisis can be attributed to increase in oil prices due to Gulf War, deterioration of trade account, adverse capital account, outflow of NRI deposits that is drying up of commercial loans, etc. and unprudent management of economy during 1987 to 1990.

1.06 Restructuring

The nature of economic system affects the living style, material prosperity, industrial activities, etc. The development of a society varies according to the nature of economic system. Economic system has stake in both generation and distribution of wealth. The material prosperity in capitalism is tremendous than in communism or socialism. Equality as a foundation of socia-lism is no more appealing but inequality as a base of capitalism has tremendous potential to bring materialism.

In equilibrium conditions, the interaction of socialism and capitalism result in socio-capitalism. But if the matrix of social and economic system is dominated by either of the ideologies then the resultant phase of socio-economic political structure will be either hypo socio-capitalism or hyper sociocapitalism. In hyposocio-capitalism, the socialism is dominating the socio-economic structure of a country with noticeable growth centres or growth pole characterizing capitalism. In hyper socio-capitalism phase capitalism is dominating the socio-economic matrix with diffusion of socialism ideologies. Hence, there ought to be three phases viz.: hyposocio-capitalism, socio-capitalism and hyper socio-capitalism.

To call socio-economic system as "mixed" or "mixed economy" tantamounts to admit the poverty of philosophy in economic realm. As stated earlier, nothing is mixed with capitalism or socialism. In fact, the refinements, transition from one stage to another means structural change of both matrix and phases of socio-economic and political system of a country. In fact, feasible socialism is never practiced, neither in Russia or any of the developing countries. The imposing of dictatorship in the name of the rule of proletariat has accelerated the natural or uncalled death of socialism. The capitalism always sees a threat to its existence from growing influence of socialism or communism. Hence, capitalism also tried to refine itself by incorporating equivalent or synonymous concepts to socialism. Hence, the diluting of capitalism was initiated at the emergence of socialism. The imperialism stage had its threshold long back. The workers participation in management was to check revolt of workers for the rule of proletariat. Similarly, modernisation concept and process was used to balance the growth of socialist concept.

The chronological events of twentieth century indicate that the Western Europe and Eastern Europe had witnessed largest revolution for change of both economic and political system. The revolts, wars and people's movement have seeded the concepts of socialism, egalitarianism, liberty, freedom, fraternity, etc. But material progress of Western Europe since World War II has surpassed the progress, if any, in Eastern Bloc Europe. As we know, westernization means capitalism and democracy (obviously military strength too) but socialism means the respect to Eastern world's economic-political system. The Eastern world has itself witnessed the large number of struggles, revolts, people's movements for more democratic rights, rights of private property, rights of freedom of speech etc. Hence, the death warrant for communism and socialism is already noticed on global scale. The countries viz.: Hungary, Poland, China, Russia, East Germany, Czechoslovakia, etc. have already seen the wrath of people. This itself gives sufficient proof that a new system called socio-capitalism is emerging on global scale.

The countries could be grouped in three economic systems that have evolved since World War II to 1989 and will be stratifiable by the end of the century. The stable structure of economy will be hyper socio-capitalism. That exists in USA, UK and their allies including Japan. The socio-capitalism is equilibrium phase and hence is liable for transition from socio-capitalism to stable structure of hyper socio-capitalism by enhancing capital investment, economies of scale and exploitation of natural resources. The economic stability and political stability has the trade off point. The hyper socio-capitalist countries are politically instable but economically stable hence, the trade off will occur by change in political structure or governing pattern of a country.

When forces reinforcing capitalism system tend to grow the forces reinforcing socialism tend to retard capitalistic growth. Similarly, when forces reinforcing socialism tend to grow then the forces reinforcing capitalism tend to retard socialistic growth. The net resultant would be the formation of phases of capitalism and socialism in such a manner that these phases are easily identifiable.

There are no stages in growth of such system but it is continuum transition from one phase to another. Therefore, there also does not exist any clear boundary when socialism can be transformed to capitalism and *vice versa.* But the transition of phase depends upon the magnitude of dictatorship, repression of people's wishes, deprivation of identical benefits elsewhere available and a nature of political governance in totalitarian nature.

The explanations on stages of growth are rudimentary, obsolete and do not fit in scientific explanation of evolution of new threshold heights of social-political behaviour. Hence, economic-political evolution is not time dependent but dependent on materialistic way of life. The materialism is basically technologically dependent and practice of capacity for accumulation of money, wealth and earnings. Hence, who earns how much and by what means is crucial aspect to determine who owns what and how much and since how long.

This way it could be possible to say that the stages of development as observed since World War-II to disintegration of USSR comprised of :

A. Capitalism	A. Communism
B. Socio capitalism	B. Socialism
C. Hyper socio-capitalism	C. Hypo socio-capitalism
D. Neoimperialism	D. Socio-capitalism

Socio-capitalism is defined as a system of political and economic governance where ideologies of socialism and capitalism coexist without conflict. But at the core of such governance the capitalism is the main driving force for socialism. The socialist ideals do not realise in such system but capitalism growth do occur no matter how small it may be. The criteria of investment as per cent of GDP do not exhibit real growth but it is import of proven technologies, economics of scale etc.

However demise of socialism in USSR and eventual disintegration of USSR itself has proved wrong both Rostow's stages of growth and Marxist stages of societal development. Though capitalism has won the cold war and emerged as ultracapitalism system of world to rule global economy, there is reason to believe that the new era is nothing but sociocapitalist era to take world in 21st century.

The drive for restructuring economic reforms, trade policies towards liberalisation, abolition of licensing mechanism, controlling and regulatory restriction at the commencement of Eighth Five Year Plan has paved the way for advent of free and fair manufacturing trading and competition. By creating suitable economic environment Government of India has taken bold steps to deal with BOP crisis. The measures initiated included fiscal correction, trade policy reforms, public sector reforms etc.

1.07 Purpose of International Monetary Fund

International Monetary Fund

One of the controversies that Indian citizens noticed was the role of the International Monetary Fund. There is a section of people who support and admire the role of IMF and there is also a section of people which terms IMF as the proxy for USA. The withdrawal of structural adjustment loan granted to India by the IMF has been branded as sale of economic sovereignty to IMF. Let us first have a look at the purposes of IMF. Purposes of the Fund are:

1. To promote international monetary cooperation through a permanent institution which provides the machinery for consultation and collaboration on international monetary problems.
2. To facilitate the expansion and balanced growth of international trade, and to contribute thereby to the promotion and maintenance of high level of employment and real income and to development of the productive resources of all members as primary objectives of economic policies.
3. To promote exchange stability, to maintain orderly exchange arrangements among members and to avoid competitive exchange depreciation.
4. To assist in the establishment of a multilateral system of payments in respect of current transactions between members and in elimination of foreign exchange restrictions which hamper the growth of world trade.
5. To give confidence to members by making the general resources of the Fund temporarily available to them under adequate safeguards, thus providing them with opportunity to correct maladjustments in their balance of payments without resorting to measures destructive of national or international prosperity.
6. In accordance with the above, to shorten the duration and loosen the degree of disequilibrium in the international balance of payments of members.
7. The Fund shall be guided in all its policies and decisions by the purposes set forth in this Article. Article I of the Funds Articles of Agreement.

1.08 Understanding Economic Crisis

Obviously IMF has become an agency of USA to intervene in financial system of USA's enemy country. Analysing economic crisis in India is not straightforward or an easy task. Because economy in general is not a single component or two components system but it is multi components system. Each component has its own influence on economic forces. But one thing is certain that the economy of any country does not show response to economic conditions imposed on it through policy instruments, if such economy is not properly integrated into international environment through trade, exchange rate, interest rate etc. Obviously the intensity of response of economic forces is not directly proportional to the imposed economic conditions. That is some economies are structure sensitive and some economies are structure insensitive. The capacity of an economy to respond to external shocks and internal shocks depends upon the industrial base, domestic policies particularly fiscal, trade, monetary and industrial policies. Over and above, the economic management and capacity to foresee the future of nation. The steps taken by the Government of India were numerous. The fiscal correction was an important step taken in 1990-91. The large budgetary deficit in the years 1987-88 to 1989-90 has caused both the problems of balance of payment and inflationary pressure. The budget deficit in 1989-90 was Rs 10,992 crores and in 1990-91 it was Rs 10,772 crores. To restore macroeconomic balance it is essential to restrain further growth in fiscal deficit. Obvious measures to curtail growth in budget deficit was to abolish export subsidies, to abolish fertilizer subsidies and raise the price of fertilizers, curtail non plan expenditure.

Import at lower cost has its own implication. Firstly, it tends to retard the growth of domestic industries. Secondly, in the absence of foreign exchange for continuous imports it would inflate the domestic prices. Thirdly, the drive for import substitution at high cost paves in. Fourthly, the export of primary items tends to rise at the cost of deprivation of those items for domestic consumption simply to earn foreign exchange to finance low cost import. Over and above such low cost imports create pressures for adjustment: technological change, competition from other products, declining demand and competition from countries besides developing ones.

In fact India's industrial growth has declined in 1990-91 and 1991-92 which was the consequence of compression in import. The curb on imports has also had adverse impact on export earning as the inputs required for export quality material were subjected to restraints due to foreign exchange crisis.

Goods, labour and capital are affected through policy instruments in differential proportion at one or other time depending upon the intensity of controls and in order of priority. Each consequent year gives an opportunity to have retrospection of past measures and shift emphasis from one aspect of industrialisation and economic development to another aspect. "Structural rigidities are a widespread problem in the industrial world. In varying degrees, they affect all countries and all markets—goods, labour and capital". Such rigidities are particularly troublesome in labour markets (*Ref.1*). The high level of unemployment is the result of lack of demand in labour market. The structural policies are concerned about the labour market. The report of the IMF clarifies that "for some times, economic analysts have debated the role of *'classical'* or *'structural factors'* relative to 'Keynesian' or demand deficiency, factors in explaining the rise in unemployment. A consensus view on this extremely controversial issue is unlikely to emerge in the foreseeable future, in part because of the difficulties associated with empirical verification of the various hypotheses for any individual country. Nevertheless, a considerable body of evidence points to the conclusion that the differences in labour market performance as between, in particular, Europe and the United States, primarily reflect classical or structural factors (*Ref.2*).

Capitalist system promotes an innate tendency for both stratification and dispersal of weak strata in spatial context. In contrast with innate tendency of hierarchial stratification process set in by capita-list system any devised process aimed at inducing people in preferential pattern or harness human potential by channelising peoples behaviour or inducement to upward mobility based on their modified values will meet through loss of indination to yield to such system meant to bring socio economic betterment by unexpectedly proliferated misconceptions against inducement, incentives, and benefits.

All the three factors of production—goods, labour and capital—are affected in varying degree in all countries at one or other time. The industrialisation and economic development shift the emphasis from one aspect to another aspect at different times. It is obvious that structural rigidities are a widespread problem in the industrial world. And such rigidities are particularly troublesome in labour markets.

---

1. *World Economic Outlook* April 1986, IMF Washington DC, pp.13.
2. *Ibid.*

The industrial scenario in the next 20 years would be entirely different from the industrial scenario that exists today or was existing 20 years back. It is simple due to the fact that the growth of industrial section is dominated by the growth of scientific and technological advancement. The world is heading for a new scientific and technological revolution. Therefore, India cannot isolate herself from the research and technological development in global context. The advent of new materials, technology, concepts of flexible manufacturing system, computer aided designs, computer aided manufacturing, application of robotics, lasers, numerical control machines, etc. is likely to dominate the future industrial base. Having achieved a moderate level of industrial base, the country has to confine her efforts to see the widespread dispersal of industries, scientific base, scientific knowledge etc. and activate the industrially backward districts of the country. The need for removal of the imbalance in terms of investment in rural and urban areas is obvious but the caution has to be taken to see that such an approach does not result in technological backwardness of the country. The environmentally sustainable growth should be reviewed keeping in view the cost of depletion of natural and non-renewable sources of the country while achieving such a growth.

Infrastructure that would be needed to sustain the economic growth, development, modernisation and technological self-reliance of the country not only in today's context but even after 20 years has to be planned from today itself. Therefore, the intensity of investment in infrastructure has to be continued at the commensurate rate of the Seventh Plan to avoid adverse effect on the future growth and expansion of industrial development. The intensity of inputs of material is gradually decreasing due to alternatives in terms of materials, products and techniques of manufacture. Therefore, the basic metal industries, construction etc. that may remain at the same level in terms of demand intensity or will be kept at moderate level.

The modernisation of industry is a continuous process and to avoid technological backwardness of industries. The policy of liberal imports of capital goods, equipment, replacement of the absolute machineries, raw materials of which no indigenous production capacity exists, etc. will be inevitable. The assimilation of imported technologies and diffusal of the indigenous technology will be complemented along with the liberal import of technologies for industrial production. The optimum strategy of import substitution and export led growth has to be adopted so that the trade deficit is minimised and the country emerges as the exporter of the manufactured goods, technologies, services, etc. in order to achieve the surplus in foreign exchange reserves. The healthy and fair competition among the industry will be the added strategy to achieve the equilibrium of competitive prices of the commodities and other goods.

The continuance of the subsidies, tax holidays and other incentives to industries tentamounts of foster the infant industry and proliferation of the protected market. This needs to be reviewed and encouraged. The industries which could sustain without such incentives, preferably by enlarging the economies of the scale, the efficient use of energy have to be encouraged.

The renewal of the commitment to promote labour intensive technologies in the country to generate more employment opportunities should not result in technological backwardness of the country. Hence, the new strategy has to be adopted in the Eighth Plan to have optimum mix of technological base in terms of labour intensity, capital intensity, technological sophistication and upgradation of technologies. The industries export obligation has to be reminded for their obligations and commitments to earn the foreign exchange by export of the more value added items. The large private enterprises including MRTP, FERA etc. should be motivated to undertake and fulfil the export obligation. In no case the export obligation should be waived off for those industries which came into existence on such principles. The infrastructure in rural areas should be developed to promote dispersal of manufacturing activities.

1.09 Losses in PSUs

In 1960s there was a drive for nationalisation of not only banks but even sick private industries. Takeover by Government the sick private industries was justified on the ground that families of employees would suffer if such sick private units were allowed for closure. Taking over by the Government all such private sick industry means pumping the money in such industries for all those economically unviable industries. Another drive in 1991 was to justify the closure of all sick and economically unviable units, no matter whether they are in private sector (i.e. under exit policy for industries) or in public sector.

Table 6 : Profile of Centre's Public Enterprises

Item	Units	1980-81	1981-82	1982-83	1983-84	1984-85	1985-86	1986-87	1987-88	1988-89	1989-90	1990-91
1	2	3	4	5	6	7	8	9	10	11	12	13
1. Number of running Public Enterprises	Number	163	188	193	201	207	211	214	221	226	233	236
2. Capital Employed	Rs Cr.	18207	21935	26526	29851	36382	42965	51835	55554	67629	84869	101797
3. Turnover	Rs Cr.	28635	36482	41989	47272	54784	62360	69088	81271	93137	106069	118355
4. Gross Margin Before Profit	Rs Cr.	2401	4012	5184	5771	7386	8230	9897	11134	13438	16412	18510
5. Depreciation	Rs Cr.	983	1358	1719	2205	2758	2983	3376	4150	4866	5790	7151
6. Gross Profit before Interest and Tax	Rs Cr.	1418	2654	3465	3565	4628	5287	6521	6984	8572	10622	11359
7. Interest	Rs Cr.	1399	1630	1923	2086	2529	3115	3420	3595	4167	5329	7539
8. Net Tax before Tax	Rs Cr.	19	1024	1524	1480	2099	2172	3101	3389	4405	5293	3820
9. Tax	Rs Cr.	222	579	928	1239	1190	1000	1330	1329	1411	1504	1452
10. Net Profit after Tax	Rs Cr.	—203	445	614	240	909	1172	1771	2060	2994	3789	2368
11. Internal Resources Generated (gross)	Rs Cr.	1225	2261	2753	3278	4251	5068	6014	6947	8915	10774	11372
12. Net Profit (after tax) Percent to Capital Employed		—1.1	2.0	2.3	0.8	2.5	2.7	3.4	3.7	4.4	4.5	2.3
13. Gross Profit (after tax)		7.8	12.1	13.1	11.9	12.7	12.3	12.6	12.6	12.7	12.5	11.2

Source : *Economic Survey of different years*

The profile of PSUs in India is given in Table 6. It is a ponderable situation. The press reports of dated November 11, 1991 indicate that decision was taken to close down eight loss making public sector units. They comprise :

1. Scooters India Ltd., Lucknow, Uttar Pradesh.
2. National Bicycle Corporation Ltd. Bombay.
3. Cycle Corporation of India, Calcutta.
4. Bharat Opthalmic Glass, Durgapur.
5. Bharat Pumps and Compressors Ltd., Allahabad.
6. Weighbird India Ltd.
7. Tanneries and Footware Corporation, Kanpur.
8. Bharat Leather Corporation, Agra.

Obviously closure of sick industries will have direct impact on employees working in all the eight public sector enterprises. Government has kept provision of Rs 250 crores (an amount equivalent to capital investment in any of the modern giant public sector) to protect the interest of workers. Perhaps inducement to voluntarily retirement would be easiest way to avoid strikes against the decision of closure of such industries. The scheme of voluntary retirement is also extended to another 30 identified public sector enterprises.

The brief financial performance of industries identified for closure is as follows :

Scooter India Ltd. was set up to manufacture the two wheelers. This was established primarily to expand market of two wheelers and break the monopoly of then two manufacturers in private sector. It was solely due to availability of scooters from this company that there was boon for domestic market for two wheeler during 1977 to 1980. Several new industries in private sectors too came into existence by seeing the success of Scooters India. Almost every State in India had set up a public sector enterprise for manufacturing scooters. For instance, Andhra Pradesh, Maharashtra, Gujarat were forerunner in manufacturing of scooters.

Unfortunately Scooters India Ltd. Unnao has started incurring losses since 1980-81. The losses as reported for some years are :

Year	*Loss (Rs crores)*
1980-81	5.0
1984-85	13.8
1987-88	27.12
1988-89	37.21
1990-91	46.00
1991-92	52.50 (estimated)

It employs over 3000 employees at the cost of Rs 52.50 crores from Government budget. Obviously continuance of such loss making unit would aggravate the budget deficit.

The National Bicycle Corporation of India, incorporated on October 27, 1980. This was accomplished by takeover of Hind Cycles Ltd. This enterprise is engaged in manufacturing of cycles and bicycle components. It has two factories, one each at Bombay and Ghaziabad with a strength of 1025 nos. of workers. The losses incurred during some of the years are as follow :

Year	*Losses (Rs crores)*
1980-81	2.25
1984-85	4.35
1987-88	6.58
1988-89	8.29
1989-90	9.82
1990-91	16.82

In November 1991, India had 58 public sector enterprises which were chronically sick with total capital of around Rs 3,000 crores and negative worth of over Rs 2600 crores. Of these 58 units 46 public sector units were earlier taken over by the Government from private sector. Because of unviability these units were identified for closure.

In all there were 98 public sector enterprises categorised as loss making units, of which 83 are said to be operating in the competitive market and 15 in the monopoly market, covering core sectors like steel, coal mines, shipyards and transport services.

131 units are termed as profit making units. May be that of these 131 units 84 units have scope for further improvement.

Table 7: Centre's Revenue Receipts and Revenue Expenditure
(As per cent of GDP)

	1980-81	1981-82	1982-83	1983-84	1984-85	1985-86	1986-87	1987-88	1988-89	1989-90	1990-91
1. Tax Revenue (Net of States share)	6.9	7.3	7.3	7.5	7.6	8.1	8.3	8.4	8.6	8.7	8.6
2. Non-Tax Revenue	2.5	2.5	2.8	2.4	2.9	3.1	3.4	3.1	2.8	3.5	2.9
3. Total Current Revenue	9.4	9.8	10.1	9.9	10.5	11.2	11.7	11.5	11.4	12.2	11.5
4. Total Current Expenditure	10.0	9.8	10.9	11.0	12.0	13.3	14.4	14.3	14.1	14.9	14.9
(a) Interest Payment	2.0	2.0	2.2	2.3	2.6	2.9	3.2	3.4	3.6	4.0	4.3
(b) Subsidies 1	1.2	1.2	1.3	1.3	1.6	1.8	1.9	1.8	2.0	2.5	1.8
(c) Defence Expenditure 2	2.6	2.6	2.7	2.7	2.8	2.9	3.4	3.0	2.9	2.7	2.4
(d) Grants to the States & Uts	2.1	1.7	2.0	2.1	2.3	2.7	2.7	2.8	2.6	2.0	2.2
(e) Others	2.2	2.4	2.6	2.5	2.8	3.0	3.3	3.3	3.0	3.8	4.2
5. Revenue Accounts Surplus(+) Deficit (—) Col. (3-4)	-0.6	—0.1	—0.8	—1.1	—1.5	—2.1	—2.7	—2.8	—2.7	—2.7	—3.4

1. Excludes subsidies on imported fertilizer up to 1985-86
2. Includes defence pension.

* R.E

Notes :

(a) The ratio in this table from 1980-81 onwards is based on the new series on GDP released by the CSO and therefore these will differ from the figures given in the earlier issues of Economic Survey.

(b) Totals may not add up because of rounding.

Sources : Economic Survey 1990-91; page 102, for the year 1981-82 Economic Survey 1987-88, page 55, ref. cd poverty, file Revenue, range al. o28

Out of 83 units, 46 units were taken over from private sector and these 46 units account for 80 per cent of employment and about 76 per cent of the capital employed. In terms of absolute number out of 3.9 lakhs employment in 83 public sector units, 3.13 lakhs were in 46 units, and capital employed in the taken over enterprises was Rs 1792.24 crores out of a total of Rs 2357.4 crores.

1.10 Government Expenditure

Federal expenditure or Central Government's expenditure is comprised of following heads of account :

1. Interest payment.
2. Subsidies.
3. Defence expenditure.
4. Grants to the States/UTs.
5. Others.

Table 7 and 8 indicate the factual position of revenue and expenditure.

Table 8 : Details of Subsidies—Interest Subsidies

Sl. No.	*Name of Public Enterprises etc.*	*Budget 1990-91*	*Revised 1990-91*	*Budget 1991-92*
1.	Garden Reach Ship Builders & Engineers	4.64	4.64	0.00
2.	Mazagaon Dock Ltd.	15.35	15.35	0.00
3.	Coal India Ltd.	58.08	58.08	58.08
4.	Industrial Reconstruction Bank of India	2.00	2.00	5.00
5.	Gaon Banks	0.10	0.10	0.10
6.	Denotified Sugar Undertakings	0.10	0.10	0.00
7.	Khadi and village Industries Commission	34.00	34.00	34.00
	(a) For Khadi Industries	23.00	23.00	23.00
	(b) For other Village Industries	11.00	11.00	11.00
8.	Burn Standard & Co. Ltd.	5.70	5.70	5.70
9.	Tungabhadra Steel Products Ltd.	0.48	0.48	0.48
10.	Interest Subsidy to Press Trust of India	0.05	0.03	0.03
11.	Bharat Refractories Ltd. (IFICO)	1.63	1.63	0.00
12.	Bharat Gold Mines Ltd.	14.00	0.00	0.00
13.	Hindustan Autibiotics Ltd.	5.15	5.15	0.00
14.	National Textile Corporation	230.00	229.68	210.00
15.	Binny & Co.	0.01	1.17	2.16
16.	Heavy Engineering Corporation	20.00	20.00	0.00
	Total—Interest Subsidies	391.29	378.11	315.55

Any attempt to reduce Government expenditure means reduction in expenditure on above five items. The defence expenditure cannot be reduced as it is the concern of nation's capability to meet the threats from external military forces. Similarly grants to States/UTs are considered to be important to maintain harmonious State-Centre relations and are governed by the sets of rules of Finance Commission. The only items that could be thought to curtail are interest payment and subsidies. The subsidies are meant to protect the interest of some industries but it leads to inefficiency and economic unviability.

The details of Centre's revenue and revenue expenditure on examination would reveal that current expenditure of the Government of India is increasing every year. As the Gross Domestic Products (GDP) of the country increases so increases the total current expenditure of the Central Government, both in absolute terms and as a proportional of GDP.

The total current expenditure in India has increased from 10 per cent in 1980-81 to 14.9 per cent in 1990-91, whereas total current revenue has increased from 9.4 per cent in 1980-81 to 11.5 per cent in 1990-91. That is Deficit in Revenue Account (see table-1) has increased from — 0.6 per cent in 1980-81 to — 3.4 per cent over a decade. Among the different heads within total current expenditure, the Interest Payment and Subsidies together have increased from 3.2 per cent of GDP in 1980-81 to 6.1 per cent of GDP in 1990-91. That is almost twice over a period of ten years. Though subsidies have declined from 2.5 per cent of GDP in 1989-90 to 1.8 per cent of GDP in 1990-91, the interest payment has increased. In fact the interest payment has increased over two times the share of GDP, over a decade. The estimated share of the interest payment of 4.3 per cent of GDP in 1990-91 is more than twice of 2.0 per cent of GDP in 1980-81.

Subsidies have increased from 1.2 per cent of GDP in 1980-81 to 1.8 per cent of GDP in 1990-91. Similarly defence expenditure is almost stationary around 2.4 per cent of GDP in 1990-91.

1.11 Liberalisation and its Impact on the Industrialisation

Today's world is not same as it was a decade ago or even three years ago. The end of cold war had paved the way for new ideas, philosophies and international economic order. This obviously means that the global changes of the contemporary world must be taken into account while framing the domestic policies. The shatter of USSR has given an indication that the centralisation of power as well as the philosophy of proliferating the means of production on collectivisation do not fulfil the socio economic obligations. The efficiency of some of the PSUs must be rewarded but not at the cost of depriving private investment. The philosophy of collective ownership of means of production is no more attractive. The globalisation of economies of the world by way of integrating and following the uniform code of economic conduct has paved the way for reformation, liberalisation and structural adjustment. Hardly one can believe that the wave of free trade open economy or market economy will sweep the whole world causing demise of orthodox ideas or socialism, indigenisation, import substitutions, nationalisation and ownership of industries by the Government. The impact of the present drive for liberalisation on industrialisation of India is very wide. To be optimistic, one can say that the changes which have been enunciated recently to overcome the Balance of Payment (BoP) crisis, fiscal deficit, trade deficit, exchange rate parity, reduction in interest rate, change in custom tariff, etc. are the determinance of free economy. Call it by any name such as liberalisation, economic reform, structural adjustments with growth, etc. they refer to the process of continuum change so that our economy responds to the internal and external shocks that might have been envisaged. In fact, the planning process was meant to avert the crisis on account of shocks. However, its performance has been questioned due to failure of planning in terms of providing the social justice to the poorest of poor. This is not to denounce the planning but to have such retrospection and initiate timely changes in it, or assign new role to it.

India has been experiencing lot of inevitable changes since the middle of 1991. These changes can be categorised in two broad categories. Primarily to accelerate the growth in the long run and secondly to keep tuned to respond to the challenges posed by the external economic environment. The first category of changes needs the review of the economic legislations, controls, statutory provisions, Acts and administrative mechanism. In order to reduce the burden on the Government as well as to avoid the frustration of dynamic entrepreneurs the licensing mechanism and control mechanism be abolished. This is what had been done by the Indian Government. It was also essential that Indian economy respond to the need of the hour particularly to attract the foreign investment. Allocation of resources and mobilising the resources had been a great challenge as resources are very scarce. If a country has to depend upon the foreign investment, technological flow, investment and remove the time lag in development, etc. then the policies of our economic development must be modified to suit the interest of not only the country but also to the investors from other countries. It has been observed that the foreign investment has been very meagre in the past decade because of restrictive policies. India has, therefore, liberalised the policies to make attractive the industrial climate for foreign investment.

The contemporary world is full of dichotomies due to the technological progress in western world. We cannot beat the western world where the technological progress is very high. The per capita income of industrial countries is very high. Similarly, the experience of newly developed countries indicates that the restrictive trade policies and licensing mechanism inhibit the industrialisation. Therefore, what has been aimed at is the economic reforms to suite the growth process in the long run.

The country has to depend upon the imports such as petroleum, raw materials for fertilizers, edible oils, newsprint and other commodities. If policies are continued to be restrictive then the country will suffer at one time or the other. The crude oil is one of the determinant factors which tilts the balance of payment position adversely. We have been practising the policies of subsidising on one or other account such as investment subsidies, food subsidies, tax subsidies, export subsidies, interest rate subsidies, transport subsidies, fertilizer subsidies, etc. It is difficult to continue this kind of subsidisation on perpetual basis. The infant industry argument does not hold valid despite the fact that India has more than 20% of share from manufacturing in the GDP. The industrial growth is very impressive and does not justify continuation of such subsidies policies. We have noticed that it causes distortion in the pricing mechanism. The impact of subsidies on trade is very adverse and obviously the views of other nations must be taken into account while framing our policies.

1.12 Structural Adjustment : Response to Measures

If structural adjustment process (i.e. approach based on conventional, orthodox and capitalistic economy concepts) is to be believed to relieve the economy from external and internal shocks, set right the prices, set right the preshock path of economic growth then the furtherance of structural theories is obvious. That is, the countries of the world could be identified or grouped into three categories viz. :

(1) Structural sensitive countries (i.e. respondable countries)

(2) Structural insensitive countries (i.e. could become in due course as respondable countries)

(3) Structural immune countries (i.e. those which cannot be made respondable or having attained mature stage).

Casting financial and economic systems of all countries into uniform and standard pattern to shape identical path of economic growth and development is unlikely to be realistic and there cannot be an all pervasive universal prescription. The level of perfection, efficiency, skillness, technological development etc. are some of the variables which influence the response of economic system. The socio-economic, socio-political, ethnic and other factors influence the response of economic measures. The response to imposed economic conditions or economic measures does not indicate the uniformity in all countries of the world. The fact one must bear in mind is that the intensity of response of economic system or economy of any nation as a whole is unlikely to be proportional to the imposed economic conditions or economic measures. Therefore, there could be at least two aspects. Firstly, in case the intensity of response in a country is proportional to the intensity of imposed economic conditions or economic measures, then such a country is structural sensitive. If the intensity of imposed conditions (through policy instruments and measures) could be integrated in a single indicator. If the year t as compared with its previous base year to It then intensity of economic response (Rt +1) could be :

$$R(t+1) \propto It$$

$$\text{or} \quad R(t+1) = K\,It$$

Where I indicates imposed conditions, R indicates response, K is the constant of proportionately or constant of structural adjustment. This constant could be derived by using efficiency of economy, that is, the rate of return of money injected in the economic system during the period of structural adjustment. This could be calculated by using capital output ratio also. The exchange rate, interest rate, fiscal deficits and balance of payment could be integrated to indicate single indicator R and the economic measures to regain the predetermined economic growth could be calculated. The value of K could also indicate the elasticity of economy as a whole with respect to imposed conditions. That is the capacity to bear the economic shocks, crisis and economic mismanagement.

The intensity of resistance, resilience, permeability of and to response economic policy measures is not treated as determinant in conventional economics but these are obviously determinant. The resistance or opposition to respond to economic measures or instruments varies from one country to another. The response of an economy to given sets of to identical policy measures varies not only from country to country but also it varies from time to time. The economic policy measures attempted at one time in one country may not yield the same result when tried at other time in other country. This is so because the socioeconomic conditions have great role in such circumstances. To prescribe the same remedial or policy measures to overcome the identified, probably identical economic problems, crisis or fiscal deficits, tantamounts to tacit presumption that all countries have identical "coefficient of structural adjustment", or "elasticity of economy", which is unlikely to be true.

Secondly, there are countries which are yet to attain requisite socioeconomic conditions, therefore, such countries are not amenable to economic discipline. The structure of economy is influenced greatly by contribution of manufacturing, trade, services and banking system. Both manufacturing and agriculture play important role but unless manufacturing grows enough to ensure acceleration of per capita income and improves the socioeconomic condition of bottom 30 per cent population. In fact, if socioeconomic condition of a country is deplorable then, such country is prone to economic crisis but attempts to revive its economy through tested economic tools may not yield the predetermined results.

A country which does not respond to the tested economic tools, policy measures and policy instruments should be then termed as "structural insensitive". The response coefficient R is then of negative value, i.e. increasing fiscal deficit, decrease or negative balance of trade, balance of payment crisis, etc. continue to prevail despite remedial measures.

1.13 Prescription to Correct Fiscal Deficit

Correction of fiscal deficit (based on IMF prescription) needs the following measures:

- — Bring down the fiscal deficit from existing 6.5 per cent in 1991-92 to 5 per cent during 1992-93
- — Budget proposals as per the framework of IMF
- — In absolute terms, the fiscal deficit has to be reduced to Rs 32,500 crores in 1992-93 as against Rs 37,727 crores in 1991-92
- — Fiscal correction was to the level of Rs 12,000 crores in 1991-92
- — Drastic cut in expenditure on government account
- — Reduction in non-Plan expenditure by 15 per cent excluding interest payment in budget of 1992-93
- — Tax reforms by broadening the base of taxation, reducing the levels of and dispersion of import duties, rationalisation of excise duties, expansion of MODVAT
- — Share of revenue through direct taxes to be enhanced
- — Reduce custom duties after enhancement of foreign exchange
- — Dependence on import duties be reduced and compensate the gap so arised by additional collection through direct taxes.

Since 1991 India is passing through a process of structural adjustment and liberalisation. Its impact on the process of industrialisation is noteworthy. In fact, the structural adjustment refers to the process of adjustment with reference to external and internal shocks, set right the prices of the commodities and adjust the path of economic growth to ensure rise in per capita income in predetermined way. Similarly, the process of liberalisation refers to removal of all the barriers and controls which are treated as impediments to the process of industrialisation, movement of goods and trade.

Keeping aside the theoretical aspects of structural adjustment process, we shall confine to the talk of liberalisation and its practical impact in Indian context. This involves the retrospection of the mechanism that has been adopted by the country during the past decade. Also this would involve the comparative changes that have been enunciated since last July 1991. To begin with, we shall confine to the following aspects :—

(1) Industrial policies.

(2) Trade policies.

(3) Shift in investment pattern.

(4) Competitiveness.

1.14 Industrial Policies

In past, the industrial policies of the Government of India had aimed to keep the major share of investment in public sector and wherever possible induce the private sector to complement the role of public sector. More than 231 public sector undertakings have been established since the independence of the country. These PSUs were treated as the core sector industries and were meant to meet the major part of the domestic demand. The proportionate share of production from public and private sectors was inclined in favour of PSUs. The infrastructural development was treated as the basic responsibility of the Government. The industries were identified where the entry of private sector was either restricted or kept at the barest minimum level.

The Industrial Development Regulation Act of 1951 stipulated the condition in Section 10 of the Act that "no person or authority other than the Central Government shall after the commencement of the IDR Act establish any new industrial undertaking, except under and in accordance with the licence issued in that behalf by the Central Government". Accordingly, it has become obligatory for an entrepreneur to seek licence for starting the industry. In other words, an entrepreneur has to seek the letter of intent and convert the same into industrial licence after commencement of the commercial production. Similarly, we had MRTP Act to safe-guard the interest of the nation. The small scale industries were exempted from industrial licensing. However, the investment limit was the criterion stipulated for identifying the unit as a small scale or a large scale industry. To comply with the requirements of IDR Act and MRTP Act, the official mechanism was set up. This office was identified as Secretariat for Industrial Approvals. The delay was obvious in processing the applications submitted for the licensing. It was also becoming essential to review the list of industries where excess capacity existed or the broad banding needed. Despite of all these efforts, the industrial growth in the country was not keeping pace with the development elsewhere in the world.

The licensing mechanism has been treated as an obstacle for the investment as the entrepreneur would know better which type of industry could be flourished and technologies could be imported than the Government's technocrats or bureaucrats. This liberalisation drive has now paved the way to remove such barriers and the new Industrial Policy envisaged the free entry and exit policies for the entrepreneurs intending to set up industrial undertakings in the country.

1.15 Trade Policies

Trade policies are interlinked with the industrial policies. The domestic production of the commodities, goods and raw materials is unlikely to be sufficient to meet the demand of the entrepreneurs and enterprises using different technologies. Therefore, the import and export are integral parts of the industrial activities. At the same time, the scarcity of raw materials (like phosphatic acid etc.) or those items for which a country does not have the natural resources a country has to depend on import. Similarly, the retrospection of import substitution policy has been proved to be counter-productive as it tantamounts to manufacture at exorbitant costs as compared with cheaper imports. The export oriented strategy has been treated as the approach towards discouraging the domestic production. However, the present wisdom of the world indicates that those items should be manufactured in the country which are likely to be manufactured at lesser cost than the cost of importation of the same item. The decision to make or to buy depends upon the relative advantages of the trade. At the same time, no country can afford to follow the closed door policies in this competitive world. Integrating the domestic economy with the international economies is likely to be a boon if the country has moderately developed industrial base. This obviously means that the present policies of import and export need to be reviewed and the tariff rates, exchange rates, custom duties, auxiliary duties, basic duties, etc. need to be set in accordance with the international accepted conventions. As we could see from last six months, various measures have been taken to make the export of the country more attractive and also liberal terms for import of the goods.

1.16 Shift in Investment Pattern

The investment pattern in past was highly based in favour of public sector undertakings. However, the chronically loss making units are the cause of concern. Despite the best brains made available to manage the public sector undertaking, the losses incurred by the public sector have been accumulating one after another year. It has also been found that the fiscal deficit is largely attributed to the losses incurred by the PSUs. Similarly, the concept of subsidy (for example, fertilizers, etc.) has been introduced to safeguard the interest of some of the public sector undertakings. In order to set right the prices, the country had to resort to the policies of administered prices etc. Though India is committed to the socialistic pattern of society, this should not tantamount to encourage the inefficiency in public sector undertakings. With the result the Government has to resort to disinvestment firstly in profit making PSUs and, if possible, to sell off the loss making PSUs to the dynamic entrepreneurs. The wave of privatisation as seen all over the globe today necessitates the shift of investment pattern in the country. It is expected that by this strategy the investment in public sector will be brought down gradually and in a phased manner so as to increase the share of investment by private sector.

The accessibility to the modern technologies will be more obvious once the strategies of privatisation are motivated. Gone are the days of admiring the investment in public sector despite the fact that those were found to be less profitable adventures. Some of the public sector enterprises were found to be non-starter for quite a long time such as Visakhapatnam Steel Plant. The project implementation period varies from 12 to 15 years which is a matter of concern. The process of basic research, applied research and commercialisation of the technologies developed indigenously were confined to only few of the PSUs. The higher investment pattern in PSUs pre-supposes that it is a primary responsibility of the Government not only to manufacture the goods but also enter into scientific research and technological development which is inappropriate. The whole process of inventions, innovation and diffusion of technologies has been negligible. With the inducement to the private sector investment it would be feasible to initiate the new process of technological transfer and trade as India is the third largest stock holder of scientific and technical man-power as well as the network of research institutions in the world.

1.17 Competitiveness

The competitiveness is the key word of the contemporary economic growth. If an industry is unable to compete not only in domestic market but also in international market, then the need to encourage the industrial activity of that enterprise is not worthwhile. In fact, supporting the inefficiency economically unviable and where technological superiority does not exist would mean to satisfy with the low return on the investment. The moral obligation of providing the employment should not be inferred as encouraging the inefficient investment in industrial activities. The number of firms, the economies of scale and trade policy determines the competitiveness of the industries. With the liberalisation drive, the country has created sufficient ground for encouraging the competitiveness. If a unit has to survive, it is imperative for it not only to improve the quality of product but also will set in the process of search for those technologies which will ensure the highest output per unit of input. Obviously, the technological choice and quality will determine the competitiveness of the industries both in domestic and international market.

Having given above background, let us have the optimistic view that would set a new pattern of development and India will face the challenges of external and internal shocks that have been experienced by the country.

2

The Stages of Political and Economic Disasters

2.01 Hypothesis of Disasters

The thesis of this book is that "advancement of both political and Economic Disasters (PED) is gradual and passes through three stages. The economic crisis and political disintegration is cumulative effect or consequence." The time elapsed in the vital decision making or premature, unwise decisions has the same effect. These three stages have been explained in this book. To prove the hypothesis of three stages of political and economic disasters (PED) or in support of the thesis the contemporary events as noticed in former USSR (and presently known as commonwealth of Independent States - CIS) and India will frequently be referred to. The events in India and former USSR reflect the interesting changes. The liberalization and reform drive in India is solely due to economic crisis and is termed in this book as Crisis-91 and refers to India alone. The disintegration of USSR is due to both economic and political disasters and mistakes committed by internationally enunciated reforms in socialism. Both India's economic crisis-91 and disintegration of USSR were contemporary or concomitant as well as with some kind of similarity. Though disintegration of USSR has nothing to do with India's crisis and the two are purely unrelated, there is international significance as India's commitment (by virtue of Constitutional obligation) to achieve socialistic pattern of society and basic concepts of socialism were inspired by USSR's economic superiority during 1950s. All the countries liberated after World War-II had cherished the dreams of socialistic pattern of the society and were committed to it by incorporating in their constitutions such ideals. Though disintegration of USSR has no direct implication or impact on India but demise of socialism in USSR has implicitly wiped off faith in socialism from India too. The similarity in the changing situation in USSR and India should be seen from posing sudden faith in capitalism, denouncing the inefficiency in public sector enterprises which was once justified (in 1960s). In contrast with drive for nationalization of giant sectors the year of 1990 has seen the wave for selling of sick and efficient public sector units to private industrialists. Private ownership and initiative was admired and all restrictions on industrial licensing and capital movements as well as trade were done away with. Obviously it was an unrestricted advent of full-fledged capitalism in both USSR and India. Obviously India was not a closed economy as was USSR but capitalism in India was subsurfaces and in USSR it was treated a vice. In Western Europe the communism was treated as undesirable system and in USSR the capitalism was treated as undesirable. Nevertheless demise of socialism and disintegration of USSR on one side and economic crisis-91 in India did not occur suddenly. Obviously it was gradual and progressed through some kinds of stages. This suggests the failure of theories of "Stages of Growth" proposed by W.W. Rostow and stages of social development proposed by Karl Marx.

To summarize, Political and Economic crisis and disasters progress through stages. This thesis of advancement of crisis and disaster have been given the shape of general theory of political and economic crisis based on the contemporary events of two big nations namely India and USSR whose economic and scientific progress attached significant importance in the world. Though the consequence differed in India and USSR, the hypothesis and theory proposed in this book is testable and valid.

If the theory of W.W. Rostow has to be believed or Karl Marx has to be believed then this theory is to be believed. The consequence leading to political and economic disasters may take shape of problems like BOP crisis, balance of trade deficit, frequent devaluation of currency, etc. or disintegration of a nation like USSR. Both USSR and India had identical and contemporary economic and political turmoil. Both economies had to give up the path of socialistic ideals and embrace the capitalism.

In international aid there is not and unlikely to be principle of benevolence or charity. The aid from one country to another has some kind of political implication. In one or other form there ought to be string attached to the aid.

The external aid means accepting dominance of donor agency, country or organization. It also tantamounts to surrender of some freedom and sovereignty of decisions, policies, trade mechanism, industrial output, etc. The acceptance of external interference in domestic policies is obvious. As political stability and economic stability are complementary to each other, any external aid on account of economic growth, stabilization, liberalization, reforms, structural adjustment, etc. is an indication of inconsistencies in political decisions, its stability and political behaviour of a country as a whole. For example, the economic crisis in India in 1991 or what could be termed as Crisis India-91, had political disturbances in the year 1989 to 1991 where chaos, caste war, civil war, etc. have erupted due to political decisions as well as change of two governments and two general elections within a span of two years. The cycle of disaster may be about 40 to 70 year depending upon socio-economic conditions of a country.

The disintegration of USSR and demise of communism on USSR soil gives ample proof that if politically impotent leaders are selected to head the nation with vast human resources, military power, economic and political mandate, etc. such a nation is likely to face same situation like USSR. Another example could be India when during 1989 and middle of 1990s, it had to face civil war, caste and communal riots etc. due to leadership prevailing then.

The events leading to Political and Economic Disasters (PED) have three stages viz.:

(1) initiation of disaster,

(2) propagation of disaster, and

(3) final disintegration

The disintegration of nation comprises civil, economic, political disturbances and coup, murders, and mass movements, and chaos. Both bloodshed and bloodless disturbances do occur in all the three stages, but pronounced effect could be found in the last stage. In general the term "crisis" is used in the context of economic crisis and "disaster" is used in the context of politics. However, in the foregoing text no rigidity is maintained and those words are used synonymously.

2.02 Initiation of Disaster

It is found that initiation of political disaster is due to wrong economic policies, particularly trade, failure of a distributive justice, wrong foreign policies, etc. The inefficient political leader responsible for disintegration of economy, initiating disaster or economic crisis, pronounced or enunciated, policies, programmes, issue order and ordain the strategies, mass movement etc. the implication of which is not understood by himself. Like Gorbachev's Perestroika which was black-book or anti-communist or anti-socialism ideological book claiming socialism's restructuring. It was rather a book on the preaching of how to destroy one's own well furnished house, because it does not look like Western style. Gorbachev was socially blind, inefficient, corrupt and morally turpitude persona-lity ever world has produced. In India too some political parties have won the elections based on political manifesto which aimed at division of people based on caste. Instead of making the whole population homogeneous there was renewed attempt to identify the group of people by their caste, religion and regions.

Disaster in USSR could be attributed to Perestroika which has caused creation of sufficient conditions to foster the forces favouring nucleation of economic crisis, incubation and initiation of disintegration process of otherwise a sound nation or what could be termed as simultaneous reinforcement of political and economic crisis. It was like injecting a slow poison or creating sufficient conditions to initiate economic crisis like that of initiating crack propagation mechanism in homogenous mass through introduction of stress. Unless the process of disintegration is arrested with suitable mechanism both intercrystalline and intracrystalline cracks travel at a specified speed so progress the economic and political crisis simultaneously, in turn there is widespread manifestation of crisis and disintegration. The unrest in the country is the consequence of initiation of either of economic crisis or political crisis or both. The ideologically inconsistent statements, policy decisions, political manifestos, decrees, reform proposals, etc. emanating or originating from Prime Minister, President, etc. are the real source of national disaster. Economic policies, trade policies, fiscal policies, industrial policies are the sources of initiating discontinuous disturbance in the economy. Market forces get signal through such policies, statements, public meetings. Like market forces the political forces too get impetus, opportunity, and stimulations to act for optimization of gains achieving the objective, aims and political goals of self determination, demand for separate statehood, plebiscite. The cumulative effect of faulty policies helps to create conducive economic environment leading to economic crisis, political crisis and national disintegration. The induced economic stresses due to national expectation (similar to theory of rational expectations) gets released through initiation of economic crisis, political crisis or national disintegration.

2.03 Propagation of Disaster

This is second stage nearing national disaster. In this stage, the ideologically inconsistent and incoherent statements, policy decisions, statements, political manifestos, etc. get undue publicity. Both party colleagues and those who are not concerned or even those who in reality are opposed to such enunciated policies, measures and strategies too extend the pretentious support. The cheap popularity is wrongly inferred as massive mandate. Justifying the wrong ideologies attains threshold heights. These factors are more and more talked about as if the leadership has invented panacea or from the theoretical and intellectual angle these are the only options available for nations's progress, growth, reform and prosperity. The response of population is mixed but general public gets immune to such propaganda and thereby gets prepared or conditioned to allow the propagation of disaster through inter and intra territory. The external forces support such movements. Like Gorbachev's perestroika which was talked, discussed and publicized to ensure propagation of his thinking (to ultimately ensure demise of communism) through support of Western media, leadership, diplomacy, etc.) to ensure smooth advent of capitalism, free trade, democracy and ultimately triumph of Western laissez-faire.

2.04 Eventual Disintegration

This is the third and final stage which is brought about by preceding two stages. In this stage while nation is disintegrated into small constituents, the people are involved in mass movement, civil unrest, coup, bloodshed (or bloodless), demonstration, military's use against population, etc. are often noticed. The moves for separate nation from central rule, declaration of independence, etc. is very much favoured in this stage. However, economic crisis is at the threshold during this stage as occurred in India. To define economic crisis we may identify the items like trade deficit, budget deficit, fiscal deficit, monetized deficit, worsening of balance of account position, drop in industrial production and growth in GDP, increasing industrial sickness, double digit inflation, excess government expenditure, unemployment, depletion of foreign exchange reserve, etc.

USSR's case is very vivid example. Gorbachev was able to manage coup against himself (from August 19, 1991 to August 21, 1991) prior to resumption of leadership and started more vigorous destructive policies.

The economic, political and military crisis propagate at very tremendous speed in third stage of disaster. Though in slow and dead society or controlled economy, incubation period for initiation of disaster may take two to three years, and propagation stage may require at least three years, the final disaster may emerge at any time after first and second stage. Where chaotic environment already exists such disasters are unpredictable after a year or two from first stage itself.

To summarize, both economic and political disintegration progress in three phases. First phase starts with massive mandate to the leader (as could be seen with Gorbachev's rise in USSR and sudden rise of V.P Singh in India). Second phase starts with enunciation of reform packages (like Mikhail Gorbachev's Perestroika in USSR and manifesto of Janata Dal in India when Mandal Commission was made as an issue of Bhartiya Janata Party's issue of Ram Janambhumi). Third and final phase of disintegration is very fast as could be seen in demise of communism in USSR, loss of presidentship by Gorbachev as well as disintegration of USSR, and civil war in India due to Mandal Commission Report leading to fall of V.P. Singh Government. It will be wrong to believe that Gorbachev has voluntarily abolished his authority because it is the situation which has made him to resign the post. Even if he would have opted to continue, the situation might have been worsened further leading to his execution. The time period between first and final phase is not more than five to six years in case of political disaster and three to four years in case of economic crisis. India's economic crisis-91 was cumulative effect of consecutive three governments' faulty policies prior to middle of 1991.

In other words, there is sufficient evidence to prove the hypothesis from the events occurred in both USSR and India that the economic and political disasters are comprised of three phases namely :

(1) Incubation and initiation of disaster through massive mandates based on cheap popularity, false promises and imprudent strategies;

(2) Propagation of imprudent, unwise and counterproductive strategies, thoughts and promises to people; and

(3) Eventual disintegration or Crisis (i.e. Eventual disintegration in the case of USSR and eventual economic crisis-91) in India when situation goes beyond control both politically and economically.

The validity of this thesis can be tested from any angle and on any country including current phasing out of apartheid in South Africa.

To furnish the chronological details of the three phases (the words 'phases' and 'stages' have been used as synonymous for the sake of convenience) the events as occurred in USSR and India will be reviewed in brief.

2.05 Retrospection of Socialism

Since March 1985, the events in USSR (the name to be buried with effect from January 1992 and new Commonwealth of Independent Republics will replace its continuity but without central command) were very turbulent. Till December 21, 1991, the entire USSR had been experiencing one or other kinds of changes, and ultimately USSR has been disintegrated in last quarter of 1991.

Declaration of independence by almost all of the 15 Republics of the Soviet Union has been contradicting to the **essence** of **perestroika** of Gorbachev. Precisely, while defending perestroika on the issue of the Union of Socialist Nations—A Unique Formation, Gorbachev said: Meeting people during (my) tours of Republics and national regions of the Soviet Union, I see myself over and over again that they appreciate and take pride in the fact that their nations belong to one big international family, that they are part and parcel of a vast and great power which plays such an important role in mankind's progress. This is exactly what Soviet patriotism in all about. We shall continue to strengthen the Union and fraternity of free nations in a free country. (Ref : Perestroika pp.

122). But all Republics whose "nationalist attitude" was referred to belong to different ethnic groups and proclaimed independence in last quarter of 1991 which was contrary to the spirit of Perestroika. In fact, Gorbachev's end or end of his tenure was very obvious on publication of his views on Glasnost and Perestroika but it was treated as internal affair of USSR. After break up or disintegration of USSR, Gorbachev had no moral right to hold the office, he should have resigned long back, had he honour, dignity and self-respect. Communism was unpleasant word for capitalist. Socialism was more mild and inconsequential term. All those countries liberated between 1947s to 1950 i.e. after World War II have shown their faith in socialism and its ideals were incorporated in the Constitutions of several countries. The admiration for collectivism has paved way for cooperative movements all over the world and banking as well as several private companies were nationalized. Several public sector undertakings were established as a source of economic growth and the concept of welfare economy came into being.

2.06 Dialectical Materialism

Marx's dialectical materialism has very great influence on each of the academic philosophies or disciplines. Marxist methodology and theory has challenged every basic concept of capitalism. Every academic discipline had to devote honourable place to Marxist philosophy. Marxist theory has been proved to be inter and intra academic disciplines including Sociology, History, Political Science, Philosophy, and Economics. Both the subjects namely, Political - economy and economics were more influenced by Marxism. The trio of Marx, Darwin and Freud have undoubtedly changed the whole course of academic streamline. Marx had influence of nineteenth-century German philosophy, "Religion is the opiate of the people" and there were no "good" or "evil" forces at work behind scene. He rejected the notions that "men could trust in the working of benevolent divine providence". Marx's philosophy was based on justified synthesis of both thesis and antithesis and called it as dialectic or struggle between two opposite or contradicting philosophies and objective material reality as dialectic materialism.

Frederick Engels stipulated principles of communism (Ref.: Selected Works, Vol. 1, pp. 81) in October or November, 1847. He replied the self-expected 25 questions explaining principles of communism. Both Karl Marx and Frederick Engels had capacity to command the reverential position as they laid the foundation not based on empty promises or pseudo intellectualism as found in perestroika but they refuted academically, intellectually, theoretically and scientifically all the theories prevailing then. In fact birth or origin of socialism and communism was based on justified philosophies for collective betterment for collective survival. But demise of socialism at the hands of ordinary person was very unexpected and without any scientific or justified academic philosophies, that too by a hoax and pseudo ideologies of personality who was not of the stature Marx was. This does not indicate the weakness of socialism or communism or nation but what it indicates is that once the process of political and economic disaster is in progress it generates enough momentum to wipe out the basic ideologies or edifice on which it was erected, no matter who the person is heading the nation. Which supports the thesis proposed here. One can imagine the kind of struggle the creators of the concept of socialism had to face in justifying feasible socialism amidst the powerful capitalism or greatest potentiality of capitalist theories and their proponents. That is why it is said that as a great ideologist Marx had to turn everything upside-down, including the religionists, jurists, politicians, etc. The manifesto of the Communist Party was written by Karl Marx and Engels in December 1847 - January 1848 which deals with all sociopolitical aspects of the societies prevailing then such as: (1) Bourgeois and Proletarians; (2) Proletarian and Communists; (3) Socialist and Communist Literature; and (4) Position of the communists in relation to the various existing opposite parties.

Three different aspects of socialism are:

(1) Reactionary Socialism
- (a) Feudal socialism
- (b) Petty-Bourgeois socialism
- (c) German or "true", socialism

(2) Conservative, or Bourgeois, socialism

(3) Critical-Utopian socialism and communism

2.07 Formation of Union

The theoretical socialism was treated as "utopian socialism" (i.e. socialism which existed nowhere) or it was infeasible to implement its ideals and ideologies for development of society as well as a system of political and economic governance of the nation but leaders then committed to socialism then have shown way to make it feasible and for advent of the formation of Union in December 1922 had paved the way for made advent of scientific and feasible socialism. In fact it was one kind of dictatorship in the pseudo name of the rule of proletariat. The dictatorship is always viewed as vice and undesirable disposition. The principle that one should work according to his "ability" and that one should get according to "needs" (i.e. basic needs) as preached in socialism did work initially. But suppression of individual's freedom and choice was also accompanied with socialism. In fact onus to ensure satisfaction of "basic needs" of lower strata of the society represent the philosophy of social justice which can be achieved through socialism. When is the social justice met? Obvious answer was that if the basic needs of the poorest of poor is met. This has then relevance to socialist ideologies. However, the "greed" for more wealth make a person to adapt dynamic approach and entrepreneurship is proliferate which ensures the satisfaction of the basic needs of the poorest of poor led to the philosophies advocating "individualism" or "fittest and ablest to survive" as seen in capitalism. The advent of socialism was seen as an alternative capitalism and obvious result was to ensure proliferation of contemporary ideologies to ensure world order conforming to strong and mostly or widely admired philosophy in the world. The struggle to achieve cultural, economic and military superiority by practicing framework of socialism and capitalism was witnessed all over the world.

The period from 1922 to 1992 has witnessed two World Wars and several struggles particularly in Europe. Till 1985, there was always a threat of third World War between East and West Europe, as USSR had emerged as one of Superpowers of the World after World War II. And USSR was always seen as protector of poor countries committed to socialistic ideals and a power to confront with eventual threat of growing imperialism. The closed door economy of the Soviet Union had kept world guessing about its real state.

The brief account of historical fact could be recapitulated here. The four independent socialist republics—Russia, the Ukraine, Byelorussia and Transcaucasian Republics were the founder members of the USSR. The Union was founded on December 30, 1922. The great October Revolution began on 25 October, 1917. As a result of the great October Socialist Revolution in Russia in 1917 ending Tsarist empire, these four States proclaimed independent Republics.

The architect of then formed Union was no less but great visionary Vladimir Ilyich Lenin and he became the founder of world's first socialist State. The idea to form a Federation of Sovereign Soviet Republics came into being in the meeting of the representatives of the four Republics in Moscow on December 30, 1922, at the first all-Union Congress of the Soviets (elected Councils) to unite on voluntary and equal terms in a single State. The Federation of Sovereign Soviet Republics gave the right of free succession from the Union and of free access to it for the existing socialist Republics and that might appear in future. This idea was formalized after two years at the second all-Union Congress of the Soviets held in Moscow on January 31, 1924. The formation of other Republics was as follows :

Year		*Republics*
1924	1.	Uzbekh Republic
	2.	Turkmen Republic
1929	3.	The Tadzik Republic
1936	4.	Kazak Republic
	5.	Kirgizh Republic Transcaucasian disbanded to
	6.	a. Azerbaijan
	7.	b. Georgia
	8.	c. Armenia
1940	9.	Lithuania
	10.	Latvia
	11.	Estonia
	12.	Moldavia

With above 12 Republics and three founders of the Unions namely Russia, the Ukraine and Byelorussia (i.e. total 15 Republics) had been incorporated in USSR. Till the proclamation of December 21, 1991 signed by three cofounder and 11 other independent Republics, the 1977 USSR's Constitution give each Republic the right to freely secede, and this clause was in operation as a part of Union Treaty.

2.08 Perishable Perestroika

Leaders are remembered for great accomplishments as well as grave mistakes they make during their tenure. In the history of mankind, whenever there would be talks of erstwhile USSR, her founder and destroyers would be certainly remembered. As Karl Marx, Engel, and Lenin would be remembered so would be Gorbachev, but former trio for their constructive work and gift of socialism to mankind whereas later for his work leading to destruction of the basic edifice on which socialism was erected and eventual demise of socialism and USSR.

Mikhail Gorbachev's Perestroika was more publicized, admired and supported in Western Europe than USSR or China. Because such an approach was more needed to Western Europe than any other nation in Third World or in USSR and its allies. Perestroika was first published in 1987, and revised version in June, 1988. By June 1991, the USSR was on the verge of total collapse. On 23rd August, 1991, Gorbachev had (managed to arrange) publicized coup against him (self) which gave general impression that there was coup against his reform policies and by the end of September, 1991, all the fifteen Republics had declared independence. In middle of December, 1991, Boris Yeltsin was able to wrest enormous power from Gorbachev, the architect of perestroika, through diplomatic, political and democratic wisdom.

During the intervening period, various goods and bads were noticed or undoings and irreparable damages have been done including historic events such as fall of Berlin Wall, reunification of Germany (both East and West Germany were divided after World War II), removal of statue of Lenin (founder of powerful USSR), removal of hammer and sickle from Russian tricolor. Gorbachev alone should not be blamed as by the time he took over leadership, USSR was a carcass of dead economy, suppressed people by own countrymen and looked like a clay tiger. He analyzed the situation and need for "efforts towards changing the structure of the national economy, transferring it on to a track of intensive development, and accelerating scientific and technological progress prompted even more urgently the need for a radical reform of the economic mechanism and for restructuring the entire system of economic management." Eventual disintegration of USSR did not prove to be coherent with Gorbachev's own advocacy which states that "Socialism and public ownership, on which it is based, hold out virtually unlimited possibilities for progressive economic processes. For this, however, we must each time find the most effective forms of socialist ownership and of the organization of the economy. Of the prime importance in this respect is for the people to be the true masters of production, rather than a master only in name. For without it, individual workers or collective are not interested, nor can they be interested, in the final results of their work."

2.09 Essence of Perestroika

Too much has been said about perestroika. In fact right from assigning blame of cause for disintegration of USSR to allegations like "it was a death sentence on socialism". Then what is perestroika all about? Gorbachev while explaining essence of perestroika says that :

1. Perestroika means overcoming the stagnation process, breaking down the braking mechanism, creating a dependable and effective mechanism, for the acceleration of social and economic progress and giving it greater dynamism.
2. Perestroika means mass initiative. It is the comprehensive development of democracy, socialist self-government, encouragement of initiative and creating endeavour, improved order and discipline, more glasnost, criticism and self-criticism in all spheres of our society. It is utmost respect for individual and consideration for personal dignity.
3. Perestroika is the all-round intensification of the Soviet economy, the revival and development of the principles of democratic centralism in running the national economy, the universal introduction of economic methods, the renunciation of management by injection and by administrative methods, and the overall encouragement of innovation and socialist enterprise.
4. Perestroika means a resolute shift to scientific methods, an ability to provide a solid scientific basis for every new initiative. It means the combination of the achievements of the scientific and technological revolution in a planned economy.
5. Perestroika means priority development of the social sphere aimed at ever better satisfaction of the Soviet people's requirements for good living and working conditions, for good rest

and recreation, education and health care. It means increasing concern for culture and spiritual wealth for the culture of every individual and society as a whole.

6. Perestroika means the elimination from society of the distortions of socialist ethics, the consistent implementation of the principles of social justice. It means the unity of words and deeds, rights and duties. It is the elevation of honest, highly qualified labour, the overcoming of levelling tendencies in pay and consumerism (Ref. Mikhail Gorbachev : Perestroika, Fontana/Collins; 1987; pp. 34-35).

About the expected results of Perestroika, as envisaged in 1987, Gorbachev says "We can hardly give a detailed, exact answer. It is not our way to engage in prophesying and trying to predestinate all the architectural elements of the public building; we will erect in the process of Perestroika". Though it is a job of Russians to evaluate Gorbachev's Perestroika, still as a spectator of global change one may like to know it. One may wonder if such underestimated efforts of reforms and restructuring are worth pursuing. Because the ideological incoherence would cause unproductive or counterproductive results out of struggle of restructuring. The efforts to give "socialism the most progressive forms of social organization" or "exposure of the humanist nature of our social, system in its crucial aspect - economic, social, political and moral" have gone into vain. Those were futile and useless. It was wrong and totally wrong still Gorbachev continued to say "I stress once again : Perestroika is not some kind of illumination or revelation. To restructure our life means to understand thè objective necessity for renovation and acceleration. And that necessity emerged in the heart of our society. The essence of Perestroika lies in the fact that it unites socialism and democracy and revives the Leninist concept of socialist construction both in theory and in practice. Such is the essence of Perestroika, which accounts for its genuine revolutionary spirit and its all-embracing scope" (Ibid). In fact, if introspection or retrospection of the events be made with publication of Perestroika, it could reveal that it has been disintegration effect and not the effect to unity or even preserve the identity of USSR, of which Gorbachev was elected as leader or General Secretary of CPSU in 1985.

Gorbachev would be remembered more for his misdeeds or harms he has done to USSR than anything good he has made for poor citizens of USSR. Seen from the remote distance of thousands of kilometres, one can easily say that the citizens or members of CPSU made him the king of Supreme Soviet, but he not only found faults the throne on which he was sitting but even in the whole motherland to which he belonged. They made him king but in turn, he made them pauper, hungry, poor and destitute. With advent of an open economy concept, the attempts to identify the number of people below the poverty line (in USSR) have also begun. They posed confidence, trust and faith in Gorbachev but he not only betrayed such people, their ideological commitment to socialism and collectivism but has become ardent admirer of capitalism and open economy of USA, thereby betrayal of basic tenets, ideologies, trust and confidence of people. Some people brand him as an agent of CIA, or spy of USA and some see in him traitor to the ideologies of Karl Marx and Lenin. It is for Russians to decide but the fact is that he has brought an eclipse to socialism and communism. The craze for materialistic life and individualism have paved way in Perestroika with the result that numerous flaws have found in socialism, communism and USSR or Union treaty of 1922. The fact is that collectivism and socialism have tremendous force and it requires great personality to manage it or else it will lead to inefficient and unproductive economy.

The peace on earth as envisaged in the process of Perestroika has Fundamental Principles with military, political, economic and humanitarian aspects.

1. In the military sphere :

   (i) renunciation by the nuclear powers of war - both nuclear and conventional - against each other or against third countries;

   (ii) prevention of an arms race in outer space, cessation of all nuclear weapons tests and the total destruction of such weapons, a ban on and the destruction of chemical weapons, and renunciation of the development of other means of mass annihilation;

   (iii) a strict controlled lowering of the levels of military capabilities of countries to limits of reasonable sufficiency;

   (iv) disbandment of military alliances, and as a stage towards this, renunciation of their enlargement and of formation of new ones; and

   (v) balanced and proportionate reduction of military budgets.

2. In the political sphere :
   (i) strict respect in international practice for the right of each people to choose the ways and forms of its development independently;
   (ii) a just political settlement of international crisis and regional conflicts;
   (iii) elaboration of a set of measures aimed at building confidence between States and the recreation of effective guarantees against attack from without and for inviolability of their frontiers;
   (iv) elaboration of effective methods of preventing international terrorism, including those ensuring the safety of international land, air and sea communications.
3. In the economic sphere :
   (i) exclusion of all forms of discrimination from international practice; renunciation of the policy of economic blockades and sanction if this is not directly envisaged in the recommendations of the world community.
   (ii) joint quests for ways of a just settlement of the problem of debts;
   (iii) establishment of a new world economic order guaranteeing equal economic security to all countries;
   (iv) elaboration of principles for utilizing part of the funds released as a result of reduction of military budgets for the good of the world community, of developing nations in the first place; and
   (v) the pooling of efforts in exploring and making peaceful use of outer space and in resolving global problems on which the destinies of civilization depend.
4. In the humanitarian sphere :
   (i) cooperation in the dissemination of the ideas of peace, disarmament and international security, greater flow of general objectives, information and broader contact between peoples for the purpose of learning about one another; reinforcement of the spirit of mutual understanding and concord in relation between them;
   (ii) extirpation of genocide, apartheid, advocacy of fascism and every other form of racial, national or religious exclusiveness, and also of discrimination against people on this basis;

(iii) extension—while respecting the laws of each country—of international cooperation in the implementation of the political, social and personal rights of the people;

(iv) solution in a humane and positive spirit to questions relating to the reuniting of families, marriage, and the promotion of contacts between people and between organizations; and

(v) strengthening of and the guests for new forms of cooperation in culture, art, science, education, and medicine.

The realities of the events indicates that none of the things occurred as envisaged in the essence of the perestroika except the fear of third World War was over and collapse of USSR has reduced the tension between USA and USSR, which was clear defeat of USSR and winnowers of USA.

Conscious reader of political events in USSR even sitting in remote corner of the globe can understand that Gorbachev has lost all his powers, wit and authority in the process of transition. The situation in USSR could be summarized as that of "no governing power and no democracy in Russia today. Democracy is unthinkable without tolerance, without respect for the views of others. Everything is falling into an abyss—the economy, finances and the people's trust. While we talk about reforms, the situation worsens catastrophically", said Russian Vice President Alexander Rutskoi. This has reference to Russian President Boris Yeltsin's approach to wrest power from Gorbachev.

2.10 Burial of USSR and Emergence of Commonwealth

On December 8, 1991, the three Republics of former USSR namely Russia, Ukraine and Byelorussia set up a commonwealth of independent States and denounced the treaty of 1922. Thereby formal burial of USSR with effect from January 1992, i.e. after a period of 70 years.

On December 21, 1991, the agreement was reached to proclaim a new commonwealth of independent States, signifying a formal end to the Soviet Union, after five hours of talks at the House of Friendship in the Kazakh capital, Alma Ata. Accordingly "The Soviet Union has ceased to exist." Leaders of 11 of the 12 Soviet Republics had signed three key documents.

First documents signed by 11 Republics (plus 4 founders) recognized all partners as cofounder on equal basis.

Second document recognizes independence of the 11 Republics of the Union and their current borders. This document is known as Alma Ata Declaration.

Third document has made temporarily provision for military command till December 31, 1991, prior to permanent arrangement.

Mr Boris Yeltsin, the architect of the new Commonwealth reiterated on December 21, 1991 that Mr Gorbachev should resign before the end of the year and retire "with dignity". Some of the words of Mr Boris Yeltsin are commendable. He said : "we respect Mr Gorbachev and we want him to resign smoothly in December, as he himself wants, and correspondingly today, we will discuss all the necessary honours." ....He further said "I think the heads of States will determine all the necessary privileges and status for him. We'd like in our civilized State to have the President of the country, who had done a lot of good as well as made mistakes, to depart with dignity, while we build the Commonwealth of the independent States." This signifies the fact that " it would be the first time since the 1917 Bolshevik Revolution that a head of State has retired peacefully." The 11 Republics who signed the December 21, 1991 documents are :

Euro-Asian Commonwealth :

1. Russia (architect country)
2. Byelorussia (Supporter of Euro-Asian Commonwealth)
3. Ukraine (supporter of Euro-Asian Commonwealth)
4. Kazakhstan
5. Turkmenistan
6. Tadzhikistan
7. Kirgizia
8. Uzbekistan
9. Moldavia
10. Armenia
11. Azerbaijan

That is out of 15 Republics following four did not sign the documents of Euro-Asian Commonwealth dated December 21, 1991 :

1. Lithuania
2. Georgia

3. Estonia
4. Latvia

2.11 Concern for Nuclear Warheads

The nuclear warheads situated in different Republics are the major cause of apprehension to NATO countries. Because instead of dealing or negotiating on nuclear warheads with one country, the breakaway nations would have to be dealt separately. However, formation of 11 nation Euro-Asian Commonwealth of December 21, 1991 has clarified that everything would be under one single command, with one button, not four. The single nuclear command and formation of the Commonwealth indicates the continuity of former Union but in different form. Nuclear Warheads in 1990 in USSR were dispersed in different Republics which have proclaimed their independence. Their number in each of the Republics were as follows :

	Republic	*Nuclear warheads (nos.)*
1.	Russia	19,000
2.	Ukraine	4,000
3.	Kazakhstan	1,800
4.	Byelorussia	1,250
5.	Lithuania*	325
6.	Georgia*	320
7.	Azerbaijan*	300
8.	Estonia*	270
9.	Armenia	200
10.	Latvia*	185
11.	Turkmenistan	125
12.	Uzbekistan	105
13.	Moldavia	90
14.	Tadzhikistan	75
15.	Kirgizia	75
	Total Nuclear Warheads	28,120

Russia seems to be the only factor in the whole struggle for power and command. Obviously, Mr Boris Yeltsin has greater advantages than any other leader of such Commonwealth. With the

* The Republics which did not sign the Euro-Asian Commonwealth documents of December 21, 1991. The total nuclear warhead in these four countries are 1,100 nos.

formation of new Commonwealth, the fears of emerging several nations with nuclear capacity or export of nuclear techno-logy were set to rest. All the nations of the world have taken a breath of relief on formation of Commonwealth. As envisaged, none of the nations of the world have any sympathy for Gorbachev and though he was alive, none bothered to wait for reactions from him, as he had no role to play or nothing to offer to the peoples of breakaway Republics of erstwhile USSR. Here ends the black book called Perestroika.

2.12 Alma-Ata Declaration of December 21, 1991

The text of the declaration signed by 11 of the 12 Republics of former USSR is as follows :

The independent States —

The Azerbaijan Republic
The Republic of Armenia
The Republic of Byelorussia
The Republic of Kazakhstan

The Republic of Kirghizia
The Republic of Moldavia
The Russian Federation
The Republic of Tadzhikistan

The Republic of Turkmenistan
The Republic of Uzbekistan, and
The Republic of Ukraine.

Seeking to build democratic law-governed States, the relations between which will develop on the basis of mutual recognition and respect for the sovereignty of the State and sovereign equality, the inalienable right to self-determination, principles of equality and non-interference in the internal affairs, the rejection of the use of force, the threat of force and economic and any other methods of pressure, a peaceful settlement of disputes, respects for human rights and freedoms, including the rights of national minorities, a conscientious fulfilment of commitments and other generally recognized principles and standards of international law.

Believing that the strengthening of the relations of friendship, good neighbourliness and mutually advantageous cooperation, which has deep historic roots needs the basic interests of nations and promotes the cause of peace and security.

Being aware of their responsibility for preservation of civilian peace and inter-ethnic accord,

Being loyal to the objectives and principles of the agreement on the creation of the Commonwealth of independent States, are making the following statement :

Cooperation between members of the Commonwealth will be carried out in accordance with the principles of equality through coordinating institutions formed on a parity basis and operating in the way established by the agreements between members.

At the death of the Soviet Union, "a democratic Commonwealth" has born. Conceptually and as agreed, there would not be any more totalitarian central control. Under the Soviet Union, all these 11 members were forced into Union either after defeat by the Red Army or annexation. Communist Party had apex centre to run the affairs of the Union. But by decree, the Communist Party has been banned, centre had been dismantled and independence was allowed to all the Republics.

In the month of August 1991, the three Baltic States had not shown any inclination or interest to join the Commonwealth but it should not matter much considering size of their economy.

One of the important aspects of the Commonwealth is that the population of 11 States may be about 284 millions and their citizenship will be determined based on geographic areas of independent States; in other words, they will be citizens of their own independent State. No citizenship of Commonwealth would be granted like that of old Soviet Union. Dual citizenship will be allowed for those who reside outside their native State. Free movement across the border without visas have been permitted. Considering the fact that prices of items of consumption which were determined by central control and central production of items of consumption, now each of the State have to face grave economic situation. That is, managing economic crisis aroused suddenly without war, flood, or natural calamity, without central budget and subsidies. Due to continuous troubles since 1987, the production of industrial and agricultural items was falling, worthless common rouble currency and advent of sudden market economy. Disappearance of items from the market, scarcity of supply, high inflation, unemployment, poverty, etc. are some of the common problems of Commonwealth of independent Republics of former Sovie Union.

2.13 Enemies of Communism and Socialism

Do communism and socialism have right to exist or not? Answer could be either of affirmative or negative. The frame of reference for answering such questions itself hinges on the ideology one subscribes to. There is no absolute frame of reference on such ideological ethics, morals and values. Both wrong and right are justified on logic and word power. As far as moral right for existence of communism and socialism is concerned, one can easily decide based on side of tossed coin one expects as outcome of social order. Seen from the side favouring just and equal social order, one can opt for socialism or communism, but seen from elite class side representing individualism and industrialism aspects of social order then socialism and communism are monsters, and represent other side to be opted for.

Who then are the enemies of communism and socialism? They are from within such societies. If just social order could not be achieved in a society dominated by communism and socialism, then blame should be assigned to those inefficient and pseudo communists who occupied such exalted positions. Say Gorbachev, who was elevated to the highest position by his own community comrades, was one of the most unreliable individuals and inefficient administrators world has ever produced. He has opted to destroy the root of a tree on which the nest of followers and enormous human strength was perched. He opted to devour the foundation of humanity for which world has experienced revolution after revolution.

Any one who has exposure to Marxism will agree that prior to Marx the theories of socioeconomic political governance were inclined to capitalism i.e. laissez-faire. The contemporaries of Marx were too advocating untiringly the capitalism. Seen from the context of division between schools of thoughts of capitalism and socialism or communism, it will reveal that all the contemporaries of Marx particularly intellectuals, academicians, theoreticians, politicians were on one side and, on opposite side were Marx and his associate Engel. These two personalities viz. Marx and Engel have generated enormous literature denouncing capitalism (or market economy as we call it today) and giving an alternate theoretical base, explanation, foundation and feasibility aspects. The "Utopian socialism" was made "feasible" for "scientific" solely due to the work of Marx, Engel and Lenin. Obviously, their revolution was associated with human bloodshed in October, 1917. Unfortunately, Gorbachev has created turbulence in USSR by his misdeeds through Perestroika and Glasnost, the words associated to unpleasant happening in USSR leading to disintegration.

Gorbachev's Perestroika is merely a collection of Western Philosophy on capitalism and signifies Gorbachev's surrender, fascination and forfeiting socialism to capitalism. Gorbachev's Perestroika is no way comparable or near to philosophy of Marx, Engel or Lenin.

The basic approach to Liberty, Equality and Fraternity involves the guarantee of control and accessibility over means of production. In other words, the continuum of the twin processes aimed at generating the economic wealth, income and prosperity at a speed to surpass the sum total of needs and wants of the growing population and distributive mechanism to ensure equality of living standards, per capita consumption expenditure, status and opportunity.

The question of Generating economic prosperity, wealth and income leads to two streamlines of thoughts, i.e. the generating income, wealth and prosperity be left to individuals (i.e. individualism) and distribution through market forces (i.e. laissez-faire); and the generating of wealth be left to government's initiative (i.e. through public sector enterprises) and distribution through identified channels and intervention by government in market forces. Liberty of citizen and liberty of economic forces is not one and the same thing. USSR has been curbing both kinds of liberty concepts. In fact, curtailing liberty of citizens means suppressing the wants, need, desires, aspirations and liberty of expression and in turn suppressing democracy. Whereas suppressing economic forces means suppressing traders, middle men, social evils, etc. In fact, communists of USSR though founders and true demonstrators (next to China) of real and workable communism or socialism (difference between socialism and communism is like a thin layer of hair thickness) have wrongly interpreted that freedom of individual is related to growth of economy (that is, suppressing freedom of individuals will accelerate growth of economy) and wrongly presumed that political stability by central rule will promote economic stability and prosperity due to which Gorbachev's Perestroika looked appealing to individual freedom. Gorbachev's phobia for USA's demonstrative effect, Japan's supremacy and progress without military supremacy during post-World War II era, has made him to have commitment or introduce reforms based on assurance of West for aid for introducing market reforms by abandoning central rule. In fact, it is irony that the throne to which Gorbachev was incarnated has been dismantled by himself alleging the blame that it had a faulty design. Of course it is for citizens of USSR to decide whether disintegration of USSR was a good or bad thing for them. Whether it has paved a way for golden era or leading to dooms days.

2.14 Chronology of Gorbachev's rise

Gorbachev took power in March, 1985 at the age of 54 and was considered to be youngest leader after Josef Stalin. He has created worldwide wave of reforms (revolutionary in nature) through Perestroika (meaning restructuring) and Glasnost (openness). Though this cannot be called as silent or bloodless revolution, it was given so publicity by Western world that Gorbachev became overnight a hero more in West than in his own country. He was so crazy for his cheap popularity that he became almost blind to understand even basic fact that events, acts, system or deeds which favour Western Europe's interest will find obvious support from the West. Gorbachev was able to wrest massive support from Western Europe because in introducing open market economy system in USSR through Gorbachev it will ensure renewed market for Western goods, new investment, expansion of industrial base etc. (i.e. pre 1917s era of imperialism) which Western world was looking for. It can obviously be said that Gorbachev was responsible (due to his own inefficiencies to manage federal and republic affairs on time tested economic model of centrally planned economy, and failure to give new dimension to socialism), for initiated crack propagating mechanism which eventually led to breakage of USSR, by allowing independence to Baltic States of Estonia, Latvia and Lithuania, Armenia and Georgia. It will not totally be wrong if some one says that Gorbachev was able to manage coup against himself to identify his opponents and eliminate them by cleverly designed drama of coup. The international level drama started with announcement that Mr Gorbachev, President of USSR was "unable to carry out his duties for health reasons". Gorbachev was on vacation in Crimea since August 5, 1991 and was removed from office on August 19, 1991.

To summarize rise of Gorbachev let us have a look on some of the important dates :

March 11, 1985 : Mikhail Gorbachev was unanimously elected as General Secretary of Central Committee of the CPSU at a special plenum of Central Committee. He was supposed to be youngest Politburo member.

June 11, 1985 : Mr Gorbachev outlined a three-pronged offensive to transform the Soviet economy.

July 29, 1985 : Mr Gorbachev announced his country's decision to suspend all nuclear explosions from August 6, 1985, the 40th anniversary of the atomic bombing of Hiroshima and called upon the US to respond to the Soviet step.

November 1985 : The first summit between President Gorbachev and US President Ronald Reagan takes place in Geneva.

January 17, 1986: Mr Gorbachev announces acceptance of NAM proposal that nuclear powers hold consultation on underground nuclear tests as well.

February 25, 1986 : Mr Gorbachev blames administration of late Mr Leonid Brezhnev for inflicting damage on Soviet society.

March 1, 1986 : Mr Gorbachev wins mandate of the rank and file of the Communist Party members with adoption by the 27th congress of the revised party programmes and amended Party Constitution.

March 6, 1986 : Mr Gorbachev reconstitutes the powerful Politburo and Party secretariat.

April 11, 1986 : Soviet Union, reacting to a US nuclear test in Nevada, withdraws its eight-month-old unilateral ban on testing nuclear weapons.

April 18, 1986 : Mr Gorbachev announces new proposals for reducing conventional military forces in Europe.

April 21, 1986 : Mr Gorbachev calls for simultaneous scrapping of the Warsaw Pact and NATO military alliances.

April 29, 1986 : Fire breaks out at Chernobyl nuclear power plant. Hundreds of casualties, thousands evacuated.

May 14, 1986 : The Soviet Union extends nuclear test moratorium till August 6, 1986 and again till Jan 1,1987.

August 23, 1986 : The U.S. and the Soviet Union sign pact on nuclear energy exchange.

December 23, 1986 : Soviet dissident scientist Andrei Sakharov and his wife return to the capital after nearly seven years in internal exile.

February 26, 1987 : The Soviet Union conducts first nuclear test since mid-1985, ending its unilateral moratorium.

August 22, 1987 : Sino-Soviet border accord signed.

December 8, 1987 : U.S. President Ronald Reagen and Mr Gorbachev sign the international Range Nuclear Forces Treaty.

1988 : Mr Gorbachev calls the first Communist Party Conference since the days of Josef Stalin to press for more radical reforms. In December, presides over the dissolution of the old Supreme Soviet, to be replaced by the Congress of People's Deputies and smaller, full time legislature, the Supreme Soviet.

1989 : Withdraws Soviet troops from Afghanistan and presides over new Parliament that elects him President.

1990 : Ends Communist Party's constitutional monopoly on power and moves to create a free market economy in Soviet Union. Wins

		Nobel Price for his role in arms treatise and ending cold war.
1991	:	Mr Gorbachev and leaders of several of the republics agree on new Union treaty to hold the country together.
August 1991	:	Alexander Yakovlev, one of the architects of Mr Gorbachev's reforms, resigns as a top aide and quits the Communist Party, warning that a coup is planned.
August 19, 1991	:	Vice - President Genady Yanayev and other hard-liners announce they are replacing Mr Gorbachev as President to prevent a "national catastrophe". They declare a state of emergency.

In fact it is for Russians to decide the good and bad sides of their leadership. But the President and Prime Minister of any country do not remain a national figure but attain the stature of international significance. The deeds, reforms and actions of such personality then have international significance and implications. The fact that world is unifying through international movements, identical actions and ideologies and urge for collective survival, the concern is obvious for aberration in one country will have implication on other.

2.15 Coup That Wasn't

Alexander Yokovlev (said to be founding father of Glasnost, i.e. policy of more open expression), the former Politburo Member, resigned from Communist Party on Friday 16th August, 1991 and charged an allegation that "Stalinist" group in the Communist Party was plotting a coup against Gorbachev. His expulsion came from Communist Central Control Commission on the ground that he indulged into "actions running counter to party rules and aimed at splitting the party". His words of caution were that : "I would like to warn society that an influential Stalinist group has formed within the leadership corps of the party, speaking against the political course since 1985 and slowing social progress in the country." The reference to misdeeds of Josef Stalin has always been part of communist ruling in USSR. Communist dictator Josef Stalin had sent millions of communist dissenters to their deaths or to hard labour. His charges also include the fact that despite its declaration, has freed itself from the democratic wing in the party and is making preparations for social revenge, a party and state coup, as party has become a hopeless bastion of anti-reform forces.

According to Moscow time the events described as coup against Gorbachev are as follows :

Sunday 4 P.M. : Presidential aide Georgi Shakhnazarov talked to Mr Gorbachev on phone about their mutual plan to return to Moscow next day.

7 P.M. : Mr Shakhnazarov's special communication line is cut off.

Monday 4 A.M. : Soviet military and KGB forces surround Mr Gorbachev's Crimean dacha and prevent his plane from leaving.

6 A.M. : Tass carries Vice President Gennady Yanayev's announcement that Mr Gorbachev is suffering from health problems and that he is assuming power as acting President.

12.50 P.M. : Russian Federation President Boris Yeltsin calls on Russians to resist the takeover and calls for general strike.

3.30 P.M. : Tass announcement that a state of emergency has been declared and eight man committee has been formed to rule the country.

5.00 P.M. : Mr Yanayev tells a news conference that Mr Gorbachev is in poor health, is undergoing treatment and might some day return to power.

7.00 P.M. : The Central TV center in Riga is occupied.

7.30 P.M. : U.S. President George Bush questions whether the Soviet people would surrender new-found freedoms and says U.S. aid to the Soviet Union is on hold.

9.00 P.M. : Latvian Interior Ministry Popular Front head-quarters are occupied.

10.15 P.M. : A man is shot and killed while driving past the Lithuanian Interior Ministry.

Tuesday 4.45 A.M.	:	Soldiers and paratroops arriving in Riga's Dom square and occupy radio buildings.
4.00 P.M.	:	About 100 tanks are seen at the Central airfield, about 4 km. from the stronghold of Mr. Yeltsin, who has spearheaded anticoup demonstrations.
5.00 P.M.	:	Mr Bush swears in Mr Robert S. Strauss as U.S. Ambassador to Moscow and sends him on a fact finding mission there.
5.30 P.M.	:	Mr Yeltsin tells British Minister John Major over the telephone that tanks are rolling even as two are speaking.
9.20 P.M.	:	The military commandant of Moscow impose a curfew on the Soviet capital.
9.30 P.M.	:	Soviet troops disarm Latvian Prime Minister's guards and seize control of the republics broadcast studios.
Midnight	:	Two people are confirmed killed when foes of the coup trap a military vehicle beneath an underpass near Mr Yeltsin's headquarters and soldiers inside the vehicle open fire.
Wednesday	:	Early Wednesday; In Tallin, Capital of Estonia, more than 100 light armoured vehicles and trucks roll into city. Estonia TV screens go blank after Soviet troops seize the studio and tower.
12.30-1.00 P.M.	:	Latvia joins neighbouring Estonia in declaring independence from Soviet Union.
1.00 P.M.	:	Tanks start driving through the main square.
3.00 P.M.	:	"Vremya" a TV newscast drops adherence to the coup-government line. Tass reports ban on reformist publications being lifted.
5.00 P.M.	:	The Communist Party denounces the takeover.
Evening	:	Leaders of national legislature demand Mr Gorbachev's reinstatement. Full legislature nullifies coup leaders emergency decrees.
8.30 P.M.	:	President Bush tells a news conference he has spoken by telephone to Mr Gorbachev who told him the coup was over.

8.30 P.M. : Troops start to leave occupied building in Riga.

9.00 P.M. : Mr Gorbachev statement that he is in control of the country is read on Soviet TV.

Thursday

2.15 A.M. : Gorbachev returns to Moscow to resume power.

The interesting thing of this coup was that Gorbachev knew when, how, and by whom coup will be made. He also declares the beginning and over of coup. After resumption of charge as President of USSR he further says that another coup by so called hardliners is in offing. That's why a cartoonist in India drew a cartoon with a caption mediamen asking Gorbachev when will next coup occur so that arrangements could be made to telecast it live.

Gorbachev perhaps was more fascinated by Western progress achieved through democracy, laissez-faire, free trade, resource mobilization, role of multinationals, etc. As demonstration effect of consumerism and charms of being a free bird as well pace of creating new needs, innovative, technological progress, glittering and glaring nudity through audiovisual electronic media etc. has made static communism of collectivism ideals an obsolete system of socioeconomic political governance. It was more a State liability to feed and meet basic needs than creating vibrant or dynamic society. The rule of proletariat or bandwagon of working class needs abandonment as it would perpetuate orthodox rule.

Therefore, move to transform from static authoritarian society of Soviet Russia to that resembling Western style social democracy through faith in individualism in contrast with collectivism of yesteryears, embracing private enterprise, allowing free trade, free market, and free people from State dependency. The urge to initiate Western pattern of governance made Gorbachev to approach USA, UK and their allies for more aid for reforms.

There was another person called Alexander Prokhanov, a right wing newspaper editor who expressed the need to seize power by the throat, as the time was ripe. According to his perceptions "Marxist-Leninists, Marxist-Stalinists, Russian Communists, social democratic liberals, extreme profascist organizations, writers, artists, the military, industrialists, monarchists and pagan" have been forming to prevent the disintegration of the Soviet Union and its economy.

Gorbachev was more concerned about his own (cheap) popularity which he was getting from Western media than making any significant contribution to the cause of USSR. The postcoup developments included the following events :

August 22, 1991 : Gorbachev returned to power after a short lived coup against him.

August 23, 1991: Lenin's monument removed from Vilnius, as a consequence of ban on communist party and KGB in Lithuania.

August 24, 1991: Gorbachev quit as CPSU Chief, disbanded Central Committee, confiscated party property and banned party cells from army, KGB and Interior (Home) Ministry.

— Ukraine declared independence from Moscow on 24th August, 1991 and became fifth Soviet Republic to break away formally from the Soviet rule.

— Other Republics declaring independence from USSR were three Baltic States namely Latvia, Estonia and Lithuania.

That is, Latvia, Estonia, The Ukraine, Byelorussia, Moldavia and Azerbaijan declared independence just within 10 days. On August 31, 1991, Uzbekhistan and Kyrghystan also declared their independence. Armenia has also announced its intention to secede under five year arrangement provided by the Soviet Constitution. As position was on August 31, 1991, the only six Republics to remain with the Soviet Union could be Russia, Kazakhstan, Kirgizia, Turkmenistan and Tadzkhistan. Russia is the largest Republic with 76.2 per cent of total land area of the USSR and representing more than 51 per cent of the total population. That is why Boris Yeltsin was considered more important to Gorbachev.

USSR with total 22.4 million square kilometers comprised of the following republics, regions and areas :

1. Union Republics 15 nos.
2. Autonomous Republics 20 nos.
3. Autonomous Regions 8 nos.
4. Autonomous Areas 10 nos.

The Union Republics of USSR prior to 10-20 August 1991 (i.e. disintegration and prior to declaration of independence from USSR) comprised of :

1. Russia
2. Ukraine
3. Byelorussia
4. Uzbekistan
5. Kozokhstan
6. Georgia
7. Azerbaijan
8. Lithuania
9. Moldavia
19. Latvia
11. Kirghizia
12. Taijikistan
13. Armenia
14. Turkmenia
15. Estonia

Responsibility of coup was assigned to Gorbachev as "the leaders of the coup were his associates, his friends and appointees". Gorbachev had tolerated, if not approved, the unconstitutional use of military personnel and equipment against civilians in Armenia, Karabagh, Lithuania, Estonia, Georgia and other Republics. He failed to condemn programmes against Armenians between 1988 and 1990 organized and encouraged by the same criminals who were ready to deploy the army against civilians in Moscow and put an end to reforms in the USSR, said Levon Ter-Petrossian, President of Armenia since August 1990 (Ref. Los Angeles: Times Syndicate dated August 27, 1991).

He further says that President Gorbachev must take full responsibility of coup. His lack of a systematic approach to economic reforms and of consistent support to democratic forces as well as his regular concessions to right wing elements, contributed directly to the failure to adapt an economic reform programme. This strengthens the position of the conservatives and the boldness of their action. In their unreserved support to these policies, Western Governments too, must assume some responsibility for the course of events.

Gorbachev will be remembered in political history of USSR, for both (little) good and (enormous) bad things. He came to power in March, 1985 at the age of 54. He was considered to be youngest leader after Josef Stalin. He has created world wide wave of reforms, though not strictly revolutionary in nature but still applauded for heading revolution. The much of his philosophy is found in Perestroika (meaning restructuring) and Glasnost (openness). Though this cannot be called as silent or bloodless revolution in USSR through Perestroika, it was given wide publicity in Western world media. Through Perestroika, Gorbachev became more popular statesman, or a hero in West than in his own homeland.

The Western media, leadership and nations do not give any such publicity unless events, acts, policies, systems or deeds unless it favours Western world. If there would have been no new opportunity or safeguard of interest of trade, economic ties, resources mobilization, capital investment, technology flow, diplomacy etc. then Western Europe would have never cared for Gorbachev and his so-called pseudo-Perestroika. Under the name of Perestroika, he has allowed his country to be disintegrate within seven years of his tenure.

2.15 Demise of Communist Rule

Soviet Union Constitution had given monopoly to CPSU rule since 1898. During the past 98 years various events have occurred in USSR. It had never witness any peaceful time. The life span of 98 years of CPSU rule prior to demise of Communist Party of the Soviet Union (CPSU) had following major developments :

1889 : First congress of the Russian Social Democratic Labour Party (RSLP) in Minsk. Its nine delegates soon arrested.

1903 : Second RSDLP congress Vladimir Lenin, insisting the party must be tightly-knit group of professional revolutionaries, lead a split between his own Bolshevik (majority) faction and Mensheviks (minority)

1905 : First Russian revolution in which some party members are prominent, crushed after several months of upheaval. RSDLP declines to an insignificant sect.

1917 : With Lenin and most other Bolshevik leaders in Siberia or in Europe, the party plays no role in the February revolution and overthrow of Tsarism. On November 7, 1917 the Bolsheviks seize power in St. Petersburg with military coup overthrowing the provisional government.

1918 : Party changes name to the Russian Communist Party (Bolsheviks). Bans other political parties; begins civil war against white anti-Bolshevik armies.

1919 : Lenin founds Communist International.

1921 : Lenin proposes new economic policy (NEP) at 10th party Congress, allowing limited private enterprise. All internal factions banned.

1924 : Lenin's death followed by several years of infighting. Joseph Stalin emerges winner. Leon Trotsky exiled.

1929 : Stalin ends NEP, begins collectivizing agriculture and breakneck industrialization.

1934 : Stalin cements personal rule at 17th party congress. Murder of Leningrad party chief Sergei Kirov launches great purge. Millions shot or sent to die in labour camp.

1952 : Leadership reorganized and name changed to Communist Party of Soviet Union (CPSU).

1953 : Stalin dies

1956 : First Secretary Nikita Khrushchev denounces Stalin at 20th party congress in "secret speech". Purge victims mostly rehabilitated.

1957 : Khrushchev foils attempt to topple him by his politburo colleagues.

1961 : Second round of de-Stalinisation. Stalin's body removed form Red Square mausoleum.

1964 : Khrushchev ousted and replaced by collective leadership under Leonid Brezhnev and Alexei Kosygin.

1968 : Warsaw Pact invades Czechoslovakia. "Brezhnev doctrine" justifies Soviet intervention to prop up communists.

1982 : Brezhnev dies. Replaced by Yuri Andropov.

1984 : Andropov dies. Replaced by Brezhnev aide Konstantin Chernenko.

1985 : Chernenko dies. Replaced by Mikhail Gorbachev.

1986 : Gorbachev begins cautious reform and renewal leadership 27th party congress. Boris Yeltsin becomes candidate politburo member.

1987 : Yeltsin resigns from top party post after row with Gorbachev and politburo colleagues.

1988 : 19th party conference. Gorbachev wins approval for multi-candidate elections and creation of new full time parliament. Start of decline in party authority.

1989 : Elections to congress of People's Deputies. Informal groups challenges Communist Party, defeat several top communist candidates, Yeltsin wins Moscow constituency with 89 percent of vote.

1990 : Creation of executive presidency, election of Gorbachev by Congress of People's Deputies, abolition of Article 6 of Soviet Constitution guaranteeing Communist Party's right to rule. Gorbachev fends off conservative assault at 28th party Congress. Yeltsin and other reformers leave party, saying it has failed to become democratic. Formation of hard-line Russian Communist Party led by Gorbachev critic Ivan Polozkov.

1991 : Gorbachev stays on as Party General Secretary, while his reformist allies urge him to quit. Yeltsin wins election as Russian President. He bans communist cells in workplaces. Gorbachev announces plans for new party congress and new reformist party programs. Gorbachev ousted by hard-liners. Communist Party prestige plumments even further when coup fails.

Gorbachev quits as party chief and announces measures effectively destroying it as political force. Yeltsin, after pivotal role in foiling coup, expands authority with string of decrees taking control of huge chunks of Soviet Government.

USSR was never a soil devoid of political uncertainties. The sins committed by Stalin were always treated as murderous communism. The progress achieved in USSR by collectivization, industrial and scientific progress, gift of economic planning etc. were never to be forgotten. The contribution to the world peace were always threatened by advancement of technology in USA. In a short tenure as President of USSR, Gorbachev had to witness numerous political events than any of his contemporaries in the world. The aims which Gorbachev wanted to achieve were not fully appreciated. It would be wrong to say that Gorbachev was not trying sincerely to reform Soviet economy, but political system of USSR was more rigid than he might have thought of. Though a person occupying seat of power is best judge to analyse the prevailing situation but he is solely held responsible for both goods and bads.

The reasons assigned for ban of CPSU were based on reasoning that CPSU had failed to denounce coup against Gorbachev. But why Gorbachev wanted CPSU to denounce is not known. The text of statement of Gorbachev read on BBC television on August 25, 1991 is as follows :

> The secretariat and politburo of the Communist Party Central Committee didn't oppose the coup d'etat. The Central Committee did not manage to take the decisive position of condemnation and resistance, did not arouse the Communists for struggle against the assault on the constitutional assault.
>
> This has put millions of communists in a false situation, many party members refused to cooperate with conspirators, condemned the coup and joined in struggle against it.
>
> No one has the moral right to accuse all communists indiscriminately and I as a President, consider myself obliged to defend them as citizens against unfounding accusations.
>
> In this situation the CPSU central committee must adopt a difficult but honourable decision on its dissolution. The fate of republican communist parties and local party organizations will be determined by them.
>
> I do consider it possible for me to continue to reform. (I was vested with the powers and) the functions (of) general secretary of the CPSU central committee and I surrender those powers.
>
> I believe that democratically inclined communists who have preserved their loyalty to constitutional legality and the course of the renewal of society set up a party on new basis which is capable, along with all progressive forces of joining actively in the continuation of radical democratic transformations in the interest of working people.

The Communist Party of the Soviet Union (CPSU), which ruled the Soviet Union for more than 70 years was suspended on August 29, 1991 and dissolved or banned on August 30, 1991. The reason being "on the basis of evidence in hand on the participation of leading organs of the CPSU in the preparation and implementation of the State coup from the 19th to 21st August, 1991, the activities of the CPSU on the entire territory of the USSR are suspended." Gorbachev resigned as party Secretary General. He urged its Central Committee to disband itself, thus leaving the party in shambles.

Russian President, Boris Yeltsin had nationalised CPSU's and Russian Communist Party's real estates, movables and investments in roubles and foreign currency in the Soviet Union and abroad, by a decree signed on Sunday and circulated today, Tass said on August 29, 1991; the property and the investments held abroad were to be distributed among the Republics after they signed Union Treaty.

Very interesting point during such pathetic disintegration of Soviet Russia was the reaction from United States of America. US President, George Bush welcomed the suspension of the Communist Party. "I frankly rejoice in that ...demise, the fall of the totalitarian non-democratic party," Mr Bush said on August 29, 1991, in Maine, where he was holding a news conference with visiting British Prime Minister, John Major.

2.17 Cost of Democracy

Democracy denotes a system of socio-political governance of a country by involving people from all segments of the society. It is a form of society devoid of discrimination, hierarchy and monarchy. It is people's involvement in every decision. Freedom of expression, faith, belief, worship, occupation, etc. follows from it.

But, it is not panacea. As no two persons can have identical thinking, perceptions and aptitude to grasp equally, so there cannot be point of coincidence. Many are the people so assembled on any platform of democracy more are divergent opinions, dissent, disagreements, and ultimately no point of convergence. In other words, democracy creates an environment of distrust, dissents, lust for power, scope for protests, walk outs, etc. This kind of chaotic society is said to be democracy.

Those who are not committed to any of the ideologies, morals, intellectual school of thoughts, or unable to infer right and wrong from society's perspective, are likely to create more hurdles in democracy than authoritarian society.

Taking example of Gorbachev, one can say that the cost to acquire democracy in communist soil of USSR has caused the disintegration of world's once most powerful (both militarily and economically) nation. What was installed since October 1917 had been shattered or reduced to dusty power during (March 1985 to August 1991) since years of rule by Gorbachev.

So-called Perestroika (i.e. restructuring) has proved to be decree of self-destruction. Due to sudden shatter of USSR into existenceless countries, one can easily predict the pace at which economy collapses if its leadership is weak. The old economic and military super power is no more to admire and fear. The mistake which Russians have made by elevating Gorbachev to the highest position of leadership will be remembered for centuries to come. The entire philosophical, intellectual and political doctrines created by Karl Marx, Frederick Engels and Lenin has been made to rot or decay due to impotent leadership that inherited power. The whole process of catastrophic demise of socialism or communism has been initiated by so-called Glasnost and Perestroika which suited most the Western Europe's imperialism than to promote harmony among the Republics of USSR. The schezophrenia of market economy has devoured the socialism, communism, central planning and collectivism. The people posed confidence, trust and faith in leadership of a crazy who has not only found faults in the system which made him to rise to elevated position but started devouring the basic fabrics to make nude first and devour one after another the parts of the human body, flesh, and blood to reveal the skeleton. Better not to have such senseless, schizophrenic, and politically important leadership and their indoctrinated mandates in the name of reforms and restructuring. Whatever may be the fate of Russians and communism ideologies, there are reasons to believe that imperialism has tremendous inertia to sweep away any kind of weak ideologies; be it socialism or communism. In a globe with socio-political environment of capitalism, democracy, free trade, secular and human rights ideologies, to keep survive the ideologies of socialism and communism, it requires the use of force to suppress unwanted tendencies in society. Obviously, suppression of both economic freedom and freedom of individual with heavy force of central command has been the essence and core of communism. Economic austerity is the need of the hour but freedom of individuals is not.

Demise of communism in USSR and fragmentation of USSR was obviously the resultant of counterproductive policies proliferated under the name of restructuring. The outcome was as envisaged on pretentious propaganda of restructuring economy. Obviously, people of USSR had posed trust and confidence in Gorbachev not for diluting the basic existence of USSR itself or allowing fragmentation of the empire but to take to further progress and prosperity. It is certainly breach of trust of millions. This happens when the leaders themselves have no commitment to the philosophies, ideologies, theories and practices of the State in which he was elevated. Reform for progress and prosperity both on short term and long term, visible and invisible, having strength in domestic affairs and international affairs, but what has been seen in USSR was its ruining through reforms and restructuring, its ultimate death. So, Gorbachev was elevated to Presidency of USSR to bid goodbye to communism.

2.18 Gorbachev's Achievements

The chronology of some of the major events during the 81-month era of Gorbachev's leadership of USSR is as follows:

March 11, 1985 : Gorbachev was named General Secretary of Soviet Communist Party following the death of Konstantin Chernenko.

February 26, 1986 : The speech to Central Committee indicating proposed restructuring of Soviet society known as "Perestroika".

December 8, 1987 : Signed Intermediate-range Nuclear Forces (INF) Treaty in Washington with President Ronald Reagan. The Treaty banned ground based missiles with ranges of 480-5600 km., with effect from June, 1, 1988.

May 15, 1988 : Withdrawal of troops from Afghanistan by USSR.

October 1, 1988 : Gorbachev replaced Andrei Gromyko as Chairman of Presidium of Supreme Soviet.

May 15, 1989 : Gorbachev's visit to China which signified stand-off between Moscow and Beijing that began since early 1960s.

May 25, 1989 : Gorbachev was elected Chairman of Supreme Soviet by Congress of People's Deputies.

February 5, 1990 : Gorbachev proposed multi-party political system and introduction of executive State Presidency at Supreme Soviet Session.

March 11, 1990	:	Lithuania, Latvia and Estonia declared Independence.
March 15, 1990	:	Gorbachev was elected as first Soviet President by Congress of People's Deputies.
March 31 to June 2, 1990	:	Gorbachev's invitation about agreement with U.S. President George Bush that led to Strategic Arms Reduction Treaty (START), reducing long-range nuclear arsenal by 30 per cent.
October 15, 1990	:	Enunciation of Winner of 1990 Nobel Peace Prize as Gorbachev.
November 17, 1990	:	Gorbachev urged signing of new union treaty, which would redefine relations between Kremlin and Government of Republics.
January 13, 1991	:	Soviet tanks attack main television tower in Vilnius, Lithuania, killing 14 people.
March 17, 1991	:	Union Treaty got approved in nationwide referendum.
April 16-20, 1991	:	Gorbachev became first Soviet leader to visit Japan and hold talks with Prime Minister Toshiki Kaifu.
June 12, 1991	:	Boris Yeltsin wins Russian Federation's first Presidential election.
July 17, 1991	:	Gorbachev became first Soviet leader to attend Group of Seven Summit of leading industrialised countries. He agreed with Bush on all aspects of START.
July 26, 1991	:	Communist leaders overwhelmingly approved Gorbachev's new party platform, abandoning decades of Marxist rule.
July 31, 1991	:	Gorbachev signed START in Moscow with Bush.
August 19, 1991	:	Gorbachev was removed from Presidency by hard-line Communist junta. National state of emergency was declared.
August 21, 1991	:	Coup fails, Gorbachev returned to Moscow.
August 24, 1991	:	Gorbachev resigned as head of Communist Party and urged it be disbanded.

September 2, 1991: US formally recognised Baltics independence.

September 6, 1991: Soviet Union recognised Baltic independence.

October, 1, 1991 : Twelve remaining Soviet Republics agreed to form new economic union.

October 18, 1991 : Gorbachev and Presidents of eight Soviet Republics signed treaty to create economic union.

November 4, 1991: Ukraine agreed to join 12 remaining Soviet Republics in new economic union.

November 14, 1991 : Seven Soviet Republics agreed in principle on new union treaty.

December 1, 1991 : Ukrainians voted overwhelmingly for independence in referendum.

December 3, 1991 : Gorbachev issued appeal for remaining Soviet Republics to sign political treaty with Kremlin or face poverty and collapse.

December 8, 1991 : Russia, Ukraine, Byelorussia declared Joint Union dead and agreed to form Commonwealth of independent States.

December 17, 1991: Gorbachev, Yeltsin agreed on dissolution of Soviet Union by the end of 1991.

December 21, 1991: Eleven of 12 Republics sign accord on formation of Commonwealth of Independent States.

December 25, 1991: Gorbachev announced resignation as Soviet President.

Above chronology is not full. In fact, the events in Poland, reunification of Germany, etc. are excluded. Western countries made fool of Gorbachev by giving him undue popularity by scribing his name on T-shirts, making dolls similar to face of Gorbachev. Quoting extract of an article of Helen Womach, we can recapitulate that "Westerners—whose admiration for the Soviet leader secured him a place in popculture and created the phenomenon known as "Gorbymania"—were never able to grasp the fact that the man whose face adorned their 'I love Gorby' buttons and T-Shirts was deeply unpopular at home. Why? His public relations problems go back to 1985 when he succeeded the geriatric Konstantin Chernenko as the General Secretary of the Communist

Party". In fact, cheap popularity has made Gorbachev so blind himself that his mistakes one after another have been admired in the West but given fatal blow to economy of USSR and created political crisis or question of identity of USSR. The phases of political crisis were so quick that within a span of six years of his tenure have caused demise of USSR in his own presence. Morally, he has no right to exist by winding up USSR. Gorbachev's reforms were like a "garbage in garbage out". Gorbachev himself acted as garbage in the process of reforms. At the same time the word "reform" is taken as an indication to a process leading to political disintegration or eroding the basic edifice on which a workable system (different from capitalistic free economy) is functioning and ensure advent of free economy.

Mikhail Gorbachev ultimately had to resign, from the post of President of the USSR on December 25, 1991. In fact, in the first week of December itself, USSR had ceased to exist as almost every Republic of USSR had proclaimed independence and agreed to form the Commonwealth without any central rule. Obviously, Gorbachev had no moral right to call himself as President of USSR whose entity and sanctity has ceased to exist. It was totally wrong to say that there was any coup against Gorbachev on August 21, 1991. It was a coup managed by himself to boost himself and seek sympathy of 280 million people by cheap method. Similarly, as he wanted to ruin communists in USSR by introducing the cheap or populist methods through propaganda of Glasnost (openness) and Perestroika (restructuring). He was more appreciated by Western Europe for his Glasnost and Perestroika than his constituent States, citizens of USSR or countries which were deriving inspiration form socialism or communism. Because capitalist countries always saw USSR and her communism as threat to capitalism and imperialism; and they could not find any better person to destroy the basic doctrine of communism from the soil of USSR than Gorbachev himself by holding the office of General Secretary of CPSU and President of USSR. That is, he has become hero in Western Europe by betraying the faith, trust, confidence of the people of USSR, socialist and communist ideals. Moreover, due to closed door economy, Western countries were unable to expand their markets, trade, technologies, international finance, etc. in USSR. Gorbachev's policies have helped all Western countries to extend helping hand to Gorbachev as Western countries were sure that whole USSR will certainly collapse within short span; or they could foresee and envisage the demise of communism, economy and end the era of Gorbachev. Therefore, to laud himself he was awarded a Nobel Price too. It was total unwise and imprudent route which Gorbachev had adopted.

With the formal resignation of Gorbachev as President of USSR, the President of Russian Federation, Boris Yeltsin has become the supreme person as the black briefcase with the Red Buttons was handed over which controls about 30,000 nuclear weapons located all over the former USSR territory. This was inevitable as Russia itself has highest nuclear weapons on its territory than any other member Republic of newly formed Commonwealth of Independent States of earlier USSR. Moreover, creation of Commonwealth of Republics without central authority has no role for so-called President of USSR.

The red flag with hammer and sickle emblem (adapted in 1924) that has furled since 70 years was replaced in Kremlin with red, white grey blue tricolour flat of Russian Republics. Therefore, Gorbachev in his live television 12 minutes address said "Due to the situation that has evolved, I hereby discontinue my activities as the President of the USSR". His other words go like this:

— The worst thing about this crisis is the collapse of statehood.
— I am concerned that the citizens of this country are ceasing to live in a great power.
— I am confident that our great civilization will find its way out of crisis and we shall one day live in a prosperous and democratic country.
— Even today, I am convinced that the democratic reforms started in spring 1985 were historically correct.
— We live in a new world.
— I leave my post with concern. But also with hope, with faith in you, in your wisdom and spiritual strength.
— We are heirs of a great civilization, and it is up to each and every one of us to see that it is reborn.
— No doubt, we could have avoided some mistakes and done many things better. But I am sure that sooner or later, our joint efforts will yield fruit and our people will live in a flourishing and democratic society.

— I will use my influence and possibilities to ensure that the Commonwealth of Independent States lives and works.

This speech is itself full of contradictions. Firstly to find a scapegoat and blame others for his own misdeeds has been easiest thing which Gorbachev could find. "Collapse of Statehood" did not come during the regime of any of the predecessors. If a leader of such superpower could not envisage the outcome of his speeches, his acts, deeds and strategies, then there cannot be anything more unfortunate than this socially, politically, economically blind. He was praising openness, open economy and Western thoughts; his advocacies have brought the resultant what was intended to be. If this eventuality was not foreseen by Gorbachev then it could be easily said he acted like an owl in a forest who ordains and ordains the things the implication of which could not understand. He held the empty ideals, thoughts and tried futile attempts to preserve fundamentals, ideologies and foundation of a fort on which USSR was built.

The Nobel Prize for Peace conferred on him was implicitly meant to praise him for setting on the fire the whole USSR and burying communist ideologies, which was a "great civilization" that has been tarnished by Gorbachev now has to be "reborn" but this does not require the ordinary person like Gorbachev but great personalities, visionary, philosopher, administrators, revolutionary, like Karl Marx, Engel and Lenin. The person like Gorbachev would make the things bad to worse or affluent society to paupers. May God save from such disaster, persons and consequences.

One thing is very clear or which could be called as hypothesis that there is a massive mandate to political person, party or individual then it is an indication that the country is on the verge of facing on one or all the fronts of political, economic, social and civilization. This could be tested from events in USSR due to sudden emergence of Gorbachev or less important person like V.P. Singh who became the Prime Minister of India bringing civil war using casteism issue. Both the persons will be in oblivion and political events were equally bad during their tenure. Their existence on the earth did not matter once they were out of office but political events thus occurred prove the hypothesis proposed in this book that the political disasters and economic crisis progress through three stages.

Indeed, question is not of imparting freedom of speech, expression, liberty to create chaos but it is a capability to hold united a country which was born after great revolutions, intellectual struggles, after laying foundation of socialism, through theoretical, philosophical and intellectual base. It was due to his several mistakes and misdeeds alone that the whole process of socialism, economic and political progress collapsed before his eyes. It is not incorrect that the observation of one woman shocked a visiting Western academic by calling Mr Gorbachev a "political prostitute". And when hard-liners tried to overthrow the Soviet leader in August, these critics said that he got what he deserved for himself protected the conservatives.

One should not be astonished if Gorbachev is offered a lectureship, job, pension not by Russian States but by USA, German, or other Western countries because during the tenure of Gorbachev, Western bloc could easily achieve without war or use of military force what they could not achieve since 1924, or keeping prepared for eventuality of war with USSR but citizens of USSR have lost the edifice what their forefathers had founded due to imprudent actions of Gorbachev. The transformation of the society or social order during Gorbachev's tenure was without any kind of bloodshed like that of Stalin's regime, for this Gorbachev must be admired.

In conclusion it could be said that the giant strides of capitalism have sweeped the Russian's socialism and her economy. The fault lies on both incapable leadership and rotten official machinery in Russia. Similarly India's economy collapsed due to strides of free trade prevailing everywhere and it made India to change its whole course of economy.

2.19 Chronology of Events in 1991

While the world was experiencing unprecedented changes, particularly demise of USSR as supreme power, eclipse of socialism and communism in USSR, unification of Germany, disintegration of constituent Republics of USSR, formation of European Common Market, consensus to have common currency in Western Europe etc., India, Sri Lanka, Pakistan, Nepal, Bangladesh etc. were facing inter and intra insurgency, militancy, terrorism, and other means of political games.

Among the major events in 1991 in India on political and economic front were instability both in elected government and established path of socio-economic development. As it is a known fact that economic stability and political stability are concomitant and complementary to each other, India was experiencing both political and economic instability in 1991. During 1989 and 1991, there have been change of two governments and both have little control over economy or political changes. The events in 1991 were significance due to the fact that changes in India cannot be isolated from global contact. While new global economic order was evolving, India was facing acute economic crisis in her history. Nevertheless, the chronology of events in India during 1991 reflects the quality of political and economic factors. One of the severe blows India had experienced was killing of Rajiv Gandhi who was seen as rising star on India's horizon.

Table 1 : Violence Marks 1991 National Scene

Restoration of democracy in several States, change of guard at the Centre and spread of terrorist violence claiming the life of former Prime Minister Rajiv Gandhi and thousands others marked the national scene in the first year of the last decade of this century.

The assumption of P.V. Narasimha Rao Government heralded far reaching changes through liberalisation in trade, financial and industrial policies opening new chapters in the history of independent India.

The year witnessed a major earthquake in Uttarkashi area resulting the death of hundreds of people and damage to property worth crores of rupees.

While the assemblies of Uttar Pradesh, Pondicherry and Kerala were dissolved, President's rule was imposed in Tamil Nadu, Haryana and Meghalaya. States like Bihar, Tamil Nadu, Assam, Arunachal Pradesh and Punjab had new Governors during the year.

The year also witnessed the loss of political leaders like Uma Shankar Dixit, S.A. Dange, C Achutha Menon, film personalities like Nutan, Durga Khote, G. Arvindan and newspaper personnel like Ramnath Goenka, Rajender Mathur and Sharad Joshi.

Following is the diary of major national events of 1991:

January 1: Khurshid Alam Khan appointed Karnataka Governor following resignation of Bhanu Pratap Singh.

Jan. 4: Justice J.C. Shah who headed Shah Commission, dies.

Jan. 5: Dr M.M. Joshi to succeed L.K. Advani as BJP president.

Jan. 10 : 22nd International Film Festival opens in Madras.

Jan. 11 : Lok Sabha Speaker Rabi Ray disqualifies eight Janata Dal-S members including five ministers.

Jan. 12 : Prime Minister Chandra Shekhar declines resignation of five Ministers disqualified by Speaker under Anti-Defection Law.

Jan. 19 : Maharashtra Chief Minister Sharad Pawar submits resignation to party president.

Jan. 20 : International Film Festival concludes in Madras.

Jan. 23 : Twenty AIADMK MLAs suspended from Tamil Nadu Assembly.

Jan. 24 : Noted Malayalam film director P.Padmarajan dies.

Jan. 25 : Bharat Ratna conferred on Morarji Desai, Ravi Naik Ministry sworn-in in Goa, Carnatic vocalist D.K. Jarayaman dies.

Jan. 26 : Baba Amte returns Padma Vibhushan and Padma Shri awards.

Jan. 30 : President's rule in Tamil Nadu following dismissal of DMK Government, Kerala's LDF sweeps district council elections.

February 8 : India and China sign trade protocol.

Feb. 9 : Thirteenth decennial census begins.

Table 1 (*Contd.*)

Feb. 13: Bihar Governor Mohammed Yunus Saleem dismissed, Bhishma Narain Singh appointed Tamil Nadu Governor following resignation of S.S. Barnala.

Feb. 15 : Fifteen people killed in Kalka Mail train accident near Allahabad.

Feb. 16 : Sitarist Balram Pathak dies.

Feb. 17 : Prime Minister Chandra Shekhar announces withdrawal of refuelling facilities to US war planes, Kannada film director N.L. Lakshminarayan dies.

Feb. 21 : Film actress Nutan passes away.

Feb. 27 : L. M. Singhvi appointed High Commissioner in London, Kalidas Samman announced for Padma Subramaniam.

March 5 : Pondicherry Assembly dissolved.

Mar. 6 : Prime Minister Chandra Shekhar resigns and recommends dissolution of Lok Sabha.

Mar. 10 : Veteran Gandhian Purabi Mukherjee dies.

Mar. 13 : Lok Sabha dissolved.

Mar. 14 : Mohammed Shafi Qureshi appointed Bihar Governor.

Mar. 15 : Lok Nath Mishra appointed Assam Governor.

Mar. 16 : Noted film director G. Aravindan dies.

Mar. 20 : S. N. Dwivedi appointed Governor of Arunachal Pradesh.

Mar. 22 : O.P. Chautala takes over as Haryana Chief Minister.

Mar. 23 : Ten people killed in bomb blast in Delhi.

Mar. 25 : Twenty-eight Air Force personnel killed in a plane crash near Bangalore.

Mar. 26 : Chautala Ministry reduced to minority.

Mar. 29 : Ustad Ali Akbar Khan to get Kalidas Samman.

Mar. 31 : West Bengal Assembly dissolved.

April 4: UP Assembly dissolved, Chimanbhai Patel launches Janata Dal-G.

Apr. 6 : Kerala Assembly dissolved.

Apr. 7 : Freedom fighter Kamlapati Tripathi dies, Telugu poet K.V. Kavi is dead, President's rule imposed in Haryana.

Apr. 9 : Fifty people killed in terrorist violence in Punjab, noted journalist Rajendra Mathur dies.

Apr. 11 : Centre decides to hold elections in Punjab and Assam.

Apr. 12 : Lok Sabha elections announced.

Apr. 17 : BJP allowed to use lotus symbol.

Apr. 24 : Poll dates for Punjab and Assam announced.

May 6 : More than 60 militants killed by Army in Jammu and Kashmir.

May 8 : Fifty people killed in cross firing in Jammu and Kashmir.

May 18 : Morarji Desai gets

Table 1 (*Contd.*)

Pakistan's highest civilian award, campaigning ends for Lok Sabha poll.

May 20 : About fifty people killed in poll violence.

May 21 : Rajiv Gandhi assassinated at Sriperumbudur.

May 22 : Second and third phase of elections postponed by 20 days, Communist leader S.A. Dange dies.

May 23 : Sonia Gandhi declines presidentship of Congress.

May 30 : Congress leader Uma Shankar Dixit dies.

June 5 : Air Marshal N.C. Suri appointed Air Chief.

June 12 : Fourteen people killed in Bihar poll violence.

June 15 : Murugan and Nalini, suspects in Rajiv assassination case arrested, militants kill 125 train passengers in Ludhiana.

June 17 : Bharat Ratna to Rajiv Gandhi and Sardar Patel.

June 20 : P.V. Narasimha Rao invited to form Government.

June 21 : Narasimha Rao Government sworn-in.

June 22 : Punjab Governor O.P. Malhotra resigns.

June 27 : L.K. Advani resigns New Delhi Lok Sabha seat, Sharad Pawar made Defence Minister.

June 28 : IOC executive director K. Doraiswamy kidnapped in Kashmir.

June 30 : Saikia Government sworn-in in Assam.

July 1 : Rupee devalued, 21 people kidnapped by ULFA.

July 3 : Rupee further devalued.

July 4 : Government announces new trade policy.

July 6 : Sonia Gandhi receives Bharat Ratna for Rajiv.

July 9 : ULFA kills Soviet engineer Sergei Grishenko.

July 10 : Shivraj Patil elected Lok Sabha Speaker.

July 15 : Narasimha Rao wins vote of confidence in Lok Sabha.

July 24 : New industrial policy announced.

July 25 : Twenty people killed in communal violence in Gujarat.

July 29 : K. Ramamurthy resigns as Labour Minister.

August 5 : Surendra Nath appointed Punjab Governor.

Aug. 8 : Indo-Soviet peace and friendship treaty renewed for another 20 years.

Aug. 13 : S. Mallikarjunaiah elected Lok Sabha Deputy Speaker.

Aug. 16 : Sixtynine people including former Manipur Chief Minister Tompak Singh killed in a plane crash near Imphal. Former Kerala Chief Minister C. Achutha Menon dies.

Aug. 21 : IOC executive director Doraiswamy released in Kashmir.

Aug. 29 : IRS-IB, India's second remote sensing satellite launched.

September 5 : Columnist Sharad Joshi Dies.

Table 1 (*Contd.*)

Sep. 7 : India recognises three Baltic republics.

Sep. 8 : T.S. Raju of ONGC and a mediator killed by ULFA.

Sep. 10 : Lok Sabha passes Places of Worship Bill, a number of dalits killed in Tsundur village of Andhra Pradesh.

Sep. 14 : Four diamond merchants kidnapped in Delhi.

Sep. 15 : Army deployed in Assam.

Sep. 18 : Parliament approves extension of President's rule in Punjab.

Sep. 22 : Actress Durga Khote dies.

Sep. 25 : Government amends reservation notification.

Sep. 28 : 37th Commonwealth Parliamentary Conference ends in Delhi. Trade Union leader Shankar Guha Niyogi murdered in Bhilai.

October 1 : Supreme Court declines to lift stay on implementation of Mandal Commission recommendations.

Oct. 3 : Supreme Court upholds the $ 470 million settlement in Bhopal gas leak case, former Governor G.D. Tapase dies, Ramnath Goenka, founder chairman of Indian Express group dies.

Oct. 5 : Ten people burnt alive at Bardol village in Karnataka.

Oct. 8 : B. B. Lyngdoh Ministry in Meghalaya loses confidence motion.

Oct. 9 : Romanian Charge d' Affaires in Delhi Liviu Radu kidnapped.

Oct. 10 : UP Government acquires 2.4 acre land in disputed Ayodhya shrine complex.

Oct. 11 : President's rule in Meghalaya. Nagpur Times resident editor R.N. Dubey shot dead.

Oct. 12 : Freedom fighter Biswanath Mukherjee dies.

Oct. 14 : O.V. Vijayan selected for Vayalar Rama Varma literary award, Dr N. K. Sehgal and Dr Iftimovici selected for Kalinga award.

Oct. 17 : Indira Gandhi award for national integration conferred on Rajiv Gandhi posthumously, more than 70 people killed in bomb explosions in Rudrapur, Nainital.

Oct. 18 : Former Minister K. Wakhloo and her husband freed from Kashmir militants.

Oct. 19 : Nine people killed and 86 injured in train accident at Pondugula station in South Central Railway, Prof. B.P. Pauthari, freedom fighter dies.

Oct. 20 : Hundreds of people killed in a severe earthquake in Uttarkashi, about 40 people killed in a fire in Gur Mandi in Ludhiana, vedic scholar Nookala Satyanarayana dies.

Oct. 24 : Urdu writer Ismat Chughtai passes away.

Oct. 26 : Twenty eight people killed in Punjab violence.

Oct. 27 : India repulses Pakistani attack in Kargil sector.

Oct. 30 : About 20 people killed in a Karnataka Express accident near Bangalore.

November 1 : Prof. Vinayak Gokak presented Jnanpith Award.

Table 1 (*Contd.*)

Nov. 2 : National Integration Council meets, surface to air missile Trishul successfully test flown.

Nov. 4 : Rikhi Jaipal, diplomat dies.

Nov. 6 : More than 30 people killed in Sura tragedy in Delhi.

Nov. 7 : Sura tragedy toll rises to 118.

Nov. 8 : At least 10 people were killed in a bomb explosion in a suburban train at Kalyan in Maharashtra, fourteen people killed in a bus accident in Hazaribagh, Bihar.

Nov. 9 : Ten people killed by militants in Sirsa, Haryana.

Nov. 12: Supreme Court upholds Anti Defection Law, Urdu poet Pannalal Srivastava passes away.

Nov. 13 : At least 10 people killed in fresh violence in Varanasi, Jawaharlal Nehru award for international understanding presented to Robert Mugabe, German Chancellor Helmut Kohl chosen for Jawaharlal Nehru Award for international understanding.

Nov. 15 : Eighteen people killed in cyclonic storm in Tamil Nadu.

Nov. 17 : Narasimha Rao wins Nandyal by-election by a huge margin, CPI-M leader A.B. Sawant dies, Asutosh Handoo, journalist dies.

Nov. 19 : Supreme Court bans employment of children in beedi manufacturing units.

Nov. 21 : Former Tamil Nadu Chief Secretary R. Nagarajan arrested.

Nov. 22 : Supreme Court quashes Cauvery ordinance of Karnataka Government, 61 people killed in a tanker accident near Dahanu, Maharashtra.

Nov. 25 : Justice K.N. Singh sworn in as Chief Justice of India, Centre accepts Supreme Court's opinion on Cauvery dispute, noted educationist V.V. John passes away.

Nov. 26 : Kidnapped Romanian diplomat L. Radu released.

Nov. 29 : About 10 people killed in spurious liquor tragedy in Rajkot.

December 5 : Government announces Legislative Assembly and Council of Ministers for Delhi.

Dec. 7 : Twenty five people killed in a train accident near Jwali, Himachal Pradesh.

Dec. 10 : Shiv Sena splits, socialist leader Pandit C.P. Pathak dies.

Dec. 11 : Chinese Premier Li Peng arrives in Delhi, twelve people killed in road accident at Mahuvej village near Surat, BJP chief M.M. Joshi starts Ekta Yatra from Kanyakumari.

Dec. 13 : Justice M.M. Kania sworn in as Chief Justice of India.

Dec. 14 : Satyajit Ray to get special Oscar award.

Dec. 16 : Death toll in December 13 Karnataka bandh rises to 16.

Dec. 17 : Fourteen people killed by terrorists in Terai region of UP.

Dec. 19 : Bomb blast kills 13 people in Ludhiana 10 police personnel killed by Naxalites in Ramavaram village in

Table 1 (*Contd.*)

Andhra Pradesh, O.R. Srivastava, journalist, dies in Lucknow, 14 people killed in a factory blast in Ahmedabad, freedom fighter Thotta Perumallu dies.

Dec. 21 : Parliament approves Delhi Assembly Bill.

Dec. 23 : Urdu writer Hussaini Shaidi dies in Hyderabad, 10 dalits killed in Gaya.

Dec. 24 : Indian Airlines chairman and managing director S.S. Ramdas resigns.

Dec. 26 : Terrorists gun down 60 train passengers in Ludhiana district, India recognises 12 Soviet Republics, Ajit Singh expelled from Janata Dal, N.S. Ramprasad, journalist, dies in Bangalore, President R. Venkataraman announces a voluntary cut of 10 per cent in his salary.

Dec. 27 : Governors announce 10 per cent cut in their salary, Ajit Singh announce plan to form a separate political party.

Dec. 28 : At least 10 people killed in a train accident at Vaswadi railway crossing near Surat.

Table 2 : Major Events in India in 1991 (When terrorists had an upper hand)

A chronology of major events that marked the year 1991 in India.

Jan. 7: M.M. Joshi replaces L.K. Advani as BJP president.

Jan. 11: Eight JD-S MPs disqualified for defection.

Jan 19 : Government outlaws NSCN and ULFA.

Jan. 22 : Two bombs explode in the police headquarters and court buildings in New Delhi, injuring 43.

Jan. 25: Forty-three-day Central rule in Goa ends as Ravi Naik sworn in as Chief Minister.

Jan. 30: President dismisses DMK Government in Tamil Nadu. Central rule imposed.

Feb. 17: Chandra Shekhar Government reverses stand on refuelling rights for Gulf-bound US warplanes.

Feb. 20 : JD's Government announces postponement of presentation of annual budget.

March. 4 : Interim budget shows Rs 9,977 crore deficit.

March. 5: Surveillance issue rocks JD-S-Congress ties.

March 6: President accepts JD-S Government's resignation.

March 8: Kashmir militants release national conference MP Saifuddin Soz's daughter, Nahida Imtiaz, after 10 days captivity.

March 13: Fifteen-month-old ninth Lok Sabha dissolved. Shekhar asked to continue as caretaker Prime Minister.

March 16: Malayalam film director G. Arvindan Dead.

March 20: Bansi Lal expelled from Congress -I for six years.

March 22: O.P. Chautala returns as Haryana Chief Minister.

March 23: Ten killed in twin bomb blast in West Delhi.

March 25: 28 IAF men killed in crash near Bangalore.

March 26: Chautala Ministry reduced to minority.

April 1: Militants abduct two Swedes in Kashmir.

April 3: V.C. Shukla rejoins Congress.

April 4 : UP Assembly dissolved. Cong-I withdraws support: Chiman Bhai Patel floats Janata Dal-G.

April 5 : Kerala Assembly dissolved.

April 6 : President's rule imposed in Haryana.

April 7 : Telugu actor Nageshwar Rao gets Phalke award.

April 12 : Election Commission announces poll dates.

April 13 : Arun Nehru, Arif Mohammad Khan quit JD.

April 17 : Chief Election Commissioner defers hearings in Lotus symbol freezing case. BJP allowed to use it in elections.

April 19 : President promulgates ordinance announcing tenth general elections and issues poll notification.

April 24: Sprint queen P.T. Usha weds. Poll dates for Punjab, Assam announced.

Table 2 (*contd.*)

April 26: 30,000 in fray as nominations close.

April 29 : With drawals close, 20,000 in fray.

May 6: Army kills 66 militants on the line of actual control at Chokibal Kashmir.

May 8: Fifty killed as security forces open fire on the funeral procession of a militant and return fire in Kashmir.

May 9: Fifty-hour army operation in Rataul village in Punjab ends with killing of eight hardcore Punjab militants held up there for a meeting.

May 13: Sudhir Kumar, MLA and son of Congress-I leader P. Shiv Shankar, released by his PWG kidnappers.

May 18: Morarji Desai gets Pakistan's highest civilian honour Nishan-e-Pakistan at his Bombay residence. Campaigning ends for 204 Lok Sabha seats that go for polling on May 20.

May 20: Fifty killed in violence in first phase polling.

May 21: Rajiv Gandhi assassinated by a woman wearing 'belt bomb' at Sriperumbudur, Tamil Nadu.

May 22: Second and third phase of polling postponed by 20 days to June 12 and 15. Veteran communist leader Shripad Amrit Dange dead.

May 23: Sonia Gandhi declines Congress-I presidentship.

May 24: Rajiv Gandhi cremated in New Delhi. Forensic experts discover that plastic explosive RDX strapped around a woman killed Rajiv.

May 27: P.V. Narasimha Rao emerges as Congress-I's consensus choice for party presidentship.

May 30: Congress-I veteran Uma Shankar Dixit dead.

June 1: Rajiv's assassin identified as Dhanu, an LTTE cadre from Vavuniya, Sri Lanka.

June 5: Air Marshal N.C. Suri new Air Chief.

June 6 and **8** : Polling held in Assam.

June 9: Forty die in record rainfall in Bombay and Thane.

June 12: Second phase polling for 113 seats held. Fourteen killed in poll violence in Bihar.

June 13: Director General Doordarshan, Shiv Sharma, shot at and injured by suspected Punjab militants in the Capital.

June 14: Nalini and Murugan, two suspects in Rajiv case arrested.

June 15: In the biggest shoot out in Punjab till date, Militants kill 125 train passengers in Ludhiana district. 25 killed in third and final phase of polling.

June 17: Rajiv Gandhi, Sardar Patel awarded Bharat Ratna.

June 20: Tenth Lok Sabha comes into being with Chief Election Commissioner's notification : President invites P.V. Narasimha Rao to form Government. Gives him four week to prove majority.

Table 2 (*contd.*)

June 21: Narasimha Rao Cabinet sworn in. Punjab elections postponed.

June 22: Punjab Governor, Gen.O. P. Malhotra, resigns.

June 25: Blast outside Capital's Indira Gandhi International Airport injures 13.

June 27: BJP leader L.K.Advani resigns New Delhi LS seat.: Sharad Pawar becomes defence Minster in Rao's Cabinet.

June 28: K. Doraiswamy, Executive Director of Indian Oil Corpn, kidnapped in Kashmir.

June 30: P. Shiv Shankar resigns as leader of Rajya Sabha: Saikia Government sworn in the Assam.

July 1: Government announces devaluation of rupee by 8.7 per cent to 9.7 per cent against four international currencies: Soviet marine engineer Sergie Grishenko and IOC and ONGC officials among 21 kidnapped by the ULFA in Assam.

July 3 : Rupee devalued by 10.58 per cent to 12.31 per cent against UD dollar taking the total two-dose devaluation to over 22 per cent; Israeli tourists Yair Yithaki set free.

July 4 : Government announces new trade policy.

July 6 : Swedish engineers Johan Johnson and Jan Ole Loman escape from the custody of Kashmir militants: Sonia Gandhi receives Bharat Ratna for Rajiv.

July 9 : ULFA kills kidnapped Soviet Sergie Grishenko.

July 10 : Shivraj Patil elected Lok Sabha Speaker.

July 15 : Rao Government wins trust vote in Lok Sabha.

July 16 : Railway budget proposes 10 per cent hike in freight rates.

July 18 : RBI admits sending 46.91 tonnes of gold to England to tide over BOP crisis.

July 24 : 1991-92 budget presented. New industrial policy announced.

July 25: Twenty killed in communal violence in Gujarat's Surendranagar district.

July 26: Key suspect in Rajiv case. N. Shanmugam, hangs himself to death. Twelve SIT men suspended.

July 28: President seeks Supreme Court's opinion on Cauvery issue.

July 29: Ramamurthi resigns as Labour Minister.

July 31: Two hundred killed in floods in Maharashtra, Gujarat.

Aug. 5: Surendra Nath appointed Punjab Governor.

Aug. 6: Government cuts down fertilizer subsidy and exempts small farmers from the hike.

Aug. 8: Indo-Soviet treaty for peace, friendship and cooperation extended by 20 years.

Aug. 9: Supreme Court upholds Chief Election Commissioner's decision to postpone Punjab polls.

Aug 12: Parliament approves

Table 2 (*contd.*)

TADA Amendment Bill extending the life of the Parent Act.

Aug. 13: BJP's S. Mallikarjunaiah elected Deputy Speaker.

Aug. 16: Former Manipur Chief Minister Tompak Singh among 69 killed in Indian Airlines air crash near Imphal: Kerala leader Achyuta Menon dead.

Aug. 21: K. Doraiswamy, IOC official abducted by Kashmir militants, freed after 54 days in captivity: Murugan an accused in the Rajiv Gandhi case, identifies Sivarasan and Subha.

Aug. 25: AIADMK and DMK win two seats each in Tamil Nadu Assembly by election.

Aug. 29: India's second remote sensing satellite IRS-IB launched successfully from Baikanur cosmodrome.

Sept. 5: Sharad Joshi, noted satirist and columnist dead.

Sept. 7: India recognises three Baltic republics.

Sept. 8: Meghalaya Speaker cancels special Assembly session where the Chief Minister was to seek a trust vote. : ULFA kills a second hostage, ONGC's T.S. Raju, and a mediator Bipul Mahanta.

Sept. 10: Lok Sabha passes Places of Worship Bill seeking to maintain status quo as Aug. 15, 1947, at all places of worship but for the Ayodhya shrine. Dalits killed in police firing on a mob in Tsundur village in Andhra Pradesh's Guntur district.

Sept. 12: Rajya Sabha passes Places of Worship Bill.

Sept. 14/15: Four Bombay-based diamond merchants abducted over two days in New Delhi.

Sept. 15: Army deployed in Assam to curb ULFA activities.

Sept. 18: Parliament approves extension of President's rule in Punjab saying polls must be held before Feb. 15, 1992.

Sept. 22: Veteran actress Durga Khote dead.

Sept. 23: Tassaduq Ahmed Deva, brother in law of Ghulam Nabi Azad, kidnapped by Kashmir militants.

Sept. 25: Rao Government issues notification amending the National Front Governments proposed 27 per cent reservations for SEBC adding ten per cent more for economically back wards: Mandal whips up passions again.

Sept. 28: 37th Commonwealth Parliamentary Conference ends in New Delhi with a call of expansion of UN Security Council: Shankar Guha Niyogi, well known trade union leader of Chhatisgarh, murdered at his residence in Bhilai.

Oct. 2: Punjab militants kill 26 relatives of policemen.

Oct 3: Supreme Court upholds the 470 million dollars settlement in Bhopal gas tragedy case and directs that prosecution against UCC be restarted.: Election Commission announces 16 Lok

Table 2 (*contd.*)

Sabha and 58 Assembly by election on November 15: Four Bombay-based diamond merchants, escape from the South Delhi hideout of their abductors.

Oct. 6: Eight securitymen killed as a pilot train derails after a blast blows up rail tracks on a drainbridge in the Amritsar-Jalandhar section.

Oct 7: Bashir Ahmed Rather, cousin of Ghulam Nabi Azad, abducted by Khwan-ul-Muslimeen Kashmir militants.

Oct. 8: Chief Minister B.B. Lyngdoh defeated in trust vote in Meghalaya Assembly.

Oct. 9: Liviu Radu, 52 year old Romanian diplomat, abducted in New Delhi.

Oct. 10: By-Poll rescheduled to November 26. U.P.'s BJP Government issues notification acquiring land housing the disputed shrine in Ayodhya.

Oct. 11: Meghalaya placed under Central rule. R.N. Dubey, Resident Editor of Nagpur Times, shot dead by a police S-I.

Oct. 17: Twin bomb blasts at Rudrapur Ramlila ground and nearby hospital kill 55.

Oct 18: Army raids a Kashmir militant hideout and rescues former J & K Tourism Minister Khemlata Wakhloo and her husband.

Oct. 20: Major earthquake rocks Uttarkashi area, killing at least 500.

Oct. 30: Twenty killed as Karnataka Express derails. Kar Sevaks hoist flags atop disputed shrine in Ayodhya, damage outer wall.

Nov. 1: Prime Minister presents 1990 Gnanpith award to Prof Vinayak Krishnan Gokak at Bombay.

Nov. 2: Lok Sabha poll in New Delhi countermanded.

Nov. 5: Sura, a methylated ayurvedic alcoholic mixture, kills 30 in the Capital on Diwali night.

Nov. 8 : Five killed in communal clashes in Varanasi.

Nov. 9 : Toll of sura victims rises to 184. Punjab militants massacre 16 in Sirsa, Haryana.

Nov. 13 : Ten killed in fresh violence in Varanasi.

Nov. 14 : Nehru Award for International Understanding for 1989 conferred on Zimbabwe Premier Robert Mugabe and for 1990 on German Chancellor Helmut Kohl.

Nov. 15 : Supreme Court orders UP Government to maintain status quo at Ayodhya.

Nov. 16: Four killed in Bihar as polling is held for bye-elections in 14 States.

Nov. 17: Prime Minister Narasimha Rao wins elections from Nandyal with a record 5.8 lakh vote margin.

Nov. 21: R. Nagarajan, former Tamil Nadu Home Secretary during DMK rule, arrested under TADA in connection with Rajiv murder case.

Nov. 22: Sixty-one people, mainly tribals, charred to death as a tanker

Table 2 (contd.)

carrying chemical catches fire in Maharashtra.

Nov. 25: K. N. Singh sworn in Supreme Court Chief Justice. Centre accepts Supreme Court's opinion on Cauvery issue. Karnataka files review petition.

Nov. 26: Kidnapped Romanian diplomat Liviu Radu returns home.

Dec. 1: Explosive device found on Air India plane.

Dec. 4: Manipur Chief Minister asks five Ministers in his coalition Ministry to resign.

Dec. 5: Government announces Legislative Assembly and Council of Ministers for Delhi. Promises elections within six to eight months.

Dec. 6: Janata Dal formally splits in Uttar Pradesh.

Dec. 7: 25 killed in train accident near Jwali, Himachal Pradesh.

Dec. 9: Manipur Chief Minister R. K. Ranbir Singh wins trust vote.

Dec. 11: Chinese Premier Li Peng arrives in Delhi. BJP president M.M. Joshi begins Ekta Yatra form Kanya Kumari.

Dec. 13. Madhukar Hiralal Kania sworn in Chief Justice of India.

Dec. 17: ULFA announces indefinite truce.

Dec. 19: ULFA release all hostages. Blast in Ludhiana kills 13.

Table 3 : Gulf war, Soviet events dominate 1991

The Year 1991 witnessed a war in the Gulf involving many countries, but the breaking up of the Soviet Union, triggered by the reforms of Mr Mikhail Gorbachev, were among major events making the year the most memorable in the recent past.

Although Mr Gorbachev plunged into oblivion by the end of the year, it remained to be seen whether he would stage a comeback or be dubbed in history as the destroyer of the powerful Soviet bloc or a saviour of suffering people.

An undeclared war in Yugoslavia, a civil war in nature, created tremors in the peaceful non-aligned European country during the year.

The year also witnessed restoration of peace in Cambodia and Angola and efforts to bring normalcy in West Asia.

Thousands of people lost their lives in earthquakes, plane crashes, cyclone and civil war during the year.

Following is the diary of important international events in 1991.

January 1: President Bush and Gorbachev condemn Iraqi conquest of Kuwait;

Jan. 5 : Soviet Union and Cuba sign agreement ending trade at easy terms;

Jan. 12: US Congress grants President Bush authority to use force to drive Iraq from Kuwait;

Jan. 13: UN Secretary-General Javier Perez de Cuellar meets Saddam Hussain in Baghdad; Soviet tanks attack Lithuanian TV station leaving 14 dead;

Jan. 15: UN deadline passes for withdrawal of Iraqi forces from Kuwait;

Jan. 16: US and coalition allies launch air strikes against targets in Iraq and Kuwait;

Jan. 17: Attack against Iraq intensifies;

Jan. 19: India launches peace initiatives to end the Gulf war;

Jan. 22: External Affairs Minister V.C Shukla holds talks with Yugoslav leaders on NAM initiative to end Gulf war;

Jan. 26: V.C. Shukla meets Iranian leaders in Teheran on Gulf war;

Jan. 29: V.C. Shukla meets Sri Lankan leaders in Colombo on Tamil problems.

February 1: Earthquake rocks Afghanistan and Pakistan killing about 200 People;

Feb. 2: India and China agree to resume border talks;

Feb. 8: India and China sign trade protocol in Beijing; Oil slick from occupied Kuwait hits Saudi coastline;

Feb. 12: Foreign Ministers of 15 Nonaligned countries meet at Belgrade to work out peace plan for Gulf;

Feb. 23: Prime Minister C. Choonhavan ousted in a coup in Thailand; Allied forces launch ground attack against Iraq;

Feb. 28: Saddam Hussain and Al-

Table 3 (*Contd.*)

lied forces suspend fighting and Iraq pledges to accept all UN resolutions on Kuwait; Bangladesh Nationalist Party of Begum Khaleda Zia emerges as largest party in Parliament elections.

March 2: Sri Lankan Defence Minister Ranjan Wijeratne killed in a bomb blast in Colombo;

Mar. 14 : Emir returns to Kuwait;

Mar. 17 : Union treaty is approved in nationwide referendum in Soviet Union;

Mar. 18 : Israel rules out return of Golan heights to Syria;

Mar. 19 : Begum Khaleda Zia appointed Bangladesh Prime Minister;

Mar. 21 : Saudi plane crashes killing 92 people;

Mar. 27 : Commandoes rescue passengers and crew of a hijacked Singapore airliner;

Mar. 29 : Italian Government collapses;

Mar. 30 : Israel restricts entry of Palestinians to Israeli territories.

April 16: Gorbachev arrives in Tokyo;

Apr. 24 : President R. Venkataraman arrives in Vietnam;

Apr. 29 : Venkataraman arrives in Manila;

Apr. 29 : Several thousand people killed in Bangla cyclone; Hundreds killed in Georgian earthquake.

May 1: Premier Hun Sen of Cambodia agrees for ceasefire;

May 2 : Pakistan lifts martial law;

May 5 : Foreign Minister of six Gulf Cooperation Council call upon UN to impose economic sanction against Iraq;

May 14 : Prime Minister K.P. Bhattarai resigns in Nepal;

May 16 : Soviet Union and China sign border agreement; First French woman Prime Minister Edith Cresson assumes office;

May 20 : UN sets a war damage fund;

May 21 : Rajiv Gandhi assassinated; Ethiopian President flees to Zimbabwe;

May 22 : Korean Prime Minister Ro Jai Bong resigns;

May 27 : Austrian Plane crashes in Thailand killing 223 people;

May 29 : G.P. Koirala Ministry sworn in Nepal;

May 31 : Angolan peace accords signed in Lisbon.

June 8: About 100 people killed in a train accident in Pakistan;

June 12 : Boris Yeltsin wins Russian Federations's first Presidential election; Former Bangladesh President H.M. Ershad sentenced to 10 years rigorous imprisonment;

June 13 : More than 165 Tamils killed in Batticaloa;

June 25 : UN team finds chemical weapon site in Iraq; Yugoslav republics of Slovenia and Croatia declare independence;

July 3 : Yugoslav military despatches troops and tanks to Croatia and Slovenia;

Table 3 (*Contd.*)

July 10 : President George Bush lifts sanctions against South Africa;

July 11 : Airliner carrying 264 Nigerian haj pilgrims crashes at Jeddah killing all aboard; Century's last eclipse of the moon;

July 17 : Prince Norodom Sihanuk announces that he will head Supreme National Council of Cambodia;

July 18 : US and Syria agree to terms for holding mideast peace talks;

July 23 : PLO announces Parliament in exile;

July 24 : Mozambiquan rebels kill about one thousand people in northern villages; Communist leaders approve Gorbachev's new party platform abandoning Marxist rule;

July 31 : Gorbachev and George Bush sign pact to reduce long range nuclear weapons at Moscow summit.

August 1: Israel accepts US formula for West Asia peace talks;

Aug. 10 : Serbs and Croats exchange prisoners for first time during their undeclared war;

Aug. 17 : Fighting shatters ceasefire in Croatia;

Aug. 19 : National state of emergency declared in the Soviet Union; Communist Junta removes Mr Gorbachev as President; Mr Yeltsin calls for general strike against coup;

Aug. 21 : Mr Gorbachev returns to Moscow after coup fails;

Aug. 24 : Mr Gorbachev resigns as Communist party chief;

Aug. 29 : Soviet law makers suspend Communist party activities and freeze its bank accounts;

Aug. 30 : Azerbaijan declares Independence;

Aug. 31 : Uzbekistan and Kirgizia declare Independence;

September 2 : US recognises Baltic republics;

Sep. 6 : Soviet union also recognises Baltic republics;

Sep. 9 : Soviet republic of Tadzhikistan declares Independence;

Sep. 15 : Sweden's social democrats suffer poll defeat;

Sep. 21 : Armenia votes for Independence;

Sep. 23 : Iraq detains UN officials in Baghdad and confiscates nuclear documents;

Sep. 25 : UN Security Council orders worldwide arms embargo against Yugoslavia;

Sep. 26 : Romanian Premier Petre Roman resigns following violent street protests; Rioting claims about 100 lives in Zaire;

Sep. 30 : Haitian President Jean Bertrand Aristide is ousted.

October 1: Twelve Soviet Republics agree to new economic union;

Oct. 4 : Member nations of Antarctic Treaty ban exploration of oil and minerals from the icy continent.

Oct. 5 : Indonesian Air Force plane crashes killing 132 people aboard;

Oct. 7 : Yugoslav Air Force jets rocket Croatia's presidential palace;

Table 3 (*Contd.*)

Oct. 14 : Myanmar's pro-democracy leader Aung San Suu Kyi wins nobel peace prize;

Oct. 17 : NATO decides to cut nuclear arsenal in Europe by 80 per cent;

Oct. 18 : Soviet Union and Israel restore diplomatic ties after 24 years; Mr Gorbachev and Presidents of eight Soviet republics sign treaty to create economic union;

Oct. 22 : Commonwealth summit ends in Harare;

Oct. 23 : Nineteen nations sign UN sponsored peace treaty for Cambodia;

Oct. 30 : West Asia peace conference begins in Madrid.

November 1: Kenneth Kaunda concedes defeat in Zambia's Presidential election;

Nov. 3 : Imelda Marcos returns to Philippines;

Nov. 5 : British publisher Robert Maxwell found dead; Kiichi Mayazawa becomes Japanese Prime Minister;

Nov. 6 : NATO leaders herald end of cold war at their summit in Rome; SAARC summit in Colombo postponed;

Nov. 12 : Troops in East Timor fire on pro-Independence demonstrators killing dozens;

Nov. 22 : Boutros Ghali of Egypt elected next UN Secretary-General;

Nov. 29 : Second summit of G-15 concludes at Caracas; Red Cross says clan battles in Somalia's capital of Mogadishu have killed more than 1,000 people;

Nov. 30 : Fighting escalates in Croatia.

December 1: Ukranians vote for Independence;

Dec. 4 : AP chief Middle East correspondent Terry Anderson freed by Shiite Muslim captors;

Dec.5 : Yugoslav President resigns;

Dec. 8 : Russia, Ukraine and Byelorussia form Commonwealth of Independent States and declare Soviet Union defunct;

Dec. 10 : Israeli and Arab negotiators resume peace talks in Washington;

Dec. 11 : European Community leaders agree to set up loose political federation with common foreign policy and single currency by 1999;

Dec. 12 : South and North Korea sign accord on non-aggression;

Dec. 15 : Egyptian Ferry sinks in Red sea killing 470 people;

Dec. 17 : Mr Gorbachev and Mr Yeltsin agree to dissolve Soviet Union and proclaim new commonwealth by year end;

Dec. 19 : Prime Minister Bob Hawke loses power in Australia;

Dec. 21 : Eleven former Soviet republics sign a commonwealth agreement;

Dec. 25 : Mr Gorbachev resigns as Soviet President;

Dec. 28 : Muslim fundamentalists secure overwhelming lead in Algeria's first free legislative election;

Dec. 30 : Leaders of new commonwealth agree to establish united command of nuclear weapons; car bomb in Beirut kills at least 30 people.

3

Lessons from Disintegration of USSR

3.01 Introduction

The comparative study of contemporary economic growth, level of civilization, living standard, freedom, liberty, coherence, in two distinct systems of social, economic and political governing of a country to the principles of capitalism and socialism, at least since World War II, will reveal the absolute truth that capitalism has assured better indicators than socialism. Similarly it is easier to manage capitalism than socialism. The socialism entrusts more power to head of the country than capitalism but execution of decisions concerning economic growth is more difficult in socialism than capitalism. The feeling of assumption that everything has to be done by the government prevails and with the result economic growth slows down. The rewarding individua-lism and entrepreneurship ensures the grassroot struggle for survival hence the free market, free trade, and freedom of choice prevail and favours surpassable growth in capitalism. The lessons from disintegration of USSR and working of socialism are numerous. To mention few are the followings:

1. Oppression of peoples's will through any kind or form of dictatorship is vice and won't last long amidst the contemporary democracy.
2. Economic and political crises are concomitant but intensity and eventualities differ depending upon the magnitude of dissent, awareness and participation of people.
3. Capitalism and imperialism have inherent nature and inate tendency of expansionism or they ought to be aggressive in

nature as a result potential to wipe out any other form of economic and political governing no matter whether it is in the form of socialism or communism. (It is a matter of time before the communism and socialism will be wiped out completely from the world.)

4. Democracy is media in which capitalism grows more faster than any other kind of media.
5. Resource allocation through soviet style planning has more hazards of bringing country at the doorstep of economic crisis inculcating inefficiency, protectionism of the capital intensive public sector and private sector industries.
6. Given them an opportunity, the people identified for quite long as a distinct race, colour, ethnic group, language, region or area would opt to declare independence, if the power was not equally distributed hitherto within such groups.
7. The ideology of "ablest and fittest to survive" has won over the ideologies of "unity is strength" or "work according to ability and get according to needs" or "cooperation for survival".
8. The natural way of governing the nation is through free economy, free trade, and democracy (or freedom, liberty and democracy) and not through dictatorship in any form or through the central authority.

Once the process of disintegration has initiated in any country, it would lead to plea for international aid. Both India and USSR have been facing financial crisis in 1991.

These countries were following the path of so-called planned economy to achieve socialist pattern of society, and lead to severe economic destability. The Soviet Union, once treated as economic and military super power had to seek international aid in 1991. Till November, 1991, the major offers of aid of Soviet Union were:

Sl. No.	*Country*	*Aid Amount (in billion $)*	*Remarks*
1.	European Community	2.4	Foreseeing the shortage in winter, for food and medical items, the package was devised.
2.	France	1.5	Of the aid amount, one third would be for food.
3.	Italy	2.0	Commercial loan

4.	Germany	400.0	Official financial commitment for loans, credit guarantee, etc. since 1989.
5.	United States	1.4 plus 2.5	To avoid famine

Thus, above $ 409.8 billion aid was necessary to avoid famine in the Soviet Union. Obviously, donor countries would like to ensure refund of their loans. This means asking the recipient country to take all measures as suggested by donor countries. With exception of Russia and Kazakhstan, all 13 former Soviet Republics have proclaimed (one after another) independence. Ukraine has 52 million population and thousands of nuclear weapons and strong industrial base. This catastrophic fall of USSR's economy has very pernicious effect on its credibility in international trade. In fact, the demise of USSR as super power on its disintegration has been very rapid as predicted on publication of Gorbachev's Perestroika. Even India's rupee currency had attained higher weightage in international market.

On December 6, 1991, just after a week of declaration of independence by Ukraine after breaking away from USSR, rouble, an official currency of USSR, has crashed drastically. The controlled exchange rate was 30 rupees to a rouble on December 6, 1991 but in open market, a rupee is sold for 4 to 5 roubles. This could be treated as wonder of economic crisis in USSR. A rouble was pegged with India's trade by USSR at an unreal exchange rate and it was arbitrary. The situation was aggravated in USSR due to inside problems due to fragmentation of USSR and advent of open economy in Soviet soil. The rupee is easily convertible to dollars. The Indian rupee may not be freely convertible in India, but it is convertible in the Soviet Union. People willing to buy the Indian rupee which is then smuggled through East Europe to the Persian Gulf where the rupee can be traded for US dollars—the ultimate dream currency for people in the Soviet Union.

The events in former USSR's Republics in forming a Commonwealth of newly independent Soviet Republics indicates that every society would like to regain its original position no matter how best is justified the post events order of the society. Even during revolution too, there aught to be forces resisting with their full vigour to retain the prerevolution position. In other words, we can conclude a hypothesis or a law that "every society is a product of long established customs, habits, traits, pattern of living, thinking and widely accepted societal harmony. It would like to continue in the same state despite its vices of orthodox, conventional, retarding, stagnant and non-progressive tendencies like myth, religion's dogma, indoctrination, rituals, traits and cults, unless it is overcome by new generation with overwhelming majority, zeal and vigour by taking into confidence both old and new generation."

Despite the fact that "unity is strength", the right to "self-determination" means isolating a segment of the population from "united" or "union" of states, etc. This kind of isolation by self created prudence under the name of "self-determination" would lead to self-imposed social, political, economic and financial crisis for the sake of acquiring leadership of the nation. Though all the Republics of Soviet Union have declared independence but majority of them have come to unite under different terms of Commonwealth. Suppressing the will of the people and suppressing the freedom of individual under Union; hence declaration of independence during the time of "Perestroika" of Gorbachev was obvious. But need to have coordination for collective security has made these independent 11 nations to form the Commonwealth. This clearly indicates the tendency to regain as far as possible the pre-revolution position. Though languages, ethnic aspects, geographic aspect differ but common behaviour of these nations is obvious.

3.02 Eclipse of Concept of Equality

Now, as both socialism and communism are on the verge of eclipse from globe, one can easily see its implication on the concept of equality. In fact, equality is generally referred to equality among equals. That is all doctorate degree holders are equal irrespective of a country, state or university or place, awarding such degree. Similarly, all master degree holders are equal, and so are bachelor's degree holders. But one cannot treat equal when the facilities are concerned. A doctorate in engineering or computer cannot be treated equal to doctorate in anthropology as far as knowledge is concerned. But for salary purpose, both doctorate should be paid equal as the duration of study is almost same. If such equality of pay is not maintained, none would like to study the branch of knowledge which is less paid. The manual labour should be paid equal irrespective of the nature of job. But skill required to perform some jobs differs with another job, therefore, the skill and experience makes the different wage structures.

The question of equal pay to barber and lawyer does not fit in economics, as division of labour or concepts of specialization will support the fact that one is semi-skilled manual labour and other is intellectual or brain work supported by university education. The western style education presupposes the illiterate man is irrational and to understand the ethics, philosophy and intricacies of civilization a man must be made rational, wise, and able to decode the written message, rules and laws of the society. The education is treated as an investment for future return. Though all men are born alike or all men are endowed with equal parts of body, or even though colour of blood flowing in the body of all men is red the eternal fact is that they differ in thinking capacity. No two men have identical thinking. Therefore, the main difference between the men is in terms of psychological factors and not in terms of physiological factors. The term equality refers to equality among the equals. It is psychological capacity which makes one bold enough to take quick decisions, risk and earn the profit. Therefore, conceptually equality breeds inequality on the ground of education, experience, skill, dexterity, intellectual content, brain work, psychological and physiological factors. Equality of opportunity and status cannot be guaranteed by law in a society dominated by inequality on account of education, experience, wealth inherited, high cost, master and slave tradition, peasants and workers, elite and rustic etc. Every society has both pleasant and unpleasant aspects in some proportion but in some societies like India unpleasant things are more than pleasant, may be due to underdevelopment. India is not only stagnant, orthodox, snake charmers' traditional and dead economy but also it continues to hold within all those characteristics to withhold such vices with inate tendency to perpetuate and foster hierarchial society. In such hierarchial society, not only casteism, dominance of one group by another, the implicit tendencies of anarchy and totalism proliferate, discrimination on the basis of caste proliferated and practice but also administration, organisational set up, bureaucratic and political functionism derive inspiration from compartmentalism, communal minded thoughts, violation of human rights, etc. The rank and file in offices still hold values of ancient cultural ethos, align themselves in groups, affiliate in a manner of official hierarchy, etc.

3.03 Capitalism Breeds Hierarchial System

Hierarchial society is a gift of capitalism in various forms. In fact, in hierarchial and stratified society, the preferential positions are preoccupied leaving the socially denounced, inferior, low paid, vulnerable and exploitative position for economically weak for furtherance of sublattice location through or for struggleful stratification. The most of the stratified positions in caste based society by birth but people are told as if those were success stories of struggle and outcome of brilliance, talent and hard work. The sporadic success stories of struggle and wealth of few individuals are wrongly projected and related or to assign the cause of economic opportunity available everywhere.

In a traditional, orthodox, feudal, caste based and capitalist society the relative positions are fixed. The capitalist society reinforces such stratified positions. Any country which accepts capitalist pattern of the development means that it accepts inequality to continue and weak or disable group have no place in the economic growth process. The hierarchial positions are fixed. These positions are not interchangeable. In caste system, the people are stratified due to birth alone and these castes are not interchangeable. Similarly, those occupations inherited from one generation to another are not interchangeable. A priest (treated in India as dignified and honourable caste by birth) no matter how poor, bad moral, ill character he may be, but he would never imagine to accept scavenger's job even if it is highly paid simply because it is supposed to be too low caste job in hierarchial society. Similarly a scavenger would never dare or would become a priest or would never accept as priest no matter how brilliant, pure, or learned (like Dr Ambedkar, who was the lone statesman, politician, academician, and intellectual of international level). This kind of social taboo, vice and discrimination exist in India as well as Indian kind of capitalism.

3.04 Starvation Amidst Plenty in India

Apart from frequent starvation in Kalahandi district of Orissa, Tripura State's tribals have been facing starvation. In fact, in Orissa too, the starvation deaths of tribals are of alarming nature.

According to press report of November 29, 1991 (Ref. The Hindustan Times, New Delhi, Saturday, November 30, 1991) "The horror of starvation in Tripura" had caused over 500 deaths due to starvation or hunger related diseases (HRD). It is very common for official sources to deny the press report and in this case, of starvation deaths in Tripura, too official sources assigned the probable cause of gastro-enteritis for such deaths not exceeding 200 numbers in Tripura State. Despite impressive growth of a nation, the remote villages in Tripura are inaccessible and distributive mechanism does not exist. "Owing to a peculiar set of circumstances, compound by corruption, official neglect and natural difficulties, it is almost impossible to deliver food to the remote hills or interior villages. In this situation, only emergency airlifting of food and other essentials by the centre had helped save thousands of tribals surviving on wild berries or snails, from certain death" says the press report. The starvation deaths in Tripura have been reported to have occurred in areas like Amarpur, Khowai, Sonamura and Gandacherra. Due to starvations, several unheard things have been practised by them to survive : the mothers selling their new born babies for as little money as Rs 50 in Sonamura and Gandacherra.

Deaths as "part of a seasonal phenomenon" has been proclamation of Chief Minister, Sudhir Ranjan Majumdar, says the press report. The Central help had been to increase the monthly supply of foodgrains to Tripura from 12,000 tonnes to 15,000 tonnes. The action taken by the State Government included increase in supply of ration by double its previous supplies, medicines and other measures.

But all these measures are ephemerals. Finding no way to earn money and failure of jhoom cultivation due to excessive rain, the mothers resorted to selling of children, women had to resort to prostitutional acts, people started begging and other immoral acts. The tribals like Reangs, Jamatias, Dabbarmas and Tripuras see vice in prostitution and begging making them to embrace death at first instance itself. People die both in home due to deprivation of food and on roads due to unability to exert after prolonged hunger. People going blind due to malnutrition, eating raw snails, roots and leaves of trees. No one dare to buy kerosene as it sells at Rs 15 to 20 a litre (i.e. more than 5 times its normal price) or equal to 4 kg. of rice to cook food.

3.05 Starvation and Subsidies (case of handloom sector)

Starvation in India has been prevailing at all time in every part of the country but officials try to deny both deaths due to starvation and deaths due to hunger related diseases. The second half of 1991 and beginning of 1992 has brought three states on the list of starvation, viz.: Orissa (particularly the district of Kalahandi), Tripura (particularly tribal community) and Andhra Pradesh (particularly handloom weavers). Starvation deaths in India during second half of 1991 and beginning of 1992 were concomitant with Crisis-91 in India. Concomitant with the drive for structural adjustment, reforms in economic and fiscal policies to overcome balance of payment crisis, liberalization of economy and trade etc. based on prescriptions of IMF to avail structural adjustment loan, India has been certainly concealing starvation, malnutrition, hunger, hunger related deaths, widespread tuberculosis, destituteness compelling people to commit suicide due to unability to purchase food adequate enough to keep soul and physical movement together not only for dependent family members but even for himself. Nevertheless, India continues to give false propaganda of her self-reliance, technological progress, success stories of literacy-drive, industrialisation, poverty eradication programmes, etc.

The handloom weavers in Andhra Pradesh have been victim of so-called modernisation programmes and mismanagement, faulty administrative policies, negligence by the government and vested interests. Instead of taking measures to avoid the deaths of remaining starving families, the officials have been searching loopholes in the terminologies of starvation, malnutrition, hunger and deaths related to these symptoms. The clinical definitions, and causes of starvation of deaths have been subjected to debates, or what causes death by starvation etc. were being debated. If postmortem report indicates not an empty stomach then the death was not attributed to starvation ignoring the act that over a month some man was starving. Press reports on January 10 to 12 indicate numerous facts of starvation deaths and cases dealt by the administration. At least ten districts namely Guntur, Prakasam, Krishna, Anantpur, Nellore, Vijaynagram, West Godavari, East Godavari, Nalgonda and Srikakulam districts of Andhra Pradesh have been seriously affected. According to press reports dated January 10, 1992, the total deaths recorded till December 15, 1991 were 113 nos. of handloom weavers. Till November 8, 1991, the number recorded was 73. Similarly, in 1989, over 50 deaths were recorded. The aggravation of this situation was due to "synchronisation with the world market, hiking yarn prices, turning a Nelson's eye to the onslaught of the powerlooms and textile mills as well as manifesting an attitude called indifference to the plight of the "under third". These are quite a few threads which go to make the weavers' tale" says the report of Chand Joshi of Hindustan Times dated January 10, 1992.

There are about 3.5 million looms (in handloom sector) supporting 17 million people, and thus next to agriculture sector. Seeing the pathetic conditions, as reported by Chand Joshi, the 77 year old Gandhian member of Rajya Sabha says : they have forgotten the weavers,... they tried even to ignore my presence in Parliament for well over a year because I am a weaver... it is with a great deal of effort that I could make our voice heard in the Rajya Sabha... the State government is quietly of callous indifference if not of natural surrender to the mills... they tell us that if yarn is diverted to the handloom sector, there will be large scale unemployment of mill labour... they are willing to condemn the self-employed weavers to perdition... the government itself asked the mills to reserve 50 per cent of the production for the handloom sector—almost every single mill defied it. Has the government taken any action? They talk of removal of subsidies but more subsidies are paid to lesser number of mill workers in the NTC mill..."

In a bid to reduce budgetary deficit, Central Government removed 20 per cent subsidy on hank yarn supplied to weavers' cooperatives and imposed a 7 per cent tax as a measure to earn tax. Andhra Pradesh Government withdrew its subsidy on 40 count yarn and reduced its commitment to the Janata Cloth Scheme by 50 per cent. This sharp increase in yarn prices because of the budgetary levies was given an upward push by shortage created by export and creation of an artificial crisis by the yearn manufacturers lobby. The prices of yarn were beyond reach of poor weavers. In the first week of January 1992, the prices prevailing were :

(1)	40s count Rs	220	to	300
(2)	60s count Rs	400	to	500
(3)	80s count Rs	550	to	650
(4)	100s count Rs	700	to	810

The twin problems comprising higher prices of yarn and government's refusal to buy the handloom cloth from weavers have aggravated the situation. The average monthly earnings of weaver family have been reported within the range of Rs 450 to 500 (for example, for 26 metres of shirting the weaver family unit gets Rs 90 and average time taken is a week).

3.06 Subsidy

It can be defined in two ways :

(i) Long run cost of products or services to government less prices at which these products or services made available to consumers or beneficiaries. That is difference between cost of production and selling prices. This difference arises due to pricing policy of the government, wherein government stipulates prices at which goods or services can be sold to consumer. The manufacturer, therefore, claims upon subsidy to overcome losses out of such pricing policy. It is assumed that manufacturing cost is higher than the selling price.

(ii) When public sector and private sector both are manufacturing identical items, government proposes the selling prices and it then affects the private sector in a situation in which equivalent services would have been provided by the private sector. This comprises pricing subsidy plus difference in cost between private and public provision of the service.

The subsidy also plays as protection for domestic industries against the import from international manufacturing industries. The multinational companies have advantages of economies of scale and have global market. Therefore, the prices of items manufactured by such MNC are less than those manufactured in developing countries. The need for import substitution and developing domestic industrial base justifies the manufacturing of items at low level and obviously cost of manufacturing is higher than price of same item in international market. Over and above, such price difference government announces the selling price of items to safeguard consumers. Therefore, subsidy has to be provided on such items.

By implication, benefits of subsidy do not reach the consumers but it is meant for producers and traders. The subsidies go on increasing and have become a part of manufacturing activity during industrialisation.

Towards liberalising of Indian economy, various steps have been initiated in July and August, 1991. The pricing policy of fertiliser was also reviewed. In fact, subsidy on fertilizer varies from 50 per cent to 100 per cent depending upon States, micronutrients, small and marginal farmer, etc. The Central subsidy on food and fertilizers for the period from 1978-79 to 1989-90 is as follows:

Table 1: Food subsidy

Year	*Food Subsidy*	*Subsidy on fertiliser*		
		Imported	*Domestic prod.*	*Total*
1978-79	5694	1710	1722	3432
1979-80	6000	2820	3208	6028
1980-81	6500	3350	1700	5050
1981-82	7000	1000	2750	3750
1982-83	7110	550	5500	6050
1983-84	8350	1480	9000	10480
1984-85	11010	7273	12000	19273
1985-86	16500	3237	16000	19237
1986-87	20000	1871	17000	18871
1987-88	22000	1140	20500	21640
1988-89*	22000	2500	30000	32500
1989-90@	22000	5300	31210	36510

@ = Budget Estimates
* = Revised Budget Estimates

Source: Fertiliser Statistics, 1988-89; Fertiliser Association of India, New Delhi; pp I-171.

The benefits of subsidy on fertiliser and food do not reach the poorest of poor or small and very small farmers. Therefore, withdrawal of subsidy on fertilisers is always pleaded with. To withdraw subsidy may have detrimental effect on production and distribution of fertiliser.

3.07 Prices of Fertilisers

Both nitrogenous and phosphate (np) and npk fertilisers were brought under statutory price control w.e.f. February 2, 1979. Depending upon the grade, the prices of fertiliser are fixed. For instance, urea ammonium phosphate of three different grades were priced as follows:

Table 2: Prices of Fertilisers

Date	*Maximum selling price for a 50 kg packing*		
		Grades	
	24-24-0	*28-28-0*	*14-35-14*
2.2.1979*	1950	2340	2230
10.3.1979**	1950	2200	2100
8.6.1980***	2600	3050	2900
11.7.1981	3050	3600	3400
29.7.1981	2800	3350	3150
31.1.1986 (in effect)	3050	3600	3400

Notes:

Prices of Fertiliser are exclusive of central & state sales tax and local taxes as shown below:

* Inclusive of 15% excise duty + 5% Auxiliary duty + special duty on excise duty w.e.f. March 1, 1978

** Inclusive of 7.5% excise duty + Auxiliary duty + 5% special duty on excise duty w.e.f. March 1, 1979

*** Excise duty; Auxiliary duty and special duty withdrawn on all fertiliser w.e.f June 7, 1980 except ammonium sulphate and calcium ammonium nitrate in which case also it was withdrawn w.e.f. Feb 28, 1983

(Source: Table 8.02 of Fertiliser Statistics 1988-89 published by FAI, pp I-145)

The Union Budget for the year 1990-91 states that : "33. In so far as fertiliser subsidies are concerned, with effect from this evening (i.e. July 24, 1991), low analysis fertilisers such as calcium ammonium nitrate, ammonium chloride, ammonium sulphate and sulphate of potash will be free from price and movement controls. There will be an increase of 40 per cent, on an average, in the price of all other fertilisers. In addition, in respect of single super phosphate, there shall also be a ceiling on the subsidy per tonne payable to producers so as to move towards total deregulation in the next few years; this should act as an incentive for all high cost units to reduce costs and improve efficiency. The necessary notifications in this regard are being issued separately, today, by the Ministry of Agriculture.

34. The economic rationale for an increase in the price of fertilisers is so obvious that it does not need to be stated. Nevertheless, I would like to draw the attention of the House to the fact that there has been no increase in fertiliser prices since July, 1981. In these ten years, there has been a continuous increase in the procurement prices of paddy and what, as also in the market prices of other crops, received by the agricultural sector. Farmers will be compensated for the proposed increase in the prices of fertilisers through suitable increase in procurement prices."

From the above text, it will be clear that subsidies on fertilisers were withdrawn and 40 per cent price increase was effected. Perhaps, it was heavy dose on poor farmers. There was dual pricing concept on fertiliser. The international prices of fertiliser were too low as compared with domestically produced fertiliser. The international competitive prices through domestic production and withdrawal of subsidies were somehow stated to be related.

3.08 Dual Pricing

That is, fertiliser sold at controlled prices plus availability of fertiliser in open market. In other words, most of the requirement of fertiliser be met through controlled market and rest of the requirement through open market. The three steps, as suggested by Yoginder K. Alagh (The Hindustan Times dated August 14, 1991) comprised of:

1. Small and marginal farmers in rainfed and dry districts should get nitrogenous fertilizers at subsidised rates up to say 40 kg./ hectare of owned land and balance fertiliser should be marketed in the open market.
2. Instead of individual retention or control prices which encourage inefficiency and corruption, fertiliser companies should get group retention prices, i.e. normative efficiency price separately worked out or gas, FC, LSHS, Naptha and coal feedstock based companies, with the open market price regulated through imports to correspond with weighted average group realisation from the subsidised and open market price.
3. Once the transitional problems of individual factory level price control as at present are resolved and the world price falls as the "Middle East" effect wears off, to implement a tariff regulated price with say a 45 per cent protection to be tapered down."

The implication of such dual pricing would be, as envisaged by Dr Y.K. Alagh in his article Fertilizer Pricing (Hindustan Times dated August 14, 1991, pp. 11) are:

(i) At the farmer level, it is genuinely promotional rather than a giveaway. It is sensible to target the subsidy at less endowed farmers and through time, only at poor farmers in poor regions. The "administrative" problems are no more complex than a list of other credit, input and investment support schemes for small and marginal farmers. Some poor farmers will sell their quota, as in the case of urban consumers selling sugar, rations but will get an income return.

(ii) The group retention prices fertiliser companies will get powerful incentives to reduce material and energy costs. Output above their levy percentage will be sold in the open market at a higher price. This will be a powerful incentive to increase capacity use and reduce energy cost. Plant level research shows that a 10 per cent increase in capacity utilisation leads to a 3 per cent to 5 per cent fall in energy consumption per tonne of ammonia produced. This leads to a powerful cost reducing effect and the need for subsidy will fall in a few years.

(iii) The policy moderates the powerful output controlling effect of a single price regime. Kirit Parikh and Narayana have reported that a 30 per cent price rise by itself would reduce wheat and rice endangering by 13 per cent thus output would go down by 15 million tonnes endangering the nation's food supply. The dual pricing policy would encourage producers whose output response rates for fertilizers are the best. In fact, the shortfall in protected fertilizer demand should not be more than half a million tonne, or around 5 to 8 per cent. According to Bhalkla Alag estimates based on experience of 280 districts across a decade, a 10 per cent decline in fertilizer application per hectare leads to a 2.5 per cent decline in agricultural yield for all crops. Thus, the output contracting effect of the present policy should at the outside be around 1.0 million tonnes of grain and much smaller amounts of other crops, which can be made up by other measures.

(iv) The policy makes a beginning of the transition to a globally competitive fertilizer producing and distribution regime which should be our objective in the next three to five years. The

Indian farmer is entitled to the best quality product at the cheapest possible price in the world.....

However, Central Government has announced the guidelines on August 14, 1991, exempting the small and marginal farmers from the price increase in fertilisers, over-ruling objections from the States on the dual pricing policy. According to guidelines dated August 14, 1991, the States have been given fixed amount for subsidising the fertilizers for the small and marginal farmers, but they would have some flexibility in developing systems of reimbursement to these farmers. The reimbursement, however, would be related to identification proof of purchase, area held, previous use and the quality of fertilisers available in a given area for subsidised supply.

The revised prices of fertilizers came into effect on August 14, 1991 and 30 per cent hike was agreed to (as against 40 per cent proposed in the Budget).

3.09 Non-plan Expenditure and Subsidies in India

Let us have a look at non-Plan expenditure of the Central Government. The Budget Estimate of 1990-91 indicates the non-Plan expenditure of Rs 68843 crores on the following heads :

Table 3 : Non-Plan Expenditure (Rs Crores)

Sl. No.	*Items*	*Budget 1990-91*	*Revised 1990-91*	*+Increase —Decrease*
1.	Interest Payment	20850	21850	1000
2.	Food Subsidy	2200	2450	250
3.	Subsidy on Indigenous Fertiliser	3250	3650	400
4.	Export Promotion and Market Development Assistance	2316	2700	384
5.	Scheme for Debt Relief to Farmer	1000	1500	500
6.	Defence Pension	1500	1670	170
7.	Loans to States Against :			
	i) Small Savings Collections	4500	6770	2270
	ii) To cover with RBI deficits	0	521	521
8.	Technical Credits to Foreign Govt.	350	1150	800
9.	Non-Plan Loans to Public Enterpr.	969	1070	101
10.	Police	1394	1581	187
11.	Write-off Loans to States	96	966	870
12.	Badarpur Thermal Power Stations	288	348	60

13.	Gulf Evacuation	0	300	300
14.	Postal Deficit	84	150	66
15.	Punjab Action Plan	20	79	59
16.	Conversion of Loans to Equity in Respect of Shipping Corporation of India	0	191	191
17.	Others	30026	29815	—211
	Total	68843	76761	7918
	Central Plan	17618	17594	—24
	Central Assistance to States and U.T. Plans	12848	12362	—486
	Grand Total	99309	107717	7408

Total subsidies were of the order of Rs 8, 516 crores in 1990-91 (B.E.) which were raised to 9550 (1990-91 R.E.) as a part of non-Plan expenditure, which comprises :

Table 4: Details of Subsidies

	Rs. Crores	
	1990-91 BE	*1990-91 RE*
Major subsidies:	8, 516	9550
A. Food Subsidy	2,200	2450
B. Fertiliser Subsidy:	4,000	4400
a. Indigenous Fertiliser	3,250	3650
b. Imported Fertiliser	750	750
C. Export Promotion	2,316	2700
Total (A+B+C):	8,516	9550
Debt Relief to Farmers	1000	1500
Interest Subsidies	391.29	378.65
Other Subsidies	716.38	692.36
Total Subsidies	10623.67	1212.01

Apart from Rs 8,516 crores (1990-91 BE) as subsidies, the provision for subsidies during the same year for railways and handloom was as follows :

Sector	*Subsidy*
A. Railway	Rs 278.75 crores
B. Mill Made and Handloom Cloth	Rs 230.50 crores
C. Interest on Subsidies	Rs 391.29 crores
Total:	Rs 900.54 crores

The details of interest subsidy are as follows :

Table 5 : Interest Subsidies in India (Rs crores)

Sl. No.	*Name of Public Enterprises etc.*	*Budget 1990-91*	*Revised 1990-91*	*Budget 1991-92*
1.	Garden Reach Ship Builders & Engineers	4.64	4.64	0.00
2.	Mazagaon Dock Ltd.	15.35	15.35	0.00
3.	Coal India Ltd.	58.08	58.08	58.08
4.	Industrial Reconstruction Bank of India	2.00	2.00	5.00
5.	Gaon Banks	0.10	0.10	0.10
6.	Denotified Sugar Undertakings	0.10	0.10	0.00
7.	Khadi and Village Industries Commission	34.00	34.00	34.00
	(a) For Khadi Industries	23.00	23.00	23.00
	(b) For Other Village Industries	11.00	11.00	11.00
8.	Burn Standard & Co. Ltd.	5.70	5.70	5.70
9.	Tungabhadra Steel Products Ltd.	0.48	0.48	0.48
10.	Interest Subsidy to Press Trust of India	0.05	0.03	0.03
11.	Bharat Refractories Ltd. (IFICO)	1.63	1.63	0.00
12.	Bharat Gold Mines Ltd.	14.00	0.00	0.00
13.	Hindustan Antibiotics Ltd.	5.15	5.15	0.00
14.	National Textile Corporation	230.00	229.68	210.00
15.	Binny & Co.	0.01	1.17	2.16
16.	Heavy Engineering Corporation	20.00	20.00	0.00
	Total — Interest Subsidies	391.29	378.11	315.55

According to scheme of subsidy which is aimed at financing from the proceeds of additional excise duties levied in textile and textile articles, the consumer is supplied with mill made controlled cloth and also dhoties and sarees produced in the handloom sector at subsidised rates. The subsidy is at Rs 2 per sq. metre for dhoties and Rs 1.5 per sq. metre for long cloth and upto Rs 3.70 per sq. metre for polyester cloth blending shirting. The scheme is to cover 700 million sq. metre of cloth in 1990-91. The provision for subsidy on handloom cloth is Rs 220.50 crores, while that for mill made cloth is Rs 10 crores. Out of Rs 220.50 crores as handloom subsidy in 1990-91 budget, the special rebate on handloom cloth was Rs 50 crores and subsidy on Janata Cloth was Rs 169 crores. The revised expenditure on subsidy on handloom sector in 1989-90 was special rebate on handloom cloth was Rs 45 crores and subsidy on Janata Cloth was Rs 110 crores and other subsidy was

Rs 2 crores. Apart from above subsidy, the price support on jute was Rs 12 crores each in 1989-90 and 1990-91 and Rs 20 crores on cotton. Subsidy on mill made cloth was Rs 10 crores in 1989-90 and 1990-91.

The percentage share of each category of nonplan expenditure is as follows:

Table 6 : Per cent Share of Different Items of Total Non-plan Expenditure

Sl. No.	Items	Budget 1990-91	Revised 1990-91	+Increase —Decrease
1.	Interest Payment	21.00	20.47	13.50
2.	Food Subsidy	2.22	2.30	3.37
3.	Subsidy on Indigenous Fertiliser	3.27	3.42	5.40
4.	Export Promotion and Market Development Assistance	2.33	2.53	5.18
5.	Scheme for Debt Relief to Farmer	1.01	1.41	6.75
6.	Defence Pension	1.51	1.56	2.29
7.	Loans to States Against:			
	i) Small Savings Collections	4.53	6.34	30.64
	ii)To Cover with RBI Deficits	0.00	0.49	7.03
8.	Technical Credits to Foreign Govt.	0.35	1.08	10.80
9.	Non-plan Loans to Public Enterpr.	0.98	1.00	1.36
10.	Police	1.40	1.48	2.52
11.	Write-off Loans to States	0.10	0.91	11.74
12.	Badarpur Thermal Power Stations	0.29	0.33	0.81
13.	Gulf Evacuation	0.00	0.28	4.05
14.	Postal Deficit	0.08	0.14	0.89
15.	Punjab Action Plan	0.02	0.07	0.80
16.	Conversion of Loans to Equity in Respect of Shipping Corporation of India	0.00	0.18	2.58
17.	Others	30.23	27.94	—2.85
	Total	69.32	71.93	106.88
	Central Plan	17.74	16.49	—0.32
	Central Assistance to States and U.T. Plans	12.94	11.58	—6.56
	Grand Total	100.00	100.00	100.00

The total provision of 7.82 per cent was made in 1990-91BE and it was 8.25 per cent in 1990-91 RE revised. The details of demand for grant of Ministry of Textiles will indicate that handloom subsidy itself is above 200 crores as shown below:

Table 7 : Handloom Subsidy

	1990-91BE	*1990-91RE*	*1991-92BE*
1. Special Rebate on Handloom cloth	50.00	50.00	65.00
2. Subsidy on Janta Cloth	169.00	136.00	137.91
3. Others	1.50	1.76	2.09
Total	220.50	187.76	205.00
4. Centrally Sponsored Scheme in Handloom	20.50	16.50	18.60
5. Other Handloom Scheme	23.36	20.70	33.65
Total Handloom Subsidy	264.36	224.96	257.25

As these schemes are supposed to help poor population below poverty line and engaged in handloom sector the amount spent on subsidies should not allow to aggravate the situation. The poverty line in India is defined as per capita monthly expenditure of Rs 131.8 for rural areas and Rs 152.13 for urban areas at 1987-88 prices. That is if a poor is able to earn Rs 131.8 and spend the same amount on consumption expenditure then he is not considered to be poor in rural areas. Obviously the estimated subsidies of Rs 264.36 crores on handloom sector as proposed in 1990-91 BE should help eradicate poverty of ($264.36 \times 10^7 / 152.13 \times 12 =$) 1448103.596 people or say feeding or meet food consumption expenditure or removal of poverty of about 14.4 lakh in a year if there is foolproof arrangement. Even if there are some "transmission losses" at least 150 lakhs people could be removed from the poverty.

Now where does such huge amount of subsidy goes ? If starvation occurs despite such a large amount of food subsidy and subsidy on handloom sector then who has to be blamed? Obviously corruption is at threshold in India. The scheme for debt relief to farmers with Rs 1,000 crores Budget provision in 1990-91 indicates political decision to import benefits to rich farmers. Similarly, fertiliser subsidy of Rs 3,250 crores in 1990-91 is aimed at fostering the rich industrialists. The scheme for export promotion and market development assistance with Rs 2,316 crores is to allow lavish expenditure of rich and white collar job people. Similarly, if we see the losses incurred by public sector enterprises, it will reveal that government is willing to pay exorbitant salary to educated employed in public sector by keeping millions destitutes, in squalor, hunger and starving. The losses incurred by some of the companies can be cited as an example:

Table 8 : Some of the Loss Making Public Sector Enterprises

	Rs Lakhs (+ profit/—loss)			
Name of the Company	*1980-81*	*1984-85*	*1986-87*	*1987-88*
1. Burn Standard Co.	—921	314	34	—1079
2. Cycle Corp. of India	—85	—855	—1034	—1210
3. National Bicycle Corporation India Ltd.	—225	—435	—604	—649
4. Braithwaite	—856	—589	—678	—892
5. Scooter India Ltd.	—490	—1380	—2335	—2712
6. Triveni Structurals	—353	—166	—186	—409
7. Cement Corporation of India Ltd.	—39	—165	—2102	—597

Like above loss making industries, there are numerous other government enterprises both in the control of Central Government and different States. But government do not want to spend a single paisa for the poor! How strange! It is really a mockery of economic development initiated in the name of poverty eradication. It is a process of cheating poor in whose name the investment of Rs 71,299 crores has been invested in 231 public sector units. It is sheer mismanagement and organised way of stealing the resources meant for poorest of poor. Even if a single person dies of hunger, then such investment is meaningless.

3.10 Sources of Corruption

There are various sources which contribute to increase in corruption. The quality of life, human value, morale values, discipline, integrity and honesty etc. are the factors which determine the commitment to nation, people and services. In economic sense, the sources of corruption are :

1. Faulty economic planning
2. Dual pricing policy and element of subsidy

3. Difference in quality and prices of products meant for domestic and international market
4. Too much control mechanism, licensing and inspectioning agencies
5. Too much state intervention causing imperfect market and haphazard growth
6. Corrupt legal, bureaucratic and administrative channels
7. Low salary structure, employment wages, unemployment, large number of dependents on earning members i.e. the relationship between total earnings and obligatory liability of dependent family members resulting in gap between wants and gets
8. Inequality of status, opportunity, distribution of income, etc.
9. Unrealistic allocation of resources.

The process called structural adjustment has direct impact on employment generation. No doubt, governments' (both at the Centre and at the State level) expenditure need to be curbed but who will be affected most? Obviously, the new job seekers, young and energetic people. On one side, the need for human resource development and on other side, the need for cutting expenditure; on one side need for better, effective and job-oriented education and training whereas other side restrains the expenditure on education and training, etc. All such juxtapositions do not go side by side in ideal situation but these have become the way of managing the economy. The option should be to select the best way of management rather than choice between them or trade off among the alternatives.

4

Vice in Economic Planning Process

4.01 Introduction

Planning process as seen in SAARC countries in general has identical approach. In 1950s all the developing countries were asked to adapt development plans to identify both priorities and needs for external assistance, aid, and mobilization of resources etc. The process of resource allocation was christened as planning process. India despite admirable progress has ultimately fallen into debt trap, economic crisis, crisis of BOP etc. So could be the fate of other SAARC countries at one or other time. Similarly the USSR has ultimately shattered despite its major base of industrial and agricultural sector. The planning process is said to be gift of USSR to achieve socialistic pattern of society but as practiced in India one can suffer from one of the major drawbacks that under the pretext or in the name of managing the economy with scarce resources, it creates a subsidies prone economy and gives an impression as if planning is devoid of foresightedness and blind to realities of dynamic society. By implication of lower targets, low level of investment, low level of inputs etc., Indian economy is wantonly retarded. The scarcity of resources, inefficient utilisation, inadequate accountability and low level of targetting has resulted in scarcity of everything. Both demand and supply side of economy are subjected to suppression hence suppression of reality. Instead of managing scarcity planning has caused planned scarcity of inputs, goods, services and dislocated circular flow at the grass root. Such planned scarcity has resulted in emergence of parallel economy, corruption, inefficient public enterprises, fostering the elite class, fostering sick enterprises etc. to retard free movement of goods, services and resources. Eventuality of such acts is retarded economic growth, accelerated economic crisis due to balance of payment deficit, continued reliance on export of primary products and goods alone. By implication, planning plays with both the life style of poor, (hungry or economically weaker section) and scarce resources of the country. Like luxury expenditure on science and technology infrastructure, planning too is a luxuriuos tool.

Earlier, for everything that was proved wrong, the blame was assigned to inefficient government or politicians. But decision-making in most of developing countries is guided by the hierarchial system. Most of the hierarchial positions are occupied by the incumbents elevated from one level to other or brought from outside as experts or Advisers or Consultant and interestingly therefore, irrespective of political set up or government such hierarchial position holders remain in the government's decision-making system. These people like shadow politicians, and proxy for politicians and being pseudo-intellectuals are always party to justifying as well as getting accepted wrong decisions and also such wrong decisions are getting implemented through various levels. The upward mobility through promotions, rewards, awards, prizes, etc. continues for such pseudo-intellectuals or pseudo-bureaucrats irrespective of their capability or commitment to national goals, etc. There is gross mismanagement as wrong people are assigned the task of economic analysis and resources allocation.

In hierarchial system, next to bureaucrats are imitators of bureaucrats like economists and engineers, occupying lower levels of decision-making. By virtue of more prominence to economic development and economic problems, the professional attached to decision-making bodies pretend like intellectuals and bureaucrats. These people are mostly opportunists with vested interest. Without sharing or accepting any responsibility, these people act like an invisible hand, or shadow prices to eventually distort the whole planning process. The nepotism, sycophancy, flattery and other such vices are at the threshold in planning process. As once a mighty nation like USSR could disintegrate one can easily conclude that the fate of all the countries following socialistic ideals and planning process as its instrument could be obvious. India's economic crisis and USSR's demise was concomitant but India could survive as it had capitalistic base alongwith lipstick of socialistic ideals. The four decades of planning not only in India but also in other countries is enough period to evaluate its merits, demerits, limitation and usefulness.

Planning process presupposes that a country has to pass through some stages of development. By implication of resource allocation process it also presupposes black box approach. The solutions to domestic problems of developing countries in general and solutions to their specific domestic problems have never came from any of the plan document; therefore it presupposes that solutions to all problems of poor countries have to come necessarily from developed countries but those are to be restated and justified in plan documents. The things written in plan document have no coherence with the world development or contemporary events of the world. It is like an imaginary and wishful thinking without any basic or fundamental research. Say for example India's planning process is in existence for over 42 years but it has not done any research or created any meaningful model of its own to keep nation ahead of her contemporary nation. What had been achieved is due solely to international agreements, technology transfer, installation of imported capital goods, manufacturing the items of which technology transfer was made by developed countries etc. But unfortunately, instead of realising the imported input content (in terms of transfer of technology, capital goods, training of personnel, foreign aid etc.), the development in India is attributed to planning process which is wrong, and this success would have been achieved without existence of such elite body. Now the questions are asked will it matter if planning process in India is abolished. Justifying the wrong things is very common for those who hold the higher position, therefore those occupying the seat of power would justify the role of planning but seen from World Bank angle planning process creates the impediments and hurdles and undue interference in working of public sector enterprises, and cause for loss making public sector units is planning process and none else.

4.02 Planning — Retrospection

The USSR, founder of economic planning, has collapsed through the process of planning itself. Planning process breeds corruption, inefficiency and initiates a mechanism of economic crisis requiring frequent revision of policies, goals and prices. Prices of essential commodities increase continuously. Where partial control over pricing mechanism exists and market forces act to counteract the statutory prices, the whole economy is distorted.

That is, planning process which is supposed to avert economic crisis through well intended actions, acts to counter-produce the effect of accelerating economic crisis. That is why, Russia has totally shattered, and India is another country to fall in trap of economic crisis. Even when there was high production of foodgrain and growth in industrial production, the prices of all commodities, industrial goods and services rose continuously in the year 1990-1991, and country faced acute problem of balance of payment.

So called "mixed economy" is a haphazardly and deliberately corrupted economy. The inefficiency, corruption, and mismanagement is much more in such economic system than would be in either of purely centrally planned economy or pure market economy. To differentiate the implication of market and planning, let us have a look on information flow:

Table 1: Comparison of Characteristics of Market vs Planning

Characteristics	*Market*	*Planning*
Major information types	Offers and counter offers	Statistical reports
	Advertising	Plan proposals and counter proposals
	Order	Plan bargaining, critique of the plan proposal
	Confirmation contract	Plan decision
	Modification of contract	Instruction or recommendations to those implementing the plan
	Payment for fulfilment of contract	
Character of reflection	The information directly reflects the real action	The information reflects real action perhaps through several transmissions
Time lag anterior	Preceding it only slightly almost simultaneously	Preceding it by considerable time (1-5-15-20 years)
Role of memory	Small, short-time horizon	Large, long time horizon

Measure	Variables measured in both physical and value term; price information has outstanding role	Variables measured in both physical and value terms; the former have outstanding role
Is the flow of goods accompanied by money flow?	Yes	No
Vertical versus horizontal flow of information	Both, but the horizontal flows are dominant	Both, but the vertical flows are dominant

Ref: Kenneth Arrow : Limited Knowledge and Economic Analysis; American Economic Review; vol. 64, No. 1, March (1974), pp. 4-6.

The pure market economy implies that "market is in itself capable of controlling the economic system. Insofar as price system meets the theoretically established requirements of optimality, it in itself will provide the basic information necessary for control. Any interference with economic process is superfluous". (Kenneth Arrow; *ibid*).

The pure planned economy implies that "the economy must be centrally regulated according to plan. If planning is of a sufficient high standard, exact and reliable, there is no need for any other control; in particular, it would be superfluous to expose the economy to fluctuations and frictions from the market." (*ibid*)

For the sake of comparing the decision making in market economy and planning let us have a look on the favourable factors.

Table 2: The Types of Decision and Combination of Market and Planning

Item	Factors which favour the market subsystem	Factors which favour planning subsystem
Degree of Concentration	Little concentration	Higher concentration
Character of Decision	standard decision (smaller modification in real variables against earlier situation)	Fundamental decision (major modification in real variables against earlier situation)

Indivisibility	The real variable controlled by the decision is continuous; there is no essential indivisibility	The real variable controlled by the decision not continuous; there are essential indivisibilities
Character of input-output functions	There are no increasing return	Increasing returns asset themselves
Time horizon	Decision can be taken with a short time horizon	Decision can be taken only on the basis of a large time horizon

Ref: Kenneth Arrow: Limited Knowledge and Economic Analysis; American Review, vol. 64, No. 1, March 1974, pp. 4-6).

The points relevant to market economy and planning are:

1. Neither the market nor planning can be reliable to control modern, complex economic system alone. In itself either one is regulator which functions in less than a completely reliable way. Therefore, on the basis of principle of multiplying information, the combined activity of the two is necessary for a satisfactory control of the system for the improvements of the performance.
2. There exist no uniform combination of the control subsystems of the market and national economic planning independent of age and endowments. Their relative weights depend primarily on the political power and ownership relations. In addition, as regards the entirety of the system, the weights are greatly influenced by economic planning (growth rates and living standards) and by the general state of the market (pressure or suction). Within a given system planning is given a greater role in more highly concentrated industries, in fundamental decisions involving greater risk and relating to indivisible major units, and in the control of effects not measurable with prices.
3. The partial market model of GE (General Equilibrium) school relying on the idea of "perfect competition" may be accelerated as an approximate presentation of the interaction between supply, demand and prices, "valid for a special, narrow class of markets". This special, narrow class is characterized, among other things, by the following properties:

1. Both demand side and the supply side consist of great number of atomized organization.
2. There exists no lasting tendency for the reproduction of market tensions, for constant disequilibrium, and for the preponderance of either side of the market.
3. There are no increasing returns. There are no large indivisible units. Production (and with its sales) can adapt continuously to small changes in needs, and conversely.
4. Prices may develop freely according to agreement between seller and buyers.

In fact, the failure of planning in Russia and India suggest that planning is not a reliable path for accelerating growth, or socio-economic development. So called complementary role of market mechanism in planning process does not hold valid. It rather aggravates the price mechanism leading to overall crisis. The market mechanism sabotages the planned action and thereby compels upward revision of every planned activity related with investment project implementation and funds required for planned activities.

Conventionally, growth process entails industrially suitable locations. The urbanisation is consequence of economic growth, trade and commercial activities. The uninterrupted four decades of planning in India had witnessed such urbanisation as pre-requisite to growth. For short spell, there was deviation in resource allocation on the plea that major portion of plan expenditure is biased in favour of urban based industries, telecommunications, and other sectors of economy. In order to have equitable distribution of resources, it was felt essential to ensure equal plan expenditure for urban and rural areas. In order to help expenditure for urban and rural areas. In order to help poorest of poor, rural farmers, and other segments of rural population the half of plan expenditure was felt essential and must be apportioned. Though it had political implication about number of rural population exceeding urban population which could be motivated in favour of parties with rural ideological base, in fact, poor population would be somehow benefited if such plan expenditure is apportioned based on rural-urban divide.

However, this basic idea was sabotaged or proved nonstarter on the ground that how can benefits be divided on urban-rural location, as almost every item like rail line, electricity poles and transmission lines, surface transport, plastics, steel, sugar, food, etc. is found to have movements in both urban and rural areas. How to divide total km. rail route on urban and rural basis. Similarly, how to measure the movements of plastics, steel, etc. and expenditure incurred on such items. Nevertheless to appease political needs some ad hoc studies were initiated for facts and figures. Those who justified earlier the sectoral allocation in the context of National Accounts Statistics have also tried to justify the rural-urban plan allocation on one or other account. That is why planning process as a whole is loosing its significance, relevance and identity. No one knows really what is the implication of planning on proliferating corruption, accelerating economic crisis and fiscal deficits.

It is said that Russia was first country to have adopted planning process. Though her prosperity reckoned in the period from 1940s to 1970s cannot be solely attributed to planning process adapted by Russia but UN's directives in 1950s to all developing countries for preparing national plan tantamounts to pose faith in planning process. But complete failure of Russia's economy in early 1991 and eventual disintegration in 1991 itself as well as discarding planning in favour of market economy levels to doubt as to whether planning is reliable at all. Similarly, India's balance of payment crisis in 1991 despite her meticulously worked out plan leads to doubt whether planning process at all is capable of yielding the intended results.

If evidence of disintegration of Russia or her total failure on economic front as well as India's perse poor performance over 40 years of planned economy are meant to convey the results of planning to avert crisis, then which is the process of accelerating failure of economy to eventually lead to economic crisis? The Germany, USA, Japan, Italy did not practise any planning but maintained economic prominence, prosperity and leadership in the world during the same era when its contemporary nations like India, Bangladesh, Pakistan, Nepal Bhutan etc. were practising planning. While Japan, Germany, Italy, United States and other nations achieved technological excellence and economic prosperity as measured from industrial output and per capita income, the countries following planned approach have deteriorated the position. Every under-developed country prepares its plan to avail external aid, but this is not mandatory for developed countries. Planning process had its useful life and now the time has come to abolish it. All developed countries have not achieved their prosperity through planning, nor industrial or scientific revolution was achieved through planning process. Neither Newton's invention nor Darwin's or Freud's theories or Einstein's invention nor any of the laws in science came into being through national planning process; therefore planning should not have any place in scientific and technological revolutions. It is a self deceptive process meant to foster the cult of nepotism under the name best brains.

Therefore, hypothesis that could be established is that planning process leads to planned approach to accelerated economic crisis, through excessive intervention, through barriers and controls, licensing mechanism, and misappropriation of resources or misallocation of resources. It also creates the parallel economy. It also helps inculcate inefficiency in first stage and justify fostering of weak and inefficient public sector enterprises created, proliferate inefficiency, corruption and justify the slow pace of poverty eradication as well as deprivation of basic needs of the poorest of poor. While subsidies given to poor are projected vociferously, the protectionism given to scientific and industrial research goes unnoticed. So called search for talents through competitive examinations, interviews and selection procedures is to deny the claims of needy, just and rightful persons and inculcate the cult of nepotism, political link up etc. All the developing countries should now reconcile the need for concept of planned development. Market economy does not believe in planning process or intervention mechanism.

To reiterate it is fact that under the pretence of managing the economy with least and scarce resources planning process in general is aimed at to create scarcity of input-output of goods, services and also create entry barriers in the industrial activities as well as it retards natural growth of economy. The problem of demand and supply side are aggravated due to intervention mechanism of planning uncalled for. So called planners (or pseudo-intellectuals) take it for granted that government's role is pervasive and they must act according to whimsical and wishful thinking by justifying wrong. Instead of allowing poor to their destiny under the name of development, poor are used like guinea pig.

4.03 Demerits of Planning

The intrinsic nature of under-developed countries in general and India in particular is very peculiar. Anything new, be it a food habit, living style, cooking methods or academic aspects, Indians rarely accept at first instance. Only by demonstrative effect and perpetual exposure or pursuasion they accept after a gap of years, that too reluctantly if convinced of proven benefits. Again, once they accept the particular system, way of living, living style, academic reasoning etc., then they do not abandon on advent of new. No matter, how best the things are justified, they would prefer to stick to old things.

Same is the case of poverty eradication process, economic system, social equality reasonings etc. Even when USSR was shattered by its own invented methods of planning, despite it had centrally command system, India had followed the footstep of USSR of planning in most unattached economy to any of the ideologies of socio-economic-political governance. India is going to eventually ruin its economy through mismanagement through non-scientific planning. It is strange but true that despite widespread poverty and hungry population, India affords to bear loss of 5,000 crores in 3 years preceding 1990-91, in 198 public sector undertakings, due to planning process.

There are numerous demerits to Indian style of planning. Those who hold the office of profit, do try to justify the planning but they little contribute of their own. The talk against and for is equal. Despite existence of over 40 years, neither any scientific model has ever been devised nor any original contribution to theoretical base has been done. Except that of technique of deducing inference to suit the political need or low targetting for production to inject inefficiency or curtailing the investment on one or other pretext, the whole exercise appears to manipulative of data. There are critique who denounce planning process not only of India but even USSR and other countries. Basically, planning is un-American or anti-laissez-faire.

There are indications to prove that poverty eradication in planning is in unidirection at predetermined rate or income of lowest 30 per cent gets increased at predetermined rate. There is also no guarantee that inflation will be determined well in advance and maintained at predetermined level during plan period. Also, the position of balance of payment and foreign exchange will be improved is not certain. Had such indication been positive then India's worsening balance of payment would not have been possible.

4.04 Failure of Planning Process

Conventional planning has been responsible for economic crisis in India. Both political and economic instability have promoted corruption of highest order. Planning (or what is plan innings) has lost its way since 1979. As a drive to liberate Indian economy from the shackles of controls and licensing at least three organisations namely Director General of Technical Development, Controller of Cement and Chief Controller of Imports and Exports have been identified for closure. As the implication of working of these offices was not conducive for liberalisation, economic reforms and allow advent of new era of free trade. Strange enough to observe why was planning body in India left secure. In fact, it is planning body and process which was responsible implicitly or explicitly to devise the policies, strategies and making allocation of unrealistic low resources with low targets, etc. which have been resulting in breeding corruption at all levels. In general, Indian type of planning process in contrast with planning in centrally command economy is more pernicious than the controlling mechanism. Obviously, controlling process came into being due to policy decision to control say cement, import-export of commodities and even restriction of entry into industrial activities. If resource allocation is less than the bare minimum needed for continuing efficient working then obviously inefficiency will emerge, low productivity and losses in public sector enterprises will also emerge. As we know, public sector enterprises came into existence by virtue of Acts of the Parliament, but planning body allocates or recommends allocation for survival of such public sector enterprises. Planning is also considered and is in fact a mechanism of intervention into market. This intervention was at the threshold due to unrealistic or whimsical planning concepts, ideas, targets and lowest possible allocation of resources, etc. This makes even the best management to get themselves demoralised at the hands of administrative machinery, controlling authorities and even lowest rung officials in planning body. Obviously, even best managerial stock of manpower are compelled to slow down the working. The efficient plans are those where there were coherence between management of public sector enterprises and other bodies with a minimum intervention from planning body. Neither it has been able to produce any new and innovative model nor any conceptual framework. Everything heard, noticed, practiced, published or said to have originated in West has been infringed in planning process. Indians in general get more attracted to the philosophies of Western intellectuals but try to find their trace into their old scriptures or antiquits. Obviously, neither going back or retrospection of 5,000 years could be proved useful nor transporting voluminous or tonnes of books, magazines, journals, etc. could help them to find workable ideas, theories, practices, sermons, hymns and rhyms to make India a developed country.

In fact, the best way of planning is not to have planning at all. It seems ridiculous to see geologists, engineers, mathematicians who have neither previously studied or exposed to economics working in India as economists. Those who were employed in international organisations occupying high positions.

This suggests why government did not thought of winding up of planning body as could be thought of Directorate of Cement and Chief Controller of Import and Export. In fact, free economy entails no role for planning. The infrastructure planning should be left to concern State Government itself. The more autonomy to State, improvised way of sharing revenue and reducing Central Government's role should go in a long way than relying on planning process.

The existence of over 40 years of planning process has proved that mere congregation or accumulation of staff from various disciplines does not promote the cause of welfare or promote socialistic pattern of society. When there was a conducive atmosphere for socialistic society to be built, it was felt that planning is at snail pace or incremental process hence, it would pay in the long run. But contrary to the expectations, the process of planning has been fatal. Let everything improve, if any, be not attributed to planning. It is really a "mixed" economic planning and not an inter disciplinary approaches to planning. It is mixing of nepotism, favouritism, corruption, with non-academicians with academicians with the result that real intellectuals are easily bypassed and harassed at the hands of pseudo-intellectuals, pseudo-economists, etc. with the result that India's planning is pseudo planning than what one might have heard in the literature. This kind of planning is responsible for all sorts of aberrations and economic mismanagement and, therefore, the role of intervention must be curtailed. There is case to disband planning to allow free market to operate.

4.05 Gold Pledging

The size of funds received and gold sold in July, 1991 was never predicted in any of the plan period. Chronological sale of gold by India is as follows:

July 4, 1991	4.8 tonnes
July 7, 1991	20.01 tonnes
July 11, 1991	10.01 tonnes
July 18, 1991	12.09 tonnes

More than Rs 4,507 crores have been drawn by India from the IMF. This includes Rs 1, 173 crores from reserve tranche between July and September, 1990. There is no reference to this amount of Rs 1,173 crores but officially, it is admitted that only US $ 1,786 million or Rs 3, 334 crores in January, 1991 have been drawn under compensatory and contingency financing facility and the first credit tranch. also SDR of 487.26 million drawn during 1990-91 is nowhere reflected.

World Bank has granted US $ 100 million loan to Industrial Development Bank of India (IDBI). Till March 31, 1991, IDBI has secured two loans, a total of $ 249 million and had succeeded in raising $ 30 million. The details of $ 249 million two lines of credit are : (i) $ 100 million for Export-Import Bank of Japan to cover specific sectors like automobile, electronics, textiles, food processing and electrical machinery; and (ii) $ 149 millions from World Bank for restructuring cement industry.

Similarly on July 13, 1991, Australian and New Zealand Banking Group has agreed to provide a short-term loan of US $ 25 million, or Rs 62 crores to SAIL to facilitate its coal import. On July 17, 1991, World Bank has acceded to request of Orissa Government's request to extend the deadline for drawing the loan for the Rs 615.92 crores for Upper Indravati Hydro-electric Project which was expired on June 30, 1991.

If planning cannot averse such crisis of BOP and funds needed for restructuring, then does it provide a reliable means to means of managing economy. After all, crisis does not occur overnight but due to cumulative mistakes over a decade or plan period.

India has started industrialisation based on the concept that public sector would generate surplus required for nation's growth. But during the past forty four years of planning experience, public sector has become a white elephant. Contrary to the expectations it needed fund huge enough that justified perpetuation of poverty. In other words at the cost of poverty and depriving basic amenities to poor, the public sector was providing white collar jobs to urban elites by raising living standard of few, promoting specialisation, increasing consumption of luxury items, etc. Obviously inefficiency, devoid of competitiveness and accountability to public has ruined the basic concept of public enterprise.

It is now widely recognised that large and public sector deficits are the main cause of macro-economic instability of a nation. India too experienced Crisis-91 due to large trade deficit and losses of public sector enterprise met through deficit financing. There were 244 central public sector enterprises with total investment of Rs 99,315 crores in 1989-90. Out of 244 central public sector enterprises, there were only 131 profit making units and 98 were loss making units. Total profits during 1989-90 aggregated to Rs 3,782 crores. The profit from 131 units was at a level of Rs 5,741 crores, while 98 loss making units have recorded loss of Rs 1,959 crores. There were 15 public sector enterprises sharing no loss no profit.

A decline in the level of public sector investment by 25 per cent will lead to a commensurate fall in private sector investment by 10 per cent and the national output will go down by 1.3 per cent as a result. The physical performance has direct impact on profit of public sector. A 5 per cent improvement in physical performance means an increase in profits of Rs 5,000 crores and as a result of this, increased efficiency in the loss making enterprises may fetch Rs 1,100 crores. According to some sources, a foreign investment inflow of US $ 1 billion a year leads to increase in GDP level by 2 per cent and increase in per capita personal disposable income by 1.5 per cent, but this is accompanied by increase in both the level of prices and trade deficit. India's imports are likely to increase by 33 per cent without commensurate exports and would cause trade deficit to go up by 25 per cent, as a consequence of recent liberalisation.

India is seeking emergency loan of US $ 300 million to overcome balance of payment crisis, prior to getting standby loan of $ 2 billion from the IMF and World Bank's structural adjustment loan of about $ 500 million. India's financial crisis has made her to avail loan of $ 220 million on July 22, 1991 and was placed under CCFF, and with such loan, India's CCFF entitlement has exhausted. Recently, World Bank has extended a loan of $ 450 million for a Rs 7,500 crores project to utilise 8.33 million cubic metres of gas which is being flared up in the Western Offshore, the Lok Sabha was informed on August 13, 1991.

Finally, a loan of $ 635 million was sanctioned on September 12, 1991, by IMF under the Compensatory and Contingency Financing Facility (CCFF) to help India to overcome its balance of payment (BOP) crisis. Prior to this loan of $ 635 million, India had already availed two credits. That is, in January 1991, India had availed the first credit of $ 1.09 billions for oil imports under CCFF. Similarly, in July 1991 and her credit of $ 220 million was granted. Thus, total allocation under CCFF has been $ 1.950 billion. Under the category of credit tranche standby arrangement for three months, IMF had made available in January 1990, a loan of $ 777 million. Another standby credit of 202 billions has been approved under Structural Adjustment Programme for 18 months beginning from July, 1991. Thus, total comes to $ 4.927 billion. However, official media indicates IMF's credit at India's disposal at over 4.7 billion dollars.

Whether planning will transform India into society like USA, UK or Sweden? At what point of time India's economic growth will surpass the prosperity and per capita income of USA, Sweden, or Germany? Or even when per capita income of average Indian will be at par with per capita income of USA, Sweden or Germany? Can such questions be answered by planning process. Or when will poverty be removed from India and casteism will be abolished from India? Whether this question can be replied by planning from India? Whether this question be replied by planning process in India. If not then what are we going to do for nation? These questions make the planning process as its target.

4.06 Impact of Economic Crisis on PSU

The impact of economic crisis-91 was so severe that Indian Government had to resort to sweeping changes in its policies including steps to disinvestment in 41 nos. out of over 200 public sector enterprises in India. On 25th November, 1991, the Cabinet Committee on Economic Affairs has approved the list of 41 nos. of public sector enterprises which were earlier established on the justification that all the public sector enterprises in core sectors of the economy would generate surplus, for nation's growth. The disinvestment is resorted to in both categories of industries namely those working efficiently as well as making no profit no loss i.e. working at break even point. The disinvestment upto 49 per cent of equity in favour of mutual funds and financial institutions. This step was enunciated in Finance Minister's Budget speech but indication then was given that up to 20 per cent of equity shares would be considered under disinvestment scheme to fetch Rs 2,500 crores, which is an amount equivalent to total investment in one public sector. In other words, disinvestment up to 20 per cent in equity would yield an amount equal to selling up one public sector unit. But as some of public sector enterprises in the list of 41 units offered for disinvestment have been proposed for disinvestment up to 49 per cent of equity, the yield from such move is expected to be between Rs 3,000 crores to Rs 3,500 crores as against initial plan of Rs 2,500 crores.

The Department of Public Enterprises has indicated 41 industrial enterprises, for disinvestment some of which are:

1. Engineers India Ltd.
2. Telecommunications India Ltd.
3. Rail India Technical and Economic Service
4. Indian Railway Construction Co.
5. Metallurgical and Engineering Construction
6. Metal Scrap Trading Corporation
7. Hindustan Petroleum Corporation
8. Minerals and Metals Trading Corporation
9. Hindustan Vegetable Oil Corporation
10. Air India
11. State Trading Corporation
12. Videsh Sanchar Nigam
13. Lubrizol India Limited
14. Shipping Corporation of India
15. Hindustan Machine Tools Corporation
16. Dredging Corporation
17. Bharat Heavy Electronics Limited
18. Bharat Electronics
19. Andrew Yule
20. Hindustan Organic Chemicals
21. Hindustan Cables
22. Indian Telephone Industries
23. Madras Refineries

24. Hindustan Photofilm
25. Indian Tourism Development Corporation
26. Uranium Corporation of India
27. Hindustan Zinc Limited
28. National Fertilizer Corporation
29. Neyveli Lignite Corporation
30. Bharat Dynamics Limited
31. National Aluminium Company
32. Fertilizers and Chemicals (Travancore Limited)
33. IPCL
34. Steel Authority of India (SAIL) with four public sector enterprises.

There is no system of assigning responsibility or blame for wrong economic policies and political decisions. In fact, what proves wrong after a long period was justified at the time of decision-making. India had cherished the dream of socialistic pattern of society which was never achieved despite her policies to foster public sector enterprises, intervention in the market by administered prices, maintaining the largest network of foodgrain distributive mechanism and railways, telephones, telecommunication, airlines, spending crores of rupees on maintaining scientific institutions and paying crores of rupees on salaries, travel expenses, etc. of third target stock of scientific manpower, etc. Perhaps, intention of achieving discriminationless, just, equitable and socialistic pattern of society was always treated as sermon without sincere attempt to make it realistic. Even plan priorities were rarely consistent with constitutional guarantees. Every wrong thing was justified in the name of poverty eradication and endeavours towards socialistic pattern of society.

Seeing the India's crisis-91 and attempts to liberate economy towards laissez-faire one can suspect whether earlier policies (industrial policies, trade policies, pricing policies, investment policies, etc. were wrong or were in the right direction at all.

Due to economic crisis-91 India had to resort to various measures, but all those enunciated decisions have been rarely implemented. There were so many changes in import-export policies that one can rarely believe that India's trade was at all working in those days.

Hotel and tourism related industries have been permitted (or to seek approval) for direct foreign investment up to 51 per cent foreign equity. The term hotel includes restaurants, beach resorts and other tourist complexes providing accommodation and/or catering and food facilities to tourists. Similarly, the term tourism related industries include among others, travel agencies, tour operating agencies and tourist operating agencies.

Automatic permission will be given to those foreign technology agreements in the hotel industry subject to the condition that technical and consultancy service fee will not exceed US $ 200,000, franching and marketing/publicity support up to 3 per cent of the gross room sales and the management fee up to 10 per cent of the foreign exchange earnings, provided the foreign party puts in 25 per cent of the equity.

The basic problems of economic development in developing countries are to achieve full employment, growth, price stability and elimination of poverty. There are theories explaining the process leading to full employment and economic growth. There is no theoretical clear and vivid inter-relationship explaining all together i.e. employment, growth, prices and poverty eradication. There is also least theoretical explanation about income distribution and its pace in relation to growth. Economic growth is prerequisite to solution of all the other problems. Had there been any empirical evidence (though it is possible to establish), the economic policies based on such theories should have been most successful in developing countries. Economic growth process entails pumping money, in the form of investment, into economy. Investment is again a function of domestic savings and, therefore, the whole process of resource allocation is treated as marginal or incremental. Obvious resultant of such process is that conditions favouring full employment, elimination of poverty and equitable distribution of income is never achieved in developing countries. Explanation to slow progress in all such vital problems is attributed to scarcity of resources.

4.07 Public Sector Enterprises—A white elephant

Public sector was treated as the source of growth in Indian economy. Government had been investing huge amount in public sector. The profile of public sector in India is as follows:

Table 3: Profile of Centre's Public Enterprises

Item	Units	1980-81	1985-86	1989-90	1990-91
1	2	3	8	12	13
1. Number of running Public Enterprises	Number	163	211	233	236
2. Capital Employed	Rs Cr.	18207	42965	84869	101797
3. Turnover	Rs Cr.	28635	62360	106069	118355
4. Gross Margin before Profit	Rs Cr.	2401	8230	16412	18510
5. Depreciation	Rs Cr.	983	2983	5790	7151
6. Gross Profit before Interest and Tax	Rs Cr.	1418	5287	10622	11359
7. Interset	Rs Cr.	1399	3115	5329	7539
8. Net Tax before Tax	Rs Cr.	19	2172	5293	3820
9. Tax	Rs Cr.	222	1000	1504	1452
10. Net Profit after Tax	Rs Cr.	—203	1172	3789	2368
11. Internal Resources Generated (gross)	Rs Cr.	1225	5068	10774	11372
12. Net Profit (aftertax) to Capital Employed	Per cent	—1.1	2.7	4.5	2.3
13. Gross Profit (aftertax) to Capital Employed	Per cent	7.8	12.3	12.5	11.2

Source: Economic Survey of different years

It will be obvious that there are both loss making and profit making units but when their profit is taken together the loss making unit's performance gets less prominence.

The basic problems from resources allocation point of view could be both production and distribution. In other words, what to produce, how much to be produced, by whom to produce, how the distributive mechanism be devised, and what kind of organisation be established to achieve aimed production and distribution. Besides Centre's public enterprises (over 222 in 1991) in India, each of the State has public sector enterprises in their control. Maharashtra State has 57 nos. of public sector enterprises. Of the 57 State sector enterprises, 27 are subsidiaries and 5 statutory corporations. In terms of performance only 10 of State enterprises are profit making and 47 are loss making. The cumulative losses of 47 State enterprises are R$ 157.14 crores (as on December 5, 1991), which included cumulative losses sustained by 25 companies had exceeded their paid up capital of Rs 68.82 crores.

The State Government has invested Rs 228.29 crores towards the paid up capital. These include 31 companies fully owned by the State Government with an investment of Rs 195.72 crores, companies jointly owned with the Central Government with the State investment of Rs 6.53 crores, 2 companies jointly owned with Central Government and private sector with the State investment of Rs 4.77 crores. The State Government has 21 subsidiaries with investment of Rs 20 lakhs along with public investment of Rs 17.32 crores. Government investment structure in different sectors roughly accounts for : Public utility enterprises — 87 per cent, commercial enterprises — 6 per cent, commercial-cum- development enterprises — 3 per cent, development enterprises — 2 per cent, and financial enterprises — 2 per cent. The criterion stipulated by Eighth Finance Corporation that profitability of commercial enterprises be 5 per cent, and financial corporations be 3 per cent. But aggregate profitability of all the 57 enterprises remained below 0.15 per cent. However, these corporations cannot meet even their administrative expenses.

The rate of return from public sector enterprises in India is not at all impressive, despite popularity believed myth that these enterprises are managed by highly educated, talented lot in the country. The rate of return, as measured by net profits to capital employed was 4.4 per cent in 1988-89. Out of Rs 2,981 crores net profit after tax generated by 222 public sector enterprises in 1988-89, Rs 2,654 crores has been generated by 22 numbers of petroleum sector enterprises. That is only Rs 417 crores of net profit after tax was from 200 numbers of public sector enterprises in non-petroleum sector. The ratio of net loss of net profits to capital employed in non-petroleum sector enterprises was less than one per cent in 1988-89.

Every integrated steel plant set up in India was considered to be based on modern technology at the time of conception and commissioning but in short span of life technological obsolescence had made steel production in India uncompetitive. Technological obsolescence, low scale of operation, high cost of inputs and higher energy consumption per tonne of steel produced, labour intensive technology, low output per man-hour or per employee etc. contributed to produce steel at higher prices than that prevailed in international market.

Other factors (as in December 1991) attributed to higher prices of steel in India are found to be (i) levies on account of engineering goods Export Assistance Fund (Rs 300 per tonne), (ii) Freight Equalisation Fund (Rs 866 per tonne); (iii) Steel Development Fund (Rs 350 to Rs 500 per tonne); and (iv) plus excise duties. Thus, the average additional burden comes to over Rs 2,000 per tonne constituting about 25 per cent of the final price of steel.

From conventional route of blast furnace — open hearth furnace there has been drastic technological change in steel making. Developed countries were able to switch over to both basic process and electric arc furnace for conversion of steel and continuous casting etc. to reduce cost, save energy and improve the quality of steel. With such technological changes, the prices in international market have drastically changed. Particularly, production cost in Japan was cut down by 29 per cent, in the United States, it was cut down by 8 per cent, and in West Germany, production cost was cut down by five per cent between 1980 and 1988. But on contrary, production cost of steel in India has shot up by 145 per cent. In switching over from open hearth process to basic oxygen convertor process would tantamount to reduce product cost by Rs 150 per tonne on account of fuel saving. Similarly, adapting continuous casting would reduce production cost. Energy consumption in India 9.53 giga calories per tonne of steel as compared with five to six giga calories in development countries.

In other words, prices of steel are comparable to or function of technology prevailing. The quality of raw material, political interference, capital investment, drive for modernisation of plant etc. contribute towards prices of items in general.

As a part of the drive to raise resources, a scheme was announced in budget 1991-92 by Indian Government that a total of Rs 2,500 crores could be raised through disinvestment. In pursuance with such drive, the Indian Government has decided to allot shares of select public sector undertakings (PSUs) to mutual funds and financial institutions to raise about Rs 1,200 crores. The department of Public Enterprises selected 31 public sector enterprises with good track record and offered part of the equity of each of these enterprises varying from five per cent to 20 per cent for sale to public sector mutual funds and financial institutions. The shares of different enterprises were bundled together into 825 separate bundles. Each of these bundles consisted of the shares of nine different public sector enterprises bids for 533 bundles for a total value of Rs 1,772 crores. The Government has evaluated these bids and has shown inclination to accept bids for 335 bundles for a total of about Rs 1,200 crores. Bids received for 198 bundles were rejected on the ground that they did not reflect the fair value of the shares as viewed by the Government. The decision of Cabinet Committee on Economic Affairs (CCEA) taken on December 25, 1991 to allot shares of profit making public sector units is based on the optimistic assumption that these 31 PSUs would continue to make profit to pay dividend and assumed appreciation value of mutual fund shares. But if these units failed or showed any loss years to come, then whole gains on short run to raise resource in 1991-92 would be total liability in the next three years. There is no guarantee that PSUs which are making profit would continue to record profit even in the wave of privatisation selling over of good public sector units, collapse of economy and under economy uncertainty. In contrast with several loss making public sector enterprises there are numerous profit making units in private sector.

To elucidate the example of success of private sectors within same industrial environment of the country, let us have a look at profit before tax of the top 20 private sector companies in the year 1989-90.

Table 4 : Profit before Tax of Top 20 Private Companies in 1989-90

Name of company	*Profit (Rs Crores)*
1. Tata	594.42
2. Birla	439.55
3. Hindustan Lever	203.73
4. Bajaj	133.86
5. ITC	122.88
6. Thapar	109.78
7. Reliance	87.36
8. Mafatlal	85.58
9. Larsen & Tubro	62.47
10 TVS Iyenger	59.80
11. Kirloskar	45.36
12. M.A. Chidamber	38.78
13. United Breweries	36.63
14. Oswal Agro	35.75
15. J.K. Singhania	35.74
16. ESSAR	34.82
17. Modi	23.09
18. Shri Ram	20.99
19. Mahindra & Mahindra	20.07
20. ACC	2.07

On one occasion or other, the role played by public sector enterprises is invariably lauded, but at the core, the performance of these enterprises is ponderable. Similarly, the PSUs are treated as a gift of socialist ideology or deriving the inspirations from policy decisions in UK in nationalising banking, coal, etc., as well as success stories of USSR, and attributing prosperity of USSR to collective ownership of means of production. The ideals as enshrined in the Constitution of India or ideals cherished in 1950s have suddenly become so bitter in 1991 that the Government has to think curtailing the role of public sector enterprises and sale of as much as possible PSUs. The ideals held true at one time become not only redundant but also treated as great mistake of that time after a lapse of say four decades. It is same as finding fault with the socialism or communism in USSR in 1991 after a gap of 72 years forgetting the fact that the revolution headed by Karl Marx and Fredrick Engel has taken so many lives and it paid its value by bringing prosperity to the nation which Gorbachev has spoiled due to his unprudent actions.

4.08 Coping with Deficits

Since June 1991-92 Budget, there are continuous efforts in India to monitor the economic growth track to deal with revenue deficit, exchange rate, interest rate and government expenditure. The revenue receipts and expenditure of government do not hold equilibrium. In order to reduce fiscal deficit, what is imperative is to reduce government expenditure. India's revenue deficit in December 1991 was exceeding Rs 20,000 crores per annum. The defence, surface transport (i.e. roads), health care, communication and irrigation need continuous investment as its growth is incremental. Dr Manmohan Singh in the capacity of Finance Minister was more effective than his earlier positions like Governor of Reserve Bank, Deputy Chairman of Planning Commission etc. His fears were genuine when he pointed out to National Development Council (NDC) held on December 23-24, 1991 that "If we continue on this path, interest and servicing debt will absorb an ever increasing share of our revenue. This has already cut down our ability to finance plan investment."

As a part of approach to reduce government expenditure, the Prime Minister of India enunciated a "major austerity drive" hitherto unprecedented in India, with a 10 per cent reduction in the senior official posts from the level of Joint Secretary, abolition of about 1,000 jobs in three government offices, 20 per cent cut in domestic and foreign travel.

Balance of payment (BOP) crisis in India during 1991 has created new opportunity for international aid donor countries. No Western donor country is benevolent. They have their own interest. The World Bank and International Monetary Fund (IMF) are the twin agencies safeguarding the interest of Group of Seven (G-7) richest countries of the world. The structural adjustment is a name of neo-colonising the economy. The days of imperialism are gone where military power was used for colonization of a weak country. Now the days of neo-imperialism and neo-colonisation are dawn to paralysis the country's economy through various economic mechanism such as interest on huge loan, royalty payment on technology transfer, sale of technology, capital goods, payment to expert, preparation of feasibility reports or detailed project reports, etc. Over and above, the game of foreign trade. The debt service ratio, balance of payment and balance of trade will favour the increasing return to develop countries than any poor country.

Donor countries under the umbrella of Aid India Consortium (which are World Bank sponsored nation) are comprised of Germany, Japan, Britain, France, the United States and the European Community). At a recently held meeting in Paris on 20th September 1991, the aid of $ 6.7 billion has been pledged to India. The aid of $ 6.7 billion included $ 2.2 billion from bilateral sources and remaining from multinational sources. The disbursement plan is as follows:

— $ 2.3 billion is in the form of grant on concessional term. It is granted under the category of fast-disbursement.

— Out of $ 2.3 billion fast-disbursing grant, the sources of aid are:

(a) $ 0.7 billion is again divided as $ 0.35 billion from Japan and $ 0.35 billion from Germany, Britain and Netherlands.

(b) $ 1.6 billion fast-disbursing is to come from World Bank and Asian Development Bank (ADB).

Aid India Consortium has so far granted aid to India as follows:

Year	*Aid in US $ Billion*
1986-87	4.4
1987-88	5.4
1988-89	6.3
1989-90	6.7
1990-91	6.5
1991-92	6.7

India received foreign aid exceeding US $ 6.7 billion. Besides the aid of $ 6.7 billion from Aid India Consortium where Japan is already a member country, the assistance of US $ 150 million was provided by Japan during June 1991 (Gulf War) to meet BOP crisis which was utilised by India to meet import bill of petroleum. Japan has also given another loan of US $ 156 million for quick disbursement to the Small Industrial Development Bank of India.

Such aid does not come simply because donor countries are benevolent to India or they believe in charity to India, but India offers good market for such countries. The failure of India's economic performance helps donor countries to tighten their grip on India's economy by way of aid and investment. India's population of over 844 million (in 1991-92) and its vast territory is of the size of over eight Japans and any assistance to India meant capturing big share of market.

It is strange that the countries like Germany and Japan which completely damaged their economy and industrial capability during World War II (and India too was liberated in post World War II era) have emerged as economic super power within less than two decades of World War II and continue to dominate world economy since then to date. Whereas India claims to have highest scientific manpower, best brain etc. still continues to be perpetual recipient country and crises are deeply now and then.

IMF has approved on July 22, 1991 to give India US $ 220 million out of the Compensatory and Contingency Financing Facilities (CCFF).

Sale of Gold by India to raise $ 400 million

July 4, 1991	4.8 tonnes of gold
July 7, 1991	20.01 tonnes of gold
July 11, 1991	10.01 tonnes of gold
July 18, 1991	12.09 tonnes of gold
Total	46.91 tonnes of gold

It will fetch $ 400 million which will be used for easing balance of payment crisis. World Bank has granted $ 100 million loan to Industrial Development Bank of India. Australian and New Zealand Banking Group would provide a short term loan of US $ 25 million. Rs 62 crores to SAIL to facilitate its coal imports on July 13,

1991. West Bengal acceded to the Orissa Government's request to extend the deadline for advancing the loan of Rs 615.92 crores for Upper Indramati Hydro-electric Project which was expiring on June 30, 1991.

Reserve Bank of India is authorised under the Reserve Bank of India Act, to keep gold up to 15 per cent of its gold holding outside India. Reserve Bank of India's gold holdings amount to 332 tonnes as on 1st July, 1991.

During 1990-91, India has drawn massive Rs 4,507 crores from IMF including Rs 1173 crores which Govt. drew silently from its reserve transfer between July and September, 1990. So long, Finance Ministry has been maintaining that it has a total of US $ 1786 million or Rs 3334 crores in January, 1991 under mix of compensatory and contingency financing facility and the first credit franche.

50 per cent investment in manufacturing activity through 1266 manufacturing projects with total investment of Rs 170,776 crores. 40 per cent into irrigation projects and the power sector or electricity project. Mining and manufacturing taken together 915 projects under implementation i.e. totalling Rs 98,000 crores and an investment of Rs 137,000 crores in 164 manufacturing projects is awaiting approval and another 250 projects involving Rs 45,500 crores are in the proposal stage.

444 irrigation projects with an outlay of Rs 64,669 crores under implementation which account for 21 per cent of the total spending. 144 electricity projects with investment of Rs 54,959 crores which account for 18 per cent of the total investment. 238 projects with investment of Rs 13,581 crores goes to transport service, which is about 4 per cent and 65 projects of Rs 10,108 crores or 3 per cent in mining. Ferrous metals will account for 34.1 per cent of ongoing projects. Of this, 6.3 per cent will be invested in steel rolling mills, rest will go to primary sector.

An organised way of neo-colonisation. The days of colonisation or imperialist rule is over but neo-colonisation and ways of extracting wealth of poor countries is found in trade, technology transfer, transfer of knowhow, licensing mechanism and royalty, etc. Trade deficit of poor/least developing countries is gradually increasing. Trade deficit of LDCs was showing positive balance of $ 13.9 billion in 1989 but has grown to US $ 24.3 billion in 1990.

5

Financial Transactions in India

5.01 Introduction

It is a very complicated subject to deal with financial transactions of the government. Nevertheless, to a curious reader, it will be helpful to give a brief idea about it. The Constitution of India has laid down detailed procedure about financial matters. Let us try to summarise them prior to going into details of actual expenditure and financial matters.

Article	Brief Subject
110	Definition of Money Bills
112	Annual Financial Statement
113	Procedure in Parliament with respect to Estimates
114	Appropriation Bills
115	Supplementary, Additional or Excess Grants
116	Votes on account, Votes of credit and Exceptional Grants
117	Special Provisions as to Financial Bills (not dealt in the discussion below)
265	Taxes not to be imposed save by authority of law
266	Consolidated Funds and Public Accounts of India and of the States
267	Contingency Fund

In fact, these are some of the Articles of the Constitution of India. There are four chapters with 36 Articles in Part XII of the Constitution on Finance, Property, Contracts and Suits which besides above deal with "Distribution of Revenues between the

Union and the States", Finance Commission, Custody of Funds, Exemption of Taxes, etc.

The matters relevant to government expenditure and fiscal deficit shall be dealt with here. The sequence of articles, explained below is to suit our discussion.

5.02 Article 265

No tax shall be levied or collected except by authority of law

According to this Article, government cannot levy any tax unless it is permitted by law. Obviously, the Parliament has to approve such proposed taxes. Obviously to raise revenue receipts to meet government expenditure through taxes such an exercise every year is inevitable.

5.03 Article 266

(1) Subject to provisions of Article 267 and to the provisions of this Chapter with respect to the assignment of the whole or part of the net proceeds of certain taxes and duties to States, all revenues received by the Government of India, all loans raised by that government by the issue of treasury bills, loans or ways and means advances and all moneys received by that government in repayments of loans shall form one consolidated fund to be entitled "the Consolidated Fund of India", and all revenues received by the Government of a State, all loans raised by that Government by the issue of treasury bills, loans or ways and means advances and all moneys received by that Government in repayment of loans shall form one consolidated fund to be entitled "Consolidated Fund of the State".

(2) All other public moneys received by or on behalf of the Government of India or the Government of a State shall be credited to the public account of India or the public account of the State, as the case may be.

(3) No money out of the Consolidated Fund of India or the Consolidated Fund of a State shall be appropriated except in accordance with law and for the purposes and in the manner provided in this Constitution.

It will be obvious from above Article with three sub-articles that both Centre and the State Governments have provisions of Consolidated Funds and are identified according to Centre's authority or State's authority. In former case, it is known as "Consolidated Fund of India" and in latter case, the "Consolidated Fund of a State". This fund is formed of money from four sources; primarily of : (1) net proceeds of certain taxes and duties; (2) all revenue receipts; (3) loans raised by issue of treasury bills, loans or ways and means advances; and (4) all moneys received in repayment of loans. However, Government cannot appropriate money out of the Consolidated Fund of India without approval of the Parliament.

5.04 Article 267

(1) Parliament may by law established a contingency Fund in the nature of an imprest to be entitled "the Contingency Fund of India" into which shall be paid from time to time such sums as may be determined by such law, and the said Fund shall be placed at the disposal of the President to enable advances of meeting unforeseen expenditure pending authorisation of such expenditure by Parliament by law under Article 115 or Article 116.

(2) The Legislature of a State may by law establish a Contingency Fund in the nature of an imprest entitled "The Contingency Fund of the State" into which shall be paid from time to time such sums as may be determined by such law, and the said Fund shall be placed at the disposal of the Governor of the State to enable advances to be made by him out of such Fund for the purposes of meeting unforeseen expenditure pending authorisation of such expenditure by the Legislature of the State by law under Article 205 or Article 206.

According to above Article 267 with two sub-articles, the constitutional provisions exist as to establishment of Contingency Fund both at Centre and the State level, which are then placed at the disposal of the President of India or Governor of the State respectively according to the authority establishing the Fund whether Centre or State.

5.05 Article 110

(1) A bill shall be deemed to be a Money Bill if it contains only provisions dealing with all or any of the following matters, namely—

(a) the imposition, abolition, remission, alteration or regulation of any tax;

(b) the regulation of the borrowing of money or the giving of any guarantee by the Government of India, or the amendment of the law with respect to any financial obligations undertaken or to be undertaken by the Government of India;

(c) the custody of the Consolidated Fund or the Contingency Fund of India, the payment of moneys into or the withdrawal of moneys from any such Fund;

(d) the appropriation of moneys out of the Consolidated Fund of India;

(e) the declaring of any expenditure to be expenditure charged on the Consolidated Fund of India or the increasing of the amount of any such expenditure;

(f) the receipt of money on account of the Consolidated Fund of India or the public account of India or the custody of issue of such money or the audit of the accounts of the Union or of a State; or

(g) any matter incidental to any of the matters specified in sub-clauses (a) to (g).

From above Article, it is clear that all matters regarding imposition, abolition, remission, alteration or regulation of any tax are called "Money Bill" and also all matters concerned with Consolidated Fund of India, Contingency Fund of India, and Public Account of India are treated under money bills" and alteration etc. in money bills of the past shall be dealt under this article.

5.06 Article 112

(1) The President shall in respect of every financial year cause to be laid before both the Houses of Parliament a statement of the estimated receipts and expenditure of the Government of India for that year, in this Part referred to as the "annual financial statement".

(2) The estimate of expenditure embodied in the annual financial statement shall show separately:

(a) the sums required to meet expenditure described by this Constitution as expenditure charged upon the Consolidated Fund of India; and

(b) the sums required to meet other expenditure proposed to be made from the Consolidated Fund of India.

and shall distinguish expenditure on revenue account from other expenditure.

(3) The following expenditure shall be expenditure charged on the Consolidated Fund of India—

(a) the emoluments and allowances of the President and other expenditure relating to his office;

(b) the salaries and allowances of the Chairman and the Deputy Chairman of the Council of States and the Speaker and the Deputy Speaker of the House of the People;

(c) debt charges for which the Government of India is liable including interest, sinking fund charges and redemption charges, and other expenditure relating to the raising of loans and the service and redemption of debt.

(d) (i) the salaries, allowances and pensions payable to or in respect of Judges of the Supreme Court;

(ii) the pensions payable to or in respect of Judges of the Federal Court;

(iii) the pensions payable to or in respect of Judges of any High Court which exercises jurisdiction in relation to any area included in the territory of India or which at any time before the commencement of this Constitution exercised jurisdiction in relation to any area included in a Governor's Province of the Dominion of India

(e) the salary, allowances and pension payable to or in respect of the Controller and Auditor General of India;

(f) any sums required to satisfy any judgement, decree of award of any court or arbitral tribunal;

(g) any other expenditure declared by this Constitution or Parliament by law to be so charged. s2.

This Article stipulates the condition that for every financial year the Government must prepare "Annual Financial Statement" which is a statement of the estimated receipts and expenditure of the Government of India for that year". This Article also explains the entries those must be incorporated while preparing Annual Financial Statement. The Constitutional Provision of "expenditure charged" upon the Consolidated Fund of India as well as "expenditure on revenue account". The items which are essentially "expenditure charged on the Consolidated Fund of India" are emoluments and allowances of the President of India and expenditure relating to his office, salaries and allowances of the Chairman, Deputy Chairman of the Council of States, Speaker and the Deputy Speaker of the Parliament Houses.

5.07 Demands for Grant

Regarding procedure in Parliament with respect to estimates, Article 113 states as follows :

Article 113

(1) So Much of the estimates as relates to expenditure charged upon the Consolidated Fund of India shall not be submitted to the Vote of Parliament, but nothing in this clause shall be construed as preventing the discussion in either House of Parliament of any of those estimates.

(2) So much of the said estimates as relates to other expenditure shall be submitted in the form of demands for grant to the House of the People, and the House of the People shall have power to assent, or to refuse to assent, to any demand, or to assent to any demand subject to a reduction of the amount specified therein.

(3) No demand for a grant shall be made except on the recommendation of the President.

In normal course expenditure charged upon the Consolidated Fund of India shall not be submitted to the Vote of Parliament, and other expenditure shall be submitted in the form of demand for grants and would be subject to assent, refuse or reduction by the Parliament.

5.08 Appropriation Bills

To withdraw money from the Consolidated Fund of India, the constitutional provision is as follows:

Article 114

(1) As seen as may be after the grants under Article 113 have been made by the House of People, there shall be introduced a Bill to provide for the appropriation out of the Consolidated Fund of India of all moneys required to meet:

(a) the grants so made by the House of the People; and

(b) the expenditure charged on the Consolidated Fund of

India but not exceeding in any case, the amount shown in the statement previously laid before Parliament.

(2) No amendment shall be proposed to any such Bill in either House of Parliament which will have the effect of varying the amount or altering the destination of any grant so made or of varying the amount of any expenditure charged on the Consolidated Fund of India, and the decision of the person presiding as to whether an amendment is inadmissible under this clause shall be final.

(3) Subject to the provision of Articles 115 and 116, no money shall be withdrawn from the Consolidated Fund of India except under appropriation made by law passed in accordance with the Provision of this Article.

In short, the Finance Minister has to introduce a "Bill to provide for the appropriations" of all moneys required to meet both "grant" and "expenditure charged" and no amendment for variation of grants is permitted.

Supplementary, additional or excess grants

In view of the Article 114(2) prohibiting amendment to Appropriation Bills, the Article 115 has provision for supplementary, additional or excess grants, as stated below:

5.09 Article 115

(1) The President shall —

(a) if the amount authorised by any law made in accordance with the provision of Article 114 to be expended for a particular service for the current financial year is found to be insufficient for the purposes of that year or when a need has arisen during the current financial year for supplementary or additional expenditure upon some new service not contemplated in the annual financial statement for that year, or

(b) if any money has been spent on any service during a financial year in excess of the amount granted for that service and for that year, cause to be laid before both the Houses of Parliament another statement showing the estimated amount of that expenditure or cause to be presented to the House of the people a demand for such excess as the case may be.

(2) The provision of Articles 112, 113 and 114 shall have effect in relation to any such statement and expenditure or demand and also to any law to be made authorising the appropria tion of moneys out of the Consolidated Fund of India to meet such expenditure or the grant in respect of such demand as they have effect in relation to the annual financial sta tement and the expenditure mentioned therein or to a demand for a grant and the law to be made for the authorisation of appropriation of moneys out of the Consolidated Fund of India to meet such expenditure or grant.

That is, supplementary, additional or excess grants are laid before the Houses of Parliament if amount authorised by law earlier is insufficient or excess for the current year. The statement and expenditure estimates or demand and law in this regard will be made authorising the appropriation of money out of Consolidated Fund of India.

Votes on account, Votes of credit and exceptional grants.

Sometimes, the expenditure to be incurred needs to be drawn prior to completion of the procedure stipulated in Article 113 to 115 above, therefore, the provision for such expenditure is essential.

5.10 Article 116

(1) Notwithstanding anything in the foregoing provisions of this Chapter, the House of the People shall have power—

(a) to make any grant in advance in respect of the estimated expenditure for a part of any financial year pending the completion of the procedure prescribed in Article 113 for the voting of such grant and the passing of the law in accordance with the provision of Article 114 in relation to that expenditure;

(b) to make a grant for meeting an unexpected demand upon the resources of India where on account of the magnitude or the definite character of the service, the demand cannot be stated with the details ordinarily given in the annual financial statement;

(c) to make an exceptional grant which forms no part of the current service of any financial year; and Parliament shall have power to authorise by law the withdrawal of moneys from the Consolidated Fund of India for the purposes for which the said grants are made.

(2) The provision of Articles 113 and 114 shall have effect in relation to the making of any grant under Clause (1) and to any law to be made under that Clause as they have effect in relation to the making of a grant with regard to any expenditure mentioned in the annual financial statement and the law to be made for the authorisation of appropriation of moneys out of the Consolidated Fund of India to meet such expenditure.

That is, under Article 116, the Parliament has power to grant in advance the estimated expenditure as well as unexpected demand for resources, as well as exceptional grants.

Having given above constitutional provisions, let us now summarise the procedure for Budget Session.

As explained above, it is Article 112 of the Constitution of India which makes obligatory to the Government of India to prepare "a statement of estimated receipts and expenditure of the Government of India" and it has to be planned before the Parliament. This exercise has to be made every financial year (i.e. from 1st April to 31st March). There are three accounts pertaining to the Government of India. They are:

(1) Consolidated Fund (as stipulated in Article 266(1)
(2) Contingency Fund (as stipulated in Article 267(1)
(3) Public Account (as stipulated in Article 266(2).

The money out of these funds cannot be withdrawn by the Government unless Parliament approves the budget proposal and authorises to withdraw money or appropriate fund as per prescribed procedure.

To iterate, the Consolidated Fund is comprised of all revenue receipts, loans raised and recoveries of loans granted by the Government. The entire expenditure incurred by the Government is met from the Consolidated Fund of India.

5.11 Measures to cut Government Expenditure

India has made its beginning for structural adjustment in June 1991 and by December 1991, it had already enunciated intention to close down or sell all or most of the public sector enterprises. It had adopted the policy of liberalisation and do away with the licensing mechanism with the result that three organisations of Central Government had to be closed down; viz. Director General of Technical Development (DGTD); Chief Controller of Import and

Export (CCIE) and Controller of Cement. The President of India has opted to forego 10 per cent of salary as a part of strategy supporting restraining government expenditure. This move was supported by various Ministers including the Prime Minister who has also enunciated to forego 10 per cent of his salary.

Uttar Pradesh Government headed by Kalyan Singh of Bhartiya Janata Party was perhaps the first to issue orders on restricting the "extravagance and undue expenses", though curb of corruption was not directly aimed at. According to press reports, the Uttar Pradesh Government issued directives on January 6, 1992 to cut "administration and unproductive expenditure in order to mobilize resources for development schemes". Certain categories of officers have been made responsible to ensure adherence of the instruction on cut off government expenditure as well as various local bodies, public enterprises, corporations, State Universities, and other departments under the control of specified or designated officers. Other measures in this direction included:

1. No direct recruitment to vacant non-technical posts of Class one, two, three and four should be made till a five per cent cut in strength of respective cadre is affected.
2. Direct recruitment to the posts of supervisory staff of Class one and Class two should be made only on the discretion of the Secretary and head of the department concerned after effecting five per cent cut in total strength.
3. Review of Plan and non-Plan expenditure to ensure surrender of unspent funds prior to close of financial year, so that savings are ensured.
4. No purchase of new vehicles be made, except ambulances, by any government department. Replacement of old vehicles by new vehicles has been permitted only with prior approval of the Finance Department of the State Government.
5. The telephones at the residence of officers below the pay scale of Rs 3700-5000 would be sanctioned only in special circumstances and the government would bear the expenditure of only the free calls allowed at residential phones of officers.
6. The norms prescribed for travel by first class, air and air-conditioned journey have been referred to for strict adherence and compliance with.

7. The officers on deputation in public undertakings should not be provided with facilities beyond what they were getting in their respective parent departments.
8. No officer/employee should be nominated for any training or seminar whatsoever.
9. Ban on display of advertisements by departments, public undertakings and autonomous bodies unless they are meant for business promotion. For other advertisements, prior approval of concerned Minister and for special publicity advertisement campaign the Chief Minister's approval would be necessary.
10. Curb the practice of employees visiting Delhi (nation's capital) frequently in connection with pending matters. Also, curb applied on journey outside State. Restrain travelling experiences. Restriction on tours of accompanying personal staff unless urgency of situation warrants it.
11. A 20 per cent cut in petrol/diesel consumption by government vehicles. No additional funds on this account would be made available.
12. Curb on the printing of greeting cards, diaries and calendars, by the government departments, public undertakings, local bodies, and autonomous institutions.
13. Ban on entertainment programmes by various departments and offices at the cost of State Exchequer, except with the prior approval of the Government.
14. Curbs on the purchase of new furniture and fresh decorations in any office with the change of incumbent.
15. The powers delegated for reappropriation of funds at various levels in this connection (item 14 above) has been withdrawn.
16. All the public undertakings, authorities and autonomous institutions have been asked not to open new guest houses, and to continue the existing ones the permission of the Chief Minister should be sought.

Above sixteen measures should hopefully cut down the government consumption at least by 3 per cent. Though the side effect of these measures would be obvious, the steps taken by the Government of Uttar Pradesh would set an example to the Central Government and other States to follow. The adverse impact could be fall of revenues of railway, air, communication, training institutions, etc. because government is major user of railway's first class, airconditioned coaches, air travels, telephones, vehicles, etc. The outgoing funds of one department forms the revenue of other or receiving Ministry. Despite the fact that telephone was invented about a century back, its accessibility utility and affordability by average Indian citizen is remote dream because of its tariffs, long waiting time and high cost of installation. With the result, telephone industry remained a government's affair for manufacturing and its demand / consumption. Similarly, government is major purchaser of trucks, buses, jeeps and staff cars for the use of government services, offices, etc. With such ban on purchase of new vehicles would mean low demand for these vehicles and obviously revenue on account of sales, excise duty, etc. would be less. That is, the curb of expenditure would also mean curb the production of those items which generate higher revenue.

Revenue deficit (in December, 1991) of both Centre and States together has exceeded Rs 20,000 crores per annum. Elimination of "political pricing" in sectors like electricity, transport, education, etc. to help States wipe out their fiscal deficits in the next three years has been another prescription.

A substantial part of the Centre's fiscal deficit could be traced to Central assistance to the States, and therefore, the States' action to reduce the deficit as States' own deficit exceeds 3.5 per cent of GDP.

The losses of State Electricity Boards exceed Rs 4,000 crores. The average rate of return on capital of the Electricity Boards was minus 14 per cent. Obviously, on one side deliberate attempt is being made to suppress the prices, and on the other side, demand for electricity is increasing. That is why Dr Manmohan Singh has rightly pointed out to National Development Council that : "no viable power generation industry could be built on such a basis. Further, private capital would not be attracted to an industry with such a "perverse incentive structure".

Reduction in 10 per cent senior officials posts from the level of Joint Secretary, abolition of about 1,000 jobs in three agencies, a 20 per cent cut in domestic and foreign travel allocation and a ban on first class air travel by the Ministers, as announced on December 24, 1991 in National Development Council Meeting called in the context of approving Draft Paper or Approach Paper on Eighth

Five Year Plan (1992-97) is basically to bring fiscal deficit and overcome economic crisis-91. That is, total 599 officials in the rank of Joint Secretaries and above including 207 officials of corresponding equivalent ranks. Ten per cent of say 600 officials would mean officials strength to be reduced by 60 numbers.

For a common man the drive for liberalisation and restructuring economy in India came to mean cuts on jobs and investment and rises in prices. Obviously, the deregulation or decontrol and abolishing licensing mechanism would mean abolishing the organisation concerned with licensing of industrial undertakings, imports and exports. The Chief Controller of Imports and Exports (CCIE), Cement Controller's office and Director General of Technical Development (DGTD), have practically no role to play if licensing mechanism is abolished. With the result, above 1,000 posts would be abolished. The reduction in 10 per cent senior officials posts from the level of Joint Secretary and correspondingly on lower categories has also been envisaged. The size of bureaucracy in India could be seen from the fact that as on December 24, 1991, there were 124 officials of Secretary rank including 44 officials of equivalent rank; 103 Additional Secretary level officials including 30 of equivalent rank officials, and 373 Joint Secretaries including 133 of the equivalent ranks.

5.12 The Outstanding Liabilities

The outstanding liabilities of Central government comprise :

1. Internal liabilities
   - A. Internal debts e.g. Market borrowing and other
   - B. External debts
2. External debt outstanding
3. Gross interest payments

Total liabilities are of the order of Rs 353,196 crores in 1991-92, which is about 58 per cent of the GDP (see table: 1).

There is nothing substantial policy framework to deal with outstanding liabilities.

5.13 Foreign Aid

The external assistance authorisation and utilisation by India since 4th plan till 1990-91 are as follows:

Table 1 : Outstanding Liabilities of the Central Government (Rs Crores)

No.	Item	1980-81	1983-84	1984-85	1985-86	1986-87	1987-88	1988-89	1989-90	1990-91	1991-92
1	2	3	4	5	6	7	8	9	10	11	12
1.	Internal liabilities (Outstanding)	48451 (35.6)	80141 (38.6)	96804 (41.8)	119331 (45.5)	146247 (49.9)	172338 (51.7)	204025 (51.7)	239849 (53.2)	279528 (52.8)	318074 (52.2)
	(a) Internal debt	30864	50264	58537	71039	86312	98646	114498	133193	151352	169584
(i)	Market borrowings	15676	26394	30470	35352	40880	46743	55161	62565	70565	78065
(ii)	Others	15188	23870	28067	35687	45432	51903	59337	70628	80787	91519
	(b) Other internal borrowings	17587 (12.9)	29877 (14.4)	38267 (16.5)	48292 (18.4)	59935 (20.5)	73692 (22.1)	89527 (22.7)	106656 (23.7)	128176 (24.2)	148490 (24.4)
2.	External Debt Outstanding	11298 (8.3)	15120 (7.3)	16637 (7.2)	18153 (6.9)	20299 (6.9)	23223 (7.0)	25746 (6.5)	28343 (6.3)	31831 (6.0)	35122 (6.8)
3.	Total Outstanding Liabilities (1+2)	59749 (43.9)	95261 (45.9)	113441 (49.0)	137484 (52.4)	166546 (56.9)	195561 (58.7)	229771 (58.3)	268192 (59.5)	311359 (58.8)	353196 (58.0)
4.	Gross interest payments	2604	4795	5749	7512	9246	11252	14278	17735	28150	27450
5.	Net interest payments	809	2127	1786	2917	3893	5497	7297	9269	12277	16441
6.	Gross interest payment as % of total expenditure	11.6	13.3	13.1	14.1	14.4	16.0	17.5	18.7	26.2	23.2
7.	Net interest payment as % of total expenditure	3.6	5.9	4.1	5.5	6.1	7.8	9.8	9.8	11.4	13.9

Table 1 (*Contd.*)

1	2	3	4	5	6	7	8	9	10	11	12
	Memorandum items: External Debt (Outstanding) (converted at year end exchange rates	13479	20214	24004	26638	32312	36578	46838	54100	660017	N.A.
		9.9	9.7	10.4	10.2	11.0	11.0	11.9	12.0	12.9	N.A

* *External debt figures represent borrowings by Central Government from external resources and are based upon historic rates of exchange*

Notes:

1. Figures in decimal are percentages to respective GDPs.
2. GDP (at current prices) for 1991-92 is estimated to grow by 15.0 per cent

(Source: Economic Survey 1991-92, part II, pp.13)

Table 2 : Overall External Assistance (Rs Crores)

Year	*Loans*	*Grants*	*Total*	*PL480*	*Grand Total*	*GDP at current yr*	*% of GDP*
1	2	3	4	5	6	7	
	Authorisation						
4th plan	9665.3	753.1	10418.4	2637.5	13055.9	67039	19.48
1974-75	1481.4	189.8	1671.2		1671.2	71201	2.35
1975-76	2192.8	440.7	2633.5	20.0	2653.5	76201	3.48
1976-77	806.7	386.1	1192.8	93.6	1286.4	76536	1.68
1977-78	1536.6	337.6	1874.2	22.8	1897.0	87351	2.17
1978-79	1894.6	441.1	2335.7		2335.7	93880	2.49
1979-80	1295.1	564.4	1859.5		1859.5	102442	1.82
1980-81	3771.2	75.8	3847.0		3847.0	122226	3.15
1981-82	2766.5	207.4	2973.9		2973.9	142976	2.08
1982-83	2549.4	423.3	2972.7		2972.7	158851	1.87
1983-84	1700.8	386.9	2087.7		2087.7	185991	1.12
1984-85	4409.3	470.7	4880.0		4880.0	207869	2.35
1985-86	5337.0	313.4	5650.4		5650.4	234159	2.41
1986-87	5730.0	429.5	6159.5		6159.5	260442	2.37
1987-88	8203.1	1062.2	9265.3		9265.3	294408	3.15
1988-89	12855.6	214.2	13069.8		13069.8	348896	3.75
1989-90	1105.8	720.2	10826.0		10826.0	401569	2.70
1990-91	7601.3	522.1	8123.4		8123.4	472599	1.72
	B. Utilisation						
4th plan	8572.6	712.7	9285.3	2636.8	11922.1	67039	17.78
1974-75	1220.4	93.9	1313.3		1314.3	71201	1.85
1975-76	1464.9	253.3	1718.2	92.3	1810.5	76201	2.38
1976-77	1285.3	245.8	1531.1	67.3	1598.4	76536	2.09
1977-78	1007.5	260.6	1268.1	21.9	1290.0	87351	1.48
1978-79	942.3	273.3	1215.6		1215.6	93880	1.29
1979-80	1048.6	304.5	1353.1		1353.1	102442	1.32
1980-81	1765.3	396.5	2161.8		2161.8	122226	1.77
1981-82	1519.4	345.5	1864.9		1864.9	142976	1.30
1982-83	1909.2	342.8	2252.0		2252.0	158851	1.42
1983-84	1962.4	303.4	2265.8		2265.8	185991	1.22
1984-85	1962.2	397.2	2359.4		2359.4	207869	1.14
1985-86	2493.1	442.9	2936.0		2936.0	234159	1.25
1986-87	3175.7	429.3	3605.0		3605.0	260442	1.38
1987-88	4574.4	477.5	5051.9		5051.9	294408	1.72
1988-89	4738.6	565.8	5304.4		5304.4	348896	1.52
1989-90	5137.8	664.7	5802.5		5802.5	401569	1.44
1990-91	6170.0	534.3	6704.3		6704.3	472599	1.42

Notes 1 : Figures of authorisation from 1974-75 onwards have been arrived at by applying the average exchange rate of the rupee with individual donor currencies. Figures for 1974-75 are at average exchange rate for the respective month, and subsequent years at current rates applicable to the dates of transactions.

2: Loan amounts are net of surrenders, de-obligations and cancellations etc. In case of PL-480 amounts are net of lapsed agreement.

3: Figure for utilisation are inclusive of suppliers credit and non-government loans upto 1977-78. Subsequent data are exclusive of suppliers credit.

The time series data were subjected to log-log analysis to find the empirical relationship. Following are the models derived using the data shown above.

Empirical model 1:

For the period from 1974-75 to 1990-91

$$\text{Log } Y = 1.68 + 1.04 \log x, \quad R^2 = 0.9$$
$$(18.95) \quad (11.51)$$

Empirical model 2:

For the period from 1980-81 to 1990-91

$$\text{Log } Y = 2.22 + 0.90 \log x, \quad R^2 = 0.9$$
$$(38.15) \quad (9.82)$$

Where Y = GDP of the country at current prices
X = utilisation of foreign aid

the figures in parentheses indicates the t value

These models explain that each per cent growth in utilisation of foreign aid would cause India's GDP to grow at 0.9 times the foreign aid utilised.

Model 2:

For the period from 1980-81 to 1990-91

$$\text{Log } Y = 2.22 + 0.90 \log x, \quad R^2 = 0.9$$
$$(38.15) \quad (9.82)$$

As could be seen from above data that India's GDP has grown at a rate of 15.1 per cent per annum over a period of last five years i.e. from 1985-86 to 1990-91. Assuming growth of GDP at 15.1 % p.a. at current prices and using model-1 the foreign aid needs (i.e. for utilisation to keep the pace of GDP) of India are:

Table 3: Projections for India's Need for Foreign Aid

Rs. Crores at 1990-91 prices			
Year	*Aid*	*Year*	*Aid*
1992-93	9826	1997-98	18581
1993-94	11161	1998-99	21106
1994-95	12678	1999-2000	21106
1995-96	14401	2000-01	27233
1996-97	16358	2001-02	30934

(Calculated using empirical model-2)

The amount shown above is exclusive of massive aid needed for structural adjustment needs. The structural needs are perceived due to political reasons and as assessed by donar agencies particularly IMF.

Earlier, it was presumed that every dollar received by developing countries as aid from developed countries was to refund later twice the aid but days to come will see that refund would be more than thrice the amount received as aid. No country in the world will lend dollars to developing country merely by benevolent attitude but such lending is accepted form of international finance, flow of capital, induced mobilisation of investment, globalisation of resources, etc.

IMF has agreed to fund India's fiscal deficit problem. India's Crisis-91 has attracted worldwide attention and so called socialistic pattern of society has suddenly opted to liberate from all constraints imposed since 44 years of her Independence. IMF's assurance or grant of $ 2.2 billions as standby loan and converting it to larger loan of $ 7 billions under Extended Fund Facility (EFF) was accompanied by policy prescriptions for India to follow. The policy prescription included bringing down its defence expenditure by 20 per cent during the next three years beginning from April 1, 1992, this may bring down fiscal deficit to 4 per cent of GDP by 1994-95, i.e. by the expiry of time stipulated for defence expenditure reduction by 20 per cent.

Of the amount sanctioned, $ 2.2 billion as standby loan, IMF may release $ 800 million on November 19, 1991 but other condition to release second instalments of $ 2.2 billion standby loan was that IMF would like to see 1992-93 budget to their satisfaction and according to their prescription. There were astronomical changes in industrial and trade policies in India since the budget of 1991-92.

On October 28, 1991, during the visit of IMF's Managing Director—Michael Camdessus, Indian Government announced further liberalisation in its policy on investment by non-resident Indian's (NRI) and overseas corporate bodies (OCBs). Actually, Michel Camdessus has expressed his opinion during his visit to India in the capacity of Managing Director of IMF that India should remove the "remaining constraints to free flow of foreign investment" to India. Imparting full benefits for repatriation of capital employed by NRI or OCBs is essential.

The investment up to 100 per cent foreign equity in high priority industries including hotels, tourism related industries, shipping and hospitals. This is in addition to the scheme of 100 per cent NRI investment in 100 per cent exported units and taking over sick units by NRI for revival. The equity participation up to 100 per cent has been permitted in various areas such as export oriented deep sea fishing, oil exploration services and advanced diagnostic centres with full repatriation benefits.

The new policy on investment by NRI and OCBs stipulates the condition that the outflow on account of dividend payments is balanced by export earnings over a period of seven years from the commencement of commercial production. The Reserve Bank of India (RBI) would, however, monitor such payments of dividends.

5.14 Concern of G-15

Group of 15 nations categorised as developing countries had recently a Summit at Caracas (Venezuela) on New International Consensus on Development. Summit was held from November 26-30, 1991. The G-15 represent the globe's major areas particularly Africa, the Americas (including the Carribean), Asia and Europe. The members comprising G-15 are :

1.	Algeria	6.	India	11.	Peru
2.	Argentina	7.	Indonesia	12.	Senegal
3.	Brazil	8.	Malaysia	13.	Venezuela
4.	Egypt	9.	Mexico	14.	Yugoslavia
5.	Jamaica	10.	Nigeria	15.	Zimbabwe

Democracy, Human Rights and Rules of Laws have been main ideals for this Summit. Similarly, directing efforts to satisfy the basic needs of food, shelter, health, literacy and employment. The rational approach had been advocated to deal with the problems of developing countries, such as poverty, unemployment, health, illiteracy, etc.

This Summit was concomitant with the transition and disintegration process of Soviet Union. Mr P.V. Narasimha Rao in his address rightly pointed out that : "There is little doubt that democracy and pluralism are going to be pattern of the future. But how meaningful will the world democracy be, if it could not deliver the goods to meet the vast needs of food, shelter, health, literacy and employment? The challenge is, therefore, not so much in establishing democratic patterns, but on making democracy work to meet the basic needs of our people. That is where the centrality of the development process must come in."

The new economic order of the world is emerging due to demise of both communist ideologies and communist supreme nation USSR. Gorbachev's so called "Perestroika" which resulted in death of communism and disintegration of USSR has tilted the entire balance of supremacy towards capitalism and capitalist nations particularly the USA. India's perception is worth appreciating that: "The countries of East Europe are following integrationist strategies. Most developing countries as part of their restructuring process are also aiming to enhance their interaction with the mainstream of the world economy. To a large extent, the globalisation of production, consumption and trade has become an imperative of technology. These processes and trends cannot be viewed in isolation. They are part of a pattern which affects all of us and the system of international economic relations within which we must all seek our economic destiny." Obviously, the process of globsaliation must be consciously made for more supportive of the emerging trend. There has to be a willingness to deal with issues like financial flows, the debt overhang, access to markets and to advances in technology, so that globalisation and interdependence can be equitably managed in the interest of all." The role envisaged for G-15 should have a bearing on above aspects. Particularly "to articulate a reasoned and pragmatic development point of view, of the emerging trends not as "demandeurs", but in the spirit of making the process underway truly beneficial for the interdependence world economy and to engage our partners in a dialogue which will enable a common understanding on these aspects.

There is explicit reference to South-South cooperation, Non-Aligned Movement (NAM), a New International Economic Order (NIEO), North-South dialogue and collective reliance. India's suggestions include : (1) the setting up of a gene bank for medicinal and aromatic plants; and (2) working out the application of solar energy in irrigation pumps, small refrigerators, cookers and dryers.

5.15 Misconceptions about IMF

IMF has been playing a role in both developed and developing countries. But in developing countries, the role of both the World Bank and International Monetary Fund (IMF) is seen as interventionist in economic management of a country. There are various points which are always treated as "misconception". Some of which are :

1. The fund applies identical remedies, irrespective of country's circumstances;
2. Fund-supported adjustment programs are antigrowth;
3. The Fund bails out the commercial banks;
4. The Fund has a market-oriented, free enterprise philosophy, which it applies in a doctrinaire manner;
5. Fund-supported programs do not work;
6. Fund-supported programs harm the poor;
7. Fund supported programs impose austerity on member countries;
8. Developing countries have no influence on fund policies;
9. The Fund has influence only over deficit countries, it does nothing about surplus countries;
10. The Fund and the World Bank collude in dealing with developing countries.

The list of points could be enlarged but above ten points have been admitted as "misconceptions" even by the World Bank.

The external aid means accepting dominance of donar agency, country or organisation. It also tantamounts to surrender of some freedom and sovereignty of decisions, policies, trade mechanism, industrial output, etc. The acceptance of external interference in domestic policies is obvious. As political stability and economic stability are complementary to each other, any external aid on account of economic growth, stabilisation, liberalisation, reforms, structural adjustment, etc. is an indication of inconsistencies in political decisions, its stability and political behaviour of a country as a whole.

6

Competitiveness

6.01 Introduction

There is no formal definition of competitiveness. Still this term is often used in international forum. Whenever export strategies are discussed, this term does get reflected not only in policy statement but also in production strategies. Due to emergence of newly industrialised countries as well as growing dominance of Japanese goods, the exports from under-developed or developing countries are becoming more and more difficult. The competition among the countries for selling their product in other countries becomes more difficult if the prices of same goods are higher. America too is facing problems due to competition from Japanese goods.

Competitiveness among the industries within the country is a little different than the competitiveness among the nations. Both domestic market and international markets are influenced by trade policies, industrial policies and fiscal policies. Other factors influencing competitiveness are economies of scale, technological advancement, exchange rate, interest rate etc.

The factors which influence the competition and affect the trade are numerous. The price, technology, labour cost, cost of input materials, cost of energy consumed, productivity per man-hour, productivity of resources, productivity of capital employed, efficiency of management, role of trade unions and so on. The technology is one of the most important factors that contribute to the productivity and cost of production. In fact, the output per unit of input is the essence of productivity and competitiveness. But when government intervenes in the economy to control the prices and investment pattern as well as to control market forces intending to distort the resources allocation then the whole concept of competitiveness gets changed.

The competitiveness of a particular industry or a group of industries is different from the competitiveness of a country. In fact, country as a whole cannot be competitive in nature unless industries within that country are competitive enough. The different sectors of the economy are affected differently through industrial policies and trade policies. Each sector of the economy has different incremental output ratio (ICOR). The rate of return on capital employed also differs from one type of industrial activity to another.

Some of the important factors that are relevant to competitiveness of the country as a whole are:

1. Level of industrial development;
2. Technology available, capacity to generate, and innovative capability;
3. Structure of the economy;
4. The macro-economic policies;
5. Budget deficit, its magnitude and rate at which it grows;
6. Human capital, utilisation, quality, level of skillness;
7. Balance of trade and nature of export;
8. Role of public sector, their accountability, capacity to generate profit or surplus and not the deficit or loss making capacity; and
9. Agricultural production, its magnitude and level of self-sufficiency.

In fact, the role of government in making decisions that would encourage export is crucial. The trade policies are basic to competitiveness. No country can afford to continue imports without export. The export of primary commodities does not fetch more foreign reserves. It is only manufactured goods which are more value added than primary goods. But the manufactured goods do not get easily marketed abroad unless those are competitive enough to be sold, and preferred over the alternate available. Therefore, competitiveness does not merely depend upon the export volume itself but on indirect inputs like industrial designing, industrial engineering, value engineering, cost-benefit analysis, financial management, etc. Over and above all these fiscal policies of the government and tax rate, import policies etc. the availability of tested raw material and capital goods are other factors which influence the competitiveness.

Competitiveness of industry could be on the basis of technological superiority, human resources, inputs and cost per unit of input and output, market size and capability to influence consumer in favour of products thus manufactured. The triumph of capitalism and emergence of socio-capitalism has created new global competitive environment. The fittest efficient and competitive enterprise to survive and sick, inefficient, disabled, and uncompetitive (i.e. seeking protection or running on protectionism theory or infant industry arguments) to exit out of industrial activity has become the theme in 1990s. Both management of economy and management of enterprises have suddenly changed basic foundation on the basis of ideals. Those which will not be able to cope up with the pace of changes all over the world, would face the closure. The factors attributing global competitiveness are numerous, such as :

(i) Identical items qualifying for living standard and international demonstrate of such items;
(ii) Common standard of performance or comparative standards;
(iii) Interchangeability standards, technological competition;
(iv) Quality and reliability at affordable prices;
(v) Accessibility to foreign capital, foreign investment, and proven new technologies;
(vi) Fluctuating exchange rate;
(vii) Improved infrastructure, transportation, communication, logistic system;
(viii) Highest rate of diffusion of technological Information;
(ix) Mobility of international resources aimed at restructuring global or economic world order;
(x) Integrating monetary and economic systems of all countries to respond or align with changing or emerging new global or international monetary systems;
(xi) Conditions favouring liberal trade and need for export oriented strategies instead of input substitutional strategies;
(xii) Need to increase direct participation by MNC or foreign investment;

(xiii) Need for entering foreign market and face direct competition;

(xiv) Need for inventions, innovation and diffusion as well as perpetuate technological development; and

(xv) Need for charges in trade policies.

There are numerous such factors relevant to competitiveness. The manufacturing alone is meaningless unless suitable trade policies are framed.

6.02 Prices and Trade Policies

Keeping in view the concepts of managing economy within the own resources, the measures initiated in India are explained below. To begin with let us have a look at some sectors of Indian economy.

Under the umbrella of "structural adjustment" and overcome of crisis 91, (i.e. BOP crisis surfaced in India since 1991), the wave of hike in prices was set in India since 1991. Railway in India is one of the biggest railways in the world but it is still to reach poorest of poor in rural and tribal areas. Nevertheless, the railway tariffs are frequently raised.

On January 8, 1991, there was hike in excess baggage rates by 30 per cent to be effective from January 16, 1991. The excess baggage charges are to be levied in excess of 35 kg. in second class, 40 kg. in air-conditioned chair car, 50 kg. in first class or 70 kg. in air-conditioned sleeper and 70 kg. in air-conditioned first class. India's Eighth Plan was to be launched in 1990-91 to 1994-95 but due to political crisis, it was to be postponed for 1992-93 and 1996-97 (both years inclusive in Plan period) was being launched amidst the crisis-91 (crisis of BOP, exchange rate, lack of resources, budget deficit, trade deficit, declining production, etc.).

The lack of resource for financing the Eighth Plan in general and sectoral allocation of budgetary support component in particular has compelled government to resort to various measures including rising prices, tariffs, taxes and curtail subsidised goods, items and services. The jurisdiction provided for raising 30 per cent excess baggage rates was that investment requirement of Railways was estimated at Rs 45,600 crores in the Eighth Plan but dwindling budgetary support, high borrowing cost and burgeoning burden of social cost they are called upon to bear etc. have forced to find critical choice to find resources, mobilize the resource to finance partly the investment requirement. The perpetual need for modernisation, upgradation, replacement, rehabilitation, addition, modification on one hand and expansion of railways' network on other hand puts pressure on resources availability and utilisation. The estimated 32,000 km track renewal by the end of 8th Five Year Plan of India was due but out of 32,000 km. track at the beginning of the Plan (i.e. 1992-93), the arrears were 12,000 km. and 11.500 km. will fall due for renewal. A surplus of Rs 560 crores was reported at the end of the Seventh Plan, after payment of Rs 3,249 crores towards dividend and appropriation of Rs 6,735 crores to depreciation reserve fund (DRF) and Rs 2,338 crores to pension fund. The corporate plan of Railways indicate that by the year 2000, the Railways would be required to carry 370 to 400 billion tonne kilometre of freight tariff, 310 to 330 billion passengers kilometre and 105 to 115 billion passenger kilometre to suburban passenger tariff.

The commodities with major import content in input would suffer setback if the prices of imported items go up. The strategies of import substitution led to higher prices of the items domestically manufactured, and it eventually gave the way for subsidies. Similarly, the export strategies lay emphasis on supply of inputs for manufacturing items for exports at much lower prices prevailing in domestic market so that its output could compete in international market, thereby paving the way for export subsidies. In other words, failure to curb price escalation of the items, irrespective of domestic or international market, reflects efficiency of economy. Subsidies are resultant of government's intention to lower the prices to meet mass demand of consumers and unability of manufacturers to supply those commodities at intended prices. That is, subsidies could be viewed as difference between government's perceptions and manufacturers' perceptions — about prices for domestic and export markets. So called "market clearing prices" are of only academic interest as all goods are sold in targetted market at one or other item at a price decided by traders. All prices are market clearing prices. There is no frame of reference to decide how market clearing prices would behave in different circumstances. Similarly, "affordable prices" prevailing in one country cannot be treated as affordable prices in another country. Technological advancement and per capita income are interrelated. What is said to be technological gap is nothing but difference between per capita income of under-developed and developed countries.

6.03 Administered Prices

As we know, in India, the prices of some of the items are regularly monitored, announced, and changed by the government. This act of the government is purely an intervention in the market. It has both merits and demerits. To "initiate open debate" on prices administered by the Indian Government, then Minister of Finance in his Budget Speech of 1986 said, "There has been a healthy debate in the country regarding the impact of administered prices on the inflationary situation. When all other prices are changing, some changes in administered prices are necessary and inevitable. But the government accepts the view that as far as possible, there is need to stabilise the prices of critical commodities. In order to clarify the issue involved, and to initiate an open debate on the appropriate approach, the government will present a policy paper on administered prices to Parliament".

In accordance with above statement, a paper was prepared on "Administered Price Policy", which explains the view point as prevails in India. In Indian economy, "large number of commodities" are governed by "formally or informally" by the government through controls of administered prices. The commodities included in administered prices famework include "either vital raw material inputs to industry or are items that are essential for final consumers." The essential commodities are invariably subjected to price controls. The logic or justification provided for governing price control is that "the prices of these commodities, therefore, have a pervasive influence on the growth and development of the economy and on the welfare of a broad cross-section of consumers. The poorer sections, in particular, are greatly dependent on a progressive pricing policy with regard to commodities essential for everyday life. A clear policy on administered prices lead to a more stable economic environment for effective planning and investment decisions both in public and the private sector."

It is difficult to relate influence of "administered prices" on "growth and development". In fact, "administered prices" in India were prevailing in one or another form since independence in 1947, or more explicit since advent of planning. As far as "welfare" of poor sections through administered prices is concerned, its benefits cannot be squarely denied. If bottom strata is deprived of wage employment, and accrual of adequate income to household is very low, or purchasing power of poor is suppressed due to low level of economic growth and development, it is obvious then that government has onus to ensure availability of essential commodities to poor sections at the prices affordable by poor. That is, the criterion of suppressing the prices at affordable level" is more valid in such a situation than allowing "free trade" to attain level of "market clearing prices". But cost of achieving and maintaining affordable prices of essential commodities is much higher than allowing trade to attain market clearing prices. Basically, infant industry which is synonymous with under-developed economy supports the argument of "affordable prices" at a commensurate level of per capita income of the country whereas "market clearing prices" support the argument of "competitive market" which is synonymous with free trade and level of industrialisation in the country.

6.04 Wholesale Price Index

Wholesale price index in India comprises price variation of 360 commodities including 55 major items whose prices are either fully administered, partially administered or subjected to different forms of voluntary and other mechanism of control. These items could be broadly categorised as follows:

Category		*WPI weight*
Overall WPI (or inflation index)		100
1.	Non-administered prices	69.149
2.	Administered prices	25.337
A1:	Core items	8.272
A2:	Other fully administered	3.229
A3:	Partially administered	13.836
3.	Petroleum and its products	5.514

The weightage of non-administered prices is 69.15 or near to 69 per cent of Wholesale Price Index (WPI) and obviously the prices of these items exert more pressure on economy. The balance of about 30.85 or say 31 per cent are monitored by the Government machinery. But as is obvious that output of one sector forms either input or intermediate product of other sector the whole economy gets proportional inflationary pressure.

The three categories of items governed under administered prices are:

A1: Core item of administered prices;

A2: Other fully administered items;

A3: Partially administered prices items;

A1 —Core items of administered prices mechanism are those items which are also termed as basic goods. These items have the weight of 8.272 per cent in WPI. The prices of these items are fully administered. In this category are the basic goods like coal, electricity fertilizers, iron and steel. Coal and electricity are the items with full monopoly of the Government. In fact industrial sector has greater stake on these items. By implication of extensive network of public sector enterprises, the Government is both major producer and consumer of both coal and electricity in industrial sector. Of the five major integrated steel plants, four are public sector enterprises and thus the share of Government in primary production of iron and steel is more or near to monopoly. Similarly production of fertilizer in Government's public sector together with cooperative sector is much more than private sector. However, users are private farmers. Hence though Government is major producer or supplier (including imported fertilizers) of fertiliser in the country. The distribution channels of iron and steel as well as fertiliser are monitored by the Government.

A2: Other fully administered items with a total weight of 3.23 per cent include at least six items such as iron ore, non ferrous metals, drugs and medicines, paper, newsprint and insecticides, which are both partly intermediate goods (like nonferrous metals and iron ores) and important final goods (like paper, newsprint and insecticides).

A3: Partially administered items includes rice, wheat, sugar, vanaspati and cement. These agro based items have been kept under "dual pricing" mechanism to contain inflation by making available in open market as well as public distribution system (PDS) simultaneously.

Above 305 commodities left out of purview of administered pricing system, that is out of 360 items only 55 items are under the purview of administered prices. The items out of purview of administered prices constitute the weight of 69.149 (in 100 WPI weight), petroleum products have weight of 5.514 and Administered prices item constitute 25.337 (on 100 point WPI scale).

Inflationary pressure is resultant of "political pricing" and "populist measure" adopted based on appeasing policies. Without any reasonable ground the prices of certain commodities, support prices, purchase of agricultural products, subsidised tarrifs for electricity, prices of diesel, petrol, kerosene, fertilizer, etc. are manipulated to suit the political thinking. Both supply side and demand side have their own interest on prices in the country. It is paradoxical that consumer wants low prices for the items of daily requirement and producers want higher profit for their initiative, investment and risk. Trade and commerce want adequate profit for ensuring optimum distribution. Trade and commerce follow the law of gravitations i.e. the goods, commodities and tradable items will flow from low profit to high profit making spatial distributive locations or channel, and also it will flow from highly competitive market to monopolistic or low competitive market.

The problem of controlling prices or setting right the prices is on both side i.e. on production (or supply) and distribution side, as well as consumption (or demand) side. On production side or supply sides one can easily see that unit cost of production is proportional to the sum total of input, assuming technology is constant. If technological efficiency is a function of production factor and it is perfectly conditioned in particular socio-economic environment of a country then only factors which influence the unit cost of production is the prices of inputs, infrastructure, interest rate, and rate of return intended, size of investment. Obviously economies of scale is another factor but it is always conditioned according to socio-economic environment of a country.

Obviously subsidised prices of inputs, infrastructure, interest rate etc. will help produce the output of lower cost. But trade and commerce will help raise prices and thereby eat away the whole subsidies. Conversely the higher the prices of inputs higher will be cost of output. That is why, technology which will ensure lower inputs cost per unit cost of output or reduce the unit cost of output for same or lower quantity of input is favoured. Though, "rate of return" and "rate of change in prices of input and cost per unit of output" are not controlled simultaneously the relationship of these two is only through technology":

For one or other reason it is observed that:

1. Prices of agricultural commodities rise continuously upward.
2. Share of agriculture in GNP is decreasing due to increase in share of other sectors.
3. External factors like import of oil and other raw material tend to raise both domestic prices.

One thing must be borne in mind that it is totally wrong to assume that control of inflationary pressure would be possible by controlling aggregate demand and managing the supply of key commodities through Government's network of public distribution system or super bazars. Because such an assumption presupposes that new demand must not be envisaged or suppressed. The demand which in extreme cases promotes starvation deaths, infant morality, rate, hunger, deprivation and total suppression of investment needed to me the just and rightful demand of the growing population. Eventuality of this could be that a country remains underdeveloped. Unless demand grows there cannot be "circular flow" of goods, commodities, services and skill nor there would be expansion of industry, investment, trade and commerce. Obviously projecting low demand as generally seen in official documents or government channel breeds proportionate corruption, malpractice, pilferage, and parallel economy. In very straightforward terms the planning process under the psuedo economic management called "mixed economy" the emergence of parallel economy or black economy is obvious.

To explain this point one can easily see the economics management in India with reference to demand for electronic goods, (colour TV, VCR and tapes) steel, coal, foodgrains, etc. particularly steel (5 under public sector and one under private sector) governed by price control and on other side there are over 500 small scale induction melting (scrap melting to get ingots) furnaces, as well as above 200 electric arc furnaces. Despite better technological performance of two public sector enterprises, the overall profitability is not high as compared with the private sector enterprises.

Steel decontrol has the implication of freight equalisation policy as its integral part. There is obvious apprehension that decontrol of steel will result in hike of steel prices in domestic market. The result of hike in steel prices would also cause inflationary pressure on economy or would cause wholesale price Index to rise. There are divergent views about decontrol. Both pro and anti decontrol groups of steel have their genuine reasoning. The integrated steel plants of SAIL, IISCO, and TISCO favour decontrol but the consumer State like J&K, Southern States (namely Tamilnadu, Karnataka, Kerala, Andhra Pradesh, Pondicherry), North Eastern States etc. oppose the move as these States do not have integrated steel plants in their control to meet fully their own requirement. Those who favour liberalisation and delicensing, also favour decontrol of steel. In fact pricing of steel has helped the private companies like TISCO and mini steel plants to earn profit much more than they expected. A two phased proposal envisaging decontrol of steel pricing and partial retention of distribution control in regard to the priority sector envisaged the first phase with proposal of decontrolling all items which do not have a premium in the sale prices in the market and raising the premium by Rs 1000 to Rs 1500 per tonne of those items which command a premium. There would be no further hike in steel prices to offset the coal and power prices increases which have raised substantively the input costs of the steel industry.

Since last several years there is control over not only licensing but even control over iron and steel pricing as well as distribution. This causes the primary producers namely SAIL, IISCO, TISCO to maintain their corporate production plan as per the targets assigned to them. Approximately 80 per cent of the rerollable are produced by mini steel plants and 20 per cent of the rerollable are contributed by the main producers. With the control on 20 per cent production of main producers and 80 per cent leaving free to earn the profit according to convenience, a mini steel plant, government is trying to suppress the profits of main producers. The premium earned by mini steel plants is very high, it is said that the mini steel plants charge about Rs 1500 to Rs 2000 per tonne over and above the prices of similar items by main producers. The pricing mechanism of steel usually results in undercharging of servis, rod and bars etc. About 20 per cent of the country's production whereas 80 per cent of the country's production from mini steel plant is allowed to charge exorbitant prices i.e. to any customer at any prices. Whenever there is shortage of production

Table 1 : Minimum Support Prices of Agricultural Commodities

Commodity	Price Category	Marketing Year*										
		1980-81	1981-82	1982-83	1983-84	1984-85	1985-86	1986-87	1987-88	1988-89	1989-90	1990-91
1. Wheat	Procurement	117	130	142	151	152	157	162	166	173	183	200
2. Paddy (Common variety)	-do-	105	115	122	132	137	142	146	150	160	185	**
3. Coarse grains	-do-	105	116	118	124	130	130	132	135	145	165	
4. Barley	Min. Support	@	105	@	122	124	130	132	135	135	145	160
5. Barley	-do-	145	@	@	235	240	@	260	280	290	325	370
6. Arhar	-do-	190	@	215	245	275	300	320	325	360	425	
7. Moong	-do-	200	@	240	250	275	300	320	325	360	425	
8. Urad	-do-	200	@	230	245	275	300	320	325	360	425	
9. Mustard	-do-	@	@	@	355	360	355	400	415	430	460	510
10. Groundnut	-do-	206	270	295	315	340	350	370	390	430	500	
11. Sunflower	-do-	183	250	250	275	325	335	350	390	450	530	
12. Soyabean (black)	-do-	183	210	220	230	240	250	255	260	275	325$	
13. Cotton	-do-	304	@	380	400***	410***	425***	430	440	500	570	
14. Sugarcane	Statutory	13.0	13.0	13.0	13.5	14.0	16.5	17.0	18.5	19.5	22	
15. Jute	-do-	160	175	175	185	195	215	225	240	250	295	@@.

Notes:

* : Marketing Year : April-March for wheat, gram, barley, and mustard June-July for Jute; August-September for cotton and October for paddy and other Kharif crops.

** : Rs 195 per quintal for fine variety and Rs 205 per quintal for superfine variety

*** : refers to F-414/H-777 variety in contrast with usual Kapas 320F/J-34 variety

@ : Not announced

@@ : Minimum support price of TD-5 variety at Nowgong in Assam

$: Rs 300 per quintal for yellow variety

from mini steel plants or prices are high, there is great pressure on mini producers to meet the whole demand of the country. Also there is always move to pressurise main producers to sell items to rerollers without ever allowing them to process for more value added projects.

6.05 Liberalising Trade

Trade is very important from export earnings point of view. Trade policy reforms are regarded as an essential element in restructuring the economy so as to achieve increased productivity, competitiveness and strong export performance. Trade policy announced on August 13, 1991 includes the following reforms/ salient features:

Advance licence would be granted within 15 days to provide exporters with duty free access to inputs. The import is commensurate with output and some norms have been established. There are about 540 items for which import output norms exist and advance licence for these items, would be given within 15 days. Where such norms do not exist, the advance licence would be granted within 45 days. By October 1991, about 1,000 items or 90 per cent of the items of export would be covered under import output norms list, and remaining 10 per cent items would be covered under the list by December, 1991.

Decanalisation of several items of both import and export has been resorted to. The items of import where decanalisation has been resorted to are 6 under Open General Licence, 14 items under REP, that is total 20 items decanalised. Similarly, 16 items were decanalised for exports. The existing procedures for bank guarantees and legal undertaking from different categories have been streamlined and liberalised, to reduce unnecessary delay and allow greater freedom to exporters in procuring essential duty free raw-materials to maintain their export competitiveness in world markets.

All Export-Oriented Units (EOUs) and Export Processing Zones (EPZs) have been made eligible for EXIM scrips at the basic rate of 30 per cent net foreign exchange earnings.

Private bonded warehouses have been allowed to establish within EPZ for stocking and sale of duty free raw-materials, components, consumables and spares.

Duty applicable on DTA (Duty-Tax-Advantages) sales from EOUs and EPZs has been reduced to 50 per cent of the normal customs duty subject to the duty payable not being less than the excise duty on the same product. In order to encourage exporters to set up EOUs and EPZs, the net foreign exchange earned by the EOUs and EPZs has been allowed to club with earnings of their parent or associated companies in the DTA for the purpose of according export house or trading house status for the latter. The International Price Reimbursement Scheme (IPRS) for supply of steel to exporters has been extended to EOUs and EPZs.

A system of automatic approval for import of capital goods has been established to fulfil new industrial policy.

State Trading Corporation (STC) and Metals and Minerals Trading Corporation (MMTC) which were canalising agencies have been reoriented to achieve the objectives of emerging as international trading houses capable of operating in a global environment. The Government pledged support to the development of export houses and trading houses as instruments for promoting exports. Exports have been allowed to open foreign currency accounts in approved banks, raise external credits, pay for export-related imports from such accounts and credit export credits to such accounts.

The Office of the Chief Controller of Imports and Exports was redesignated as the Directorate General of International Trade, and functions assigned include promotion of exports and facilitate imports to promote export trade.

Improvement in EXIM scrip has been made to allow certain value-added agricultural products, all electronics products, high technology engineering products (to be notified separately), and certain drugs and intermediaries, eligible for an additional EXIM scrips (REP) entitlement of 10 per cent IOB value. Other than these products, the EXIM scrip rate of 30 per cent would prevail.

Steel was one of the items governed by the policies of administered prices. Price of steel was linked to another scheme known as "Freight Equalisation Scheme" which ensured same prices all over the country irrespective of distance involved to transport from integrated steel plants to consumer industries. On January 16, 1991, both control on the prices of iron and steel items and freight equalisation scheme were done away. Decontrol of iron and steel was always sought by the public sector enterprises, for their profitability. Freight equalisation scheme was in practice since 1956, but it was treated as obstacle for integrated steel plants' profitability.

Decontrol of iron and steel was also accompanied with abolition of distribution mechanism of Joint Plant Committee (JPC) which was set up in 1964, and reduction of import duty. The details of reduction in import duty were as follows:

— Pig iron's import duty reduced from 55 per cent to 25 per cent

— Import duty on billets and H.R. Coils has been reduced from 65 per cent to 45 per cent each and

— Import duty has been reduced from 35 per cent to 10 per cent.

There was fear that abolition of freight equalisation scheme would not affect consumers in Southern, Western and Northern States. But it was clarified that steel from integrated steel plants would make steel available at the present freight rates if the freight element was more than Rs 956 per tonne as fixed for FES Scheme and Rs 645 per tonne of pig iron.

The partial distribution was felt essential to cater to the needs of sensitive sectors like defence, exporters of engineering goods and North Eastern region. As a measure of liberalisation of economy, decontrol of steel prices was felt essential. This measure would also contribute to improve efficiency and international competitiveness, on one hand and on other hand, it would promote conducive industrial climate to create new capacities in the private sector for meeting the increasing requirements of the future.

Due to inflation and budget for 1991-92, there was general phobia of price increase on every item. The public sector enterprises were no exception to raise the price of their output. Salem Steel Plant has raised prices of its stainless steel with effect from August 1, 1991. The price hike is as follows :

Stainless steel Quantity (No.)	*Price hike Rs/Kg.*
304	17
316	23
310	40

These stainless steel grades are used for manufacturing stainless steel utensils.

The prices of alloy steel have been raised w.e.f. August 13, 1991 by Rs 2,000 to Rs 2,500 per tonne. This being a second price rise for alloy steels. The first price rise was announced in mid-June when price rise was Rs 1,500 per tonne. The reason quoted is that the higher prices of imported scrap, following devaluation of rupee are responsible for the second dose of hike in alloy steel prices.

6.06 Trade Policies/Decanalisation

In a bid to "bring capital goods and many more raw materials under the Open General Licence (OGL)" and switch over of the items from canalised list to OGL, 14 items of imports were put under REP, 6 items were added to the list of OGL, and 16 export items decanalised on August 14, 1991. These are in addition to all measures announced in Budget 1991-92.

A. Items decanalised and put under OGL (6 Nos.) :

1.	silk worms	4.	fluorospar
2.	sodium borate	5.	platinum
3.	old ships	6.	palladium

B. Items of imports to be decanalised and put under REP (14 Nos.) :

1.	jute pulp	8.	eleic
2.	manila hemp	9.	stearic acid
3.	raw sisal fibre	10.	palamitic acid
4.	raw jute	11.	palm fatty acid
5.	alkyl benzene	12.	palm acid oil
6.	floppy diskettes	13.	other fatty acids
7.	lauric acid	14.	pure or mixed including acid cils and soap stocks

C. List of export items decanalised (16 Nos.) :

1. Castor oil
2. Polythene (LD)
3. Coal and coke
4. Colour picture tubes

5. Sub-assemblies of colour TV containing colour TV picture tube
6. Ethyl alcohol or rectified spirit of any proof degree whether denatured or not
7. Exposed cinematographic films and video tube cinema films
8. Khandari molasses
9. Molasses
10. Milk scale scrap
11. Bimetal ore
12. Railway passenger coaches and locomotives
13. Raw jute, mesta and jute cuttings
14. Sugar
15. Iron ore of redi-origin
16. Iron ore from Goa when exported to China or Europe in addition to Japan, South Korea and Taiwan
17. Laws grade bauxite of the west coast origin

6.07 Licensing Policy

Restructuring economy and liberalising the economy to avert crisis has made India to review industrial licensing policy, and 34 industries were identified to get automatic clearance for foreign tie-ups or foreign technology agreement w.e.f. August 14, 1991. The industries identified are :

1. Metallurgical industries;
2. Boilers and steam generating plants;
3. Prime movers (other than electrical generators);
4. Electrical equipment;
5. Transportation;
6. Industrial machinery;
7. Machine tools and industrial robuts and their controls and accessories;
8. Agricultural machinery;
9. Earth moving machinery;
10. Industrial instruments;

11. Scientific and electromedical instruments and laboratory equipments;
12. Nitrogenous and phosphatic fertilisers;
13. Chemicals (other than fertilisers);
14. Drugs and pharmaceuticals;
15. Paper and pulp including paper products;
16. Automobile tyres and tubes;
17. Plate glass;
18. Ceramics;
19. Cement products;
20. High technology reproduction and multiplication equipment;
21. Carbon and carbon products;
22. Pretensioned high pressure RCC pipes;
23. Rubber machinery;
24. Printing machinery;
25. Welding electrodes (other than those for welding mild steel);
26. Industrial synthetic diamonds;
27. Photosynthesis imprevers etc.;
28. Extraction and upgrading of minor oils;
29. Prefabricated building materials;
30. Soya products;
31. Certified high yielding hybrid seeds and synthetic seeds;
32. All food processing industries (other than milkfood, malted foods and flour but excluding the items reserved for the small scale sector);
33. All items of packing of food processing industries (excluding the items reserved for small scale sector);
34. Hotel and tourism related industries.

These industries qualify for automatic approval of foreign technology agreements. Beside automatic clearance for foreign tie-ups, procedure for foreign tie-ups has been liberalized to complement Industrial Policy of July 24, 1991. According to procedure announced, automatic permission will be given for foreign technology agreements in high priority industries up to a lumpsum payment of Rs one crore, five per cent royalty for domestic sales and eight per cent for exports, subject to total payments of 6 per cent of sales over a ten-year period from the date of agreement or seven years from commencement of production.

6.08 Foreign Exchange Release

Foreign exchange release under blanket permission would not be subjected to any restriction or per diem rates and duration of engagement, etc. The guidelines for foreign exchange release as delegated to authorised dealers include:

1. Where duration of the engagement of foreign technicians does not exceed 12 months by a company in a year with no single technician exceeding 3 months;
2. Where the payment to the foreign technician does not exceed US $ 500 per day, regardless of whether the local costs on board and lodging and other items are met by the Indian company or not; and
3. Wherein the case of company to company payment by the Indian company to the foreign company does not exceed US $ 50,000 in a year.

Consequent upon devaluation of the rupee, all those products with imported inputs mainly raw-material had upward revision of prices of output. The worst affected items were drugs and medicines. The shortage of drugs was observed in September, October, 1991, in Indian market. It was due to the fact that most of the drugs are governed under Act and these are subjected to price revision according to Drug Price Control Order, 1987. Due to rise in inputs cost of imported materials, the upward revision of prices at commensurate rate of devaluation was necessary but this was not immediately possible. There was perhaps postponement of the announcement of the new drug policy, due to which leading manufacturers in private sector have either stopped manufacturing for want of sufficient return due to cost escalation of imported raw material or producing at below normal production capacity.

More than 70 per cent of drugs marketed in India were governed by Price Control Orders till October 26, 1991, and perhaps, it would be brought down to 40 per cent. That is out of 148 drugs under price control, the list of drugs subjected to price control would be 62 drugs. The list of 62 drugs would cover all 21 drugs included in Category I of Price Control Order, 1987 and 41 drugs of Category II of the same control order. The Category I drugs totalling 21 numbers are connected with National Health Programmes.

The mechanism of automatic price revision of drugs governed under Price Control Order has been thought of. Taking wholesale price index as the basis, manufacturers may be allowed to automatically revise prices to the extent of seventy per cent of the total cost increase on the basis of the wholesale price index.

Earlier, after devaluation of the rupee, the government did allow price increase for 54 drugs on the assumption that the cost of the imported component had gone up correspondingly but this did not avert the problem of shortage as seen in September-October, 1991. The drugs subjected to price control includes 46 bulk drugs which are totally imported and 60 drugs with import content from 1 per cent to 95 per cent are manufactured indigenously.

6.09 Sugar Industry

On November 8, 1991, the government has issued new guidelines for licensing of new and expansion of existing sugar factories for the year 1991-92 and for the Eighth Plan.

Though as a part of liberalising economy and induce investment, the licensing mechanism has been done away within India in post budget period of 1991, sugar industry was continued to be governed under licensing mechanism. The new guidelines issued on November 8, 1991 indicate continuance of licensing of sugar industry for minimum economic capacity of 2,500 tonnes cane crushing per day. No criteria of maximum limit of capacity has been fixed.

Interesting feature of this policy is that licensing of cooperative and public sector would be allowed for initial capacity of 1,750 TCP if such proposal is for establishing sugar unit in industrially backward area as notified by the government and certified by Indian Council of Agricultural Research to be agro-climatically suited for development of sugarcane, however, the initial capacity of 1,750 TCD licensed has to be expanded to 2,500 TCD within a period of five years of going into production.

Another criterion for licensing of sugar industries would be the distance between two sugar units. That is, licences to be issued for new sugar units will be subjected to condition that the distance between existing sugar unit and proposed new unit would not be less than 25 kms., however, if availability of sugar cane is adequate enough to justify the distance between new and existing unit of less than 25 then the relaxation of distance criterion would be possible, and as a special case, the reduced distance of 15 kms. would be allowed.

The viability of sugar unit would be judged from availability of sugarcane and potential for development of sugarcane would also be another important criterion. The preference order for licensing would be cooperative sector, public sector and the private sector. Obviously, such policy is contrary to the expectation of the liberalising mechanism.

In general prices go up continuously for majority of items. Except for the items of international trade where prices are most volatile, the items of domestic trade and distribution show upward trend. The rise in prices is gradual, continuous and steep depending upon the demand supply gap. The general tendency of non-reversible hike in price is very common in developing countries. It is said that "prices" are like "animal" which graze the commodities in short supply. There is no way to keep prices constant for decades and it is unlikely to find a way for stabilising prices for decades. Prices do change in every corner of the world over a period.

6.10 Privatising Tourism

Lakshadweep (literally meaning of lakhs of islands) is the Union Territory with above 36 islands including only 10 inhabitated by 40,000 people. From Kerala coast, these islands are at a distance of about 200-400 km. in the Arabian sea. Government of India decided on January 16, 1992 to lease out to private parties for development as "tourist resorts". The two islands identified for tourist resort are "Thinakkara" and "Cheriyam". The length and breadth of these islands is 1360 x 307 and 2960 x 153 metres respectively, and area would be 41.80 hectares for Thinakkara and Cheriyam is above 45.55 hectares. Thinakkar island is triangular in shape with a crystal clear lagoon having an estimated area of 95 sq. kms. There is a reef separating the islands from the open sea.

Similarly, Cheriyam has a lagoon with an estimated area of 20 sq. kms. It is surrounded by a coral reef which separates the island and the lagoon from the open sea.

In fact, some people call it selling of Indian territory to private parties or even foreigners under the name of privatizing the tourism. Pledging of over 42 tonnes gold, selling of profit making public sector enterprises, closure of loss making units and removal of subsidies where poorest of poor are gainfully employed etc., raising the prices of essential commodities, doing away with the licensing mechanism, indiscriminate foreign investment etc. are some of the measures India has to adapt to overcome the economic crisis which emerged in 1991. The liberalizing trade, restructuring whole economy, transition from conventional planning to so-called indicative planning, thrice devaluation of Indian currency, exchange rate, interest rate, curtailing government expenditure etc. was felt essential due to the fact that India was following to a great extent closed economy strategies. The price it had paid by adapting mixed policies of capitalism and socialism simultaneously was so heavy that neither it has emerged as "self-reliant" nor "industria-lized" but cover of industrial giants had demonstrative effect to conceal in the widespread poverty, acute starvation, deprivation, proliferation of inequality etc. The price it had to pay for maintaining democracy was so heavy that government expenditure and inefficiency of economy has made it not only vulnerable but even bankrupt.

7

Role of Subsidies

7.01 Introduction

Subsidies are found in almost every aspect of economy. Be it agriculture, industry, trade, transport, public health, education etc. in every economic activity, some kinds of subsidies are prevailing. Both 'for and against' arguments on subsidies are found in literature. Both infant industry and protectionism arguments support the role of subsidies but distortion of prices and emergence of dual economy are attributed to subsidies as one of the numerous causes hence arguments to withdraw subsidies are not uncommon. "Free trade", "Laissez-faire", "open or market economy", "liberalisation", "restructuring with growth", "privatisation per-se", shift from public sector enterprises or nationalization to privatization of manufacturing, etc. are the concepts which see subsidies as source of budget deficits, economic crisis, distortions of prices, distortion of trade, balance of payment, balance of trade, exchange rate, interest rate, devaluation of currency, etc.

7.02 Definitions of Subsidy

It can be defined in two ways :

(i) Long run cost of products or services to government less prices at which these products or services are made available to consumers or beneficiaries. That is difference between cost of production and selling prices. This difference arises due to pricing policy of the government, wherein government stipulates prices at which goods or services can be sold to consumer. The manufacturer, therefore, claims subsidy to overcome losses out of such pricing policy. It is assumed that manufacturing cost is higher than the selling price (*Ref.*: [1].

(ii) When public sector and private sector both are manufacturing identical items, government proposes the selling prices and it then affects the private sector in a situation in which equivalent services would have been provided by the private sector. This comprises of pricing subsidy plus difference in cost between private and public provision of the service. (*Ref.* [2])

The subsidy also plays as protection for domestic industries against the import from international manufacturing industries. The multinational companies have advantages of economies of scale and have global market. Therefore, the prices of items manufactured by such MNC are less than those manufactured in developing countries. The need for import substitution and developing domestic industrial base justifies the manufacturing of items at low level and obviously cost of manufacturing is higher than price of same items in international market. Over and above such price difference government announces the selling price of items to safeguard consumers. Therefore, subsidy has to be provided on such items.

There are numerous definitions of the term "subsidy". Some of them are as follows:

1. United Nations' definition in the context of A System of National Accounts is as follows:

Subsidies include all grants on current account which private industries receive from government. These are transfers which, in view of the basis on which they are made, represent additions to the income of the producers from current production. The grants may, for example, be based on the amount or value of the commodities produced, exported or consumed, the labour or land employed in production, or the manner in which production is organised and carried on. Transfers by public authorities to private industries for investment purposes or to cover destruction, damage and other losses in capital and working assets are classed as capital transfers rather than as subsidies .... Subsidies also include all grants on current account which government makes to public corporations, for example, compensation for operating losses (negating operating surplus). In the case of government enterprises, transfers on current account should be treated as subsidies when it is clear that the transfers are the consequences of the policy of the government to maintain prices at a level at which the proceeds of the enterprise will not cover the current costs of production (*Ref.* [3]).

2. Definition adapted by the U.S. Joint Economic Committee (1965) is as follows:

   An act by a governmental unit involving either (1) a payment, (2) a remission of charge, or (3) supplying commodities or services at less than cost or market price, with the intent of achieving a particular economic objective, most usually the supplying to a general market a product or service which would be supplied in as great quantity only at a higher price in the absence of the payment or remission of charges.

3. Herald Malmgren's definition:

   Any government action which causes a firm's or a particular industry's total net private costs of production to be below the level of costs that would have been incurred in the course of producing the same level of output in absence of government action (*Ref.* [4]).

4. Any kinds of government interference with an idealised free market economy must be regarded as subsidy.
5. Subsidies implies any special favour, benefit, advantage, or inducement conferred by the government, even if it is given as a release from the burden and is not a direct charge on the Treasury, is fairly included in the idea and meaning of an indirect bounty.
6. A subsidy might be considered to be any government action which causes a firm's or a particular industry's total net private cost of production to be below the level of cost that would have been incurred in the course of producing the same level of output in the absence of government action.

7.03 Schools of Thought on Subsidies

Subsidies tend to nullify trade liberalisation. Subsidies can frustrate the benefits of tariff or other trade concessions obtained through multilateral bargaining. Subsidies tend to increase as more items are covered under its scope

European school of thought views "subsidies to be second best correction to the market that should be penalised only when they cause injury", whereas US school of thought views subsidies as "generally undesirable, efficiency reducing distortions resulting from special interest group" (*Ref.* [5]).

The intermediate view has emerged between two conceptions in Tokyo Round which stipulates the "practice of applying countervailing duties only when injury exists" as accepted by us, in exchange for European acceptance of the principle that "subsidies, ostensibly for domestic purposes, are also subjected to countervailing if they cause trade injury".

The Tokyo Round subsidies "code has two tracks". On the first, a country may impose "countervailing duties" against another country's "domestic" or export subsidies if they cause "material injury", a relatively high threshold of damage associated with falling sales and employment, rising import shares, and a price depressing effect of imports. On the second track, there can be multilateral authorisation of countervailing duties or other offsetting measures when the subsidy in question is clearly an export subsidy, even though the threshold of injury is low ("adverse effects") and the subsidizing country can avoid such action only by disproving that any such "adverse effects" exist which is quite difficult to do." "Countervailing duties are the accepted means of offsetting subsidies..... CVDs are special import duties levied by individual governments to cancel out the effects of foreign subsidies on the levying countries trade. They may equal, but not exceed, the value of the original subsidy" (*Ref.* [6]).

Dumping refers to an act by which product of one country are introduced into the commerce of another country at less than the normal value of the products. A product can be introduced into commerce of an importing country at less than its normal value, if the product is exported from one country to another.

(a) is less than the comparable price, in the ordinary course of trade for the like product when destined for consumption in the exporting country, or

(b) in absence of such domestic price, is less than either

  (i) the highest comparable price for the like product for export to any third country in the ordinary course of trade, or

  (ii) the cost of production of the product in the country of origin plus a reasonable addition for selling cost and profit.

7.04 Prices and Subsidies

It is very popular in economics to use the term "get prices right" in the context of development policy. But we have little knowledge about the mechanism which distorts prices. Obviously, output cost and input cost relevant to production, goods and services have their own law of distortion of prices at slow and steady rate of increase. To get prices right some intervention is necessary. Subsidies is one such instrument. Some element of subsidy exists in almost every sector of the economy. Whether it is agriculture, fertiliser, coal, electricity generation and distribution, textile (handloom, powerloom, sericulture or handicraft), shipbuilding, steel, aluminium, smelting, aircraft, automobile, computers.

Pre-requisite to economic management of the country is to "set right the prices". But it is difficult to measure whether prices are right, sensible or appropriate. The right prices are those which will clear market for the goods or commodities; or the prices which can be afforded by buyers. When the cost of production is higher than selling prices then losses incurred must be born by government. This creates the need for subsidies.

Market forces, if not intervened at appropriate time, tend to exert inflationary pressure and accelerate economy towards economic crisis by destabilising manufacturing, trade due to differential rate of growth in prices of input and output on one hand and on other hand by pushing prices high enough to create revolt in tranquillity of consumers of goods and services. As a policy instrument subsidies play an important role of intervention in market forces. Basically, the pricing mechanism is mostly affected due to subsidies. Subsidies are treated as intervention mechanism to correct market imperfections; but it also leads to "dual economy" and foster economically unviables at high cost to be borne by the government. Both domestic and international prices are monitored, affected and set right through policy instrument of subsidies. Due to pernicious effect of subsidies, an international trade of various other countries due to subsidies in domestic activities of one country, GATT has invariable reference to subsidies.

Developing countries while availing international aid or domestic industries operating at small scale manufacturing plead for preferential treatment under the argument that they need protection being "infant industry". The essence of the infant industry is that the industry under consideration is not competitive in world markets today but it may in due course of time become competitive in world market through appropriate government support in terms of policies of protectionism, subsidies in various forms, kinds, types, etc. In the context of international trade both countervailing duties (CVDs) and countervailing subsidies play important role. While the countervailing duties refer to duties imposed by one country on imports from another country to offset the other country's subsidies, the countervailing subsidies refer to subsidies granted by one country on its exports to offset the subsidies previously granted by another country. In other words, former is to restrain imports and latter to promote export and both are contradictory to each other in implication concerning international trade. Some terms connected with market forces and market failure (*Ref.* [7]) necessitating intervention by the government are :

1. the market does not function properly — the case of market imperfection:
2. the market result is incorrect — the case of externalities;
3. no market exists for the relevant activity — the case of public goods; and
4. the market yields undesirable results in terms of objectives other than resource allocation. In these cases of market failure, market prices do not exist, or do not reflect the true value, or are irrelevant.

It is rightly stated that "a state of underdevelopment is in large measure synonymous with pervasive market imperfection. A variety of market imperfection can reduce the efficiency of private market performance" (*Ref.* [8]). The efficiency of resources allocation is also affected due to market imperfection. Market distortions and imperfections are consequences of misallocation of resources, differential price structure and excessive intervention in market. All the mechanisms of interventions create impact on prices in one or other way. The demand-supply equilibrium as envisaged by the government agency is invariably faulty and creates scarcity of commodities thereby pushing up the prices, eventually to suppress the free demand. It is a kind of mechanism which creates continuous disturbance in an economy. The users charges are sometimes introduced for one or other reasons which are much less than real charges to be collected, if those were to be charged at market prices. For a variety of purposes, a government may introduce on a commodity or service by making a payment to the producer, or by the remission of charges, or by supplying the commodity or service at less than cost or market price. A subsidy may be introduced to stimulate development or consumption of some desired activity or service, to stimulate development of a particular area, to redress deficiencies in income distribution, to reduce risk of speculative activity such as research and development, or to encourage an activity that yields external economies (*Ref.* [9]).

There are criticisms of subsidies on the ground that "subsidies may lead to unanticipated distortions elsewhere in the economy, may require counter-subsidies to offset distortion created, may become burdensome administratively, may inhibit incentives of efficiency, may give unwarranted market protection and may be difficult to terminate". This is what actually is seen in India and other developing countries. The subsidies introduced at one time become legitimate demand of a particular sector of economy.

Virtually, any sort of government assistance to industry could be folded into a general definition of subsidies, whether the assistance takes the form of an outright grant, interest-free loan, protection from imports, or is bestowed less visibly through tax exemption (for example, for export earnings) or relaxed health and safety or environment regulations (*Ref.* [10]).

Two hypothesis relevant to subsidies are "falling water level" and "rising reef". The first hypothesis, namely "falling water level" implies that "as tariffs and other forms of protection decline, the remaining trade distortions have a more visible effect. Subsidies are a prominent distortion, and national differences in subsidy practices have perhaps become more apparent as the general level of protection has declined" (*Ref.* [11]). The second hypothesis, namely, "rising reef hypothesis" implies that "subsidies and surrogate practices have escalated rapidly as industrial nations have responded to rising energy prices, slow growth, and antiquated factories. This hypothesis suggests that "government subsidies have taken a sharp upward tilt" (*Ref.* [12]).

By implication, benefits of subsidy do not reach the consumers but it is meant for producers and traders. The subsidies go on increasing and have become a part of manufacturing activity during industrialisation.

Towards liberalising of Indian economy, various steps were initiated in July and August, 1991. The pricing policy of fertilizer was also reviewed. In fact, subsidy on fertilizer varies from 50 per cent to 100 per cent depending upon States, micronutrients, small and marginal farmer, etc. The Central subsidy on food and fertilizers for the period from 1978-79 to 1989-90 is as follows :

Table 1: Subsidies on Food and Fertilisers (Rs Million)

Year	*Food Subsidy*	*Subsidy on Fertiliser*		
		Imported	*Domestic*	*Total*
1	2	3	4	5
1978-79	5694	1710	1722	3432
1979-80	6000	2820	3208	6028
1980-81	6500	3350	1700	5050
1981-82	7000	1000	2750	3750
1982-83	7110	550	5500	6050
1983-84	8350	1480	9000	10480
1984-85	11010	7273	12000	19273
1985-86	16500	3237	16000	19237
1986-87	20000 *	1971	17000	18971
1987-88	22000 *	1140	20500	21640
1988-89 *	22000	2500	30000	32500
1989-90 @	22000 @	5300	31210	36510

Notes:
@ Budget Estimates
* Revised Budget Estimates

(Source: Fertiliser Statistics; 1988-89; FAI New Delhi pp. I-171)

The simple regression of time scale data shown above bears following relationships (Using 1978-79 = 1 and 1989-90 = 11 years):

1. simple regression
X = time in years
Y = subsidy on food in Rs million

Regression Output :

Constant	618.7
Std Err of Y Est	2508.7
R Squared	0.9
No. of Observations	11.0
Degrees of Freedom	9.0
X Coefficient(s)	1899.4
Std Err of Coeff.	239.2

2. simple regression
X = time in years
Y = subsidy on imported fert. in Rs million

Regression Output :

Constant	2223.4
Std Err of Y Est	1938.2
R Squared	0.0
No. of Observations	11.0
Degrees of Freedom	9.0
X Coefficient(s)	39.0
Std Err of Coeff.	184.8

2. simple regression		3. simple regression	
X = time in years		X = time in years	
Y = subsidy on dome fer. in Rs million		Y = total subsidy on food plus fertiliser in (Rs Million)	
Regression Output:		Regression Output:	
Constant	—4935.9	Constant	—2712.5
Std Err of Y Est	3107.7	Std Err of Y Est	3754.8
R Squared	0.9	R Squared	0.9
No. of Observations	11.0	No. of Observations	11.0
Degrees of Freedom	9.0	Degrees of Freedom	9.0
X Coefficient(s) 2631.4		X Coefficient(s) 2670.4	
Std Err of Coeff. 296.3		Std Err of Coeff. 358.0	

The benefits of subsidy on fertiliser and food do not reach the poorest of poor or small and very small farmers. Therefore, withdrawal of subsidy on fertilisers is always pleaded with. To withdraw subsidy may have detrimental effect on production and distribution of fertiliser.

Both nitrogenous and phosphate (np) and npk fertilisers were brought under statutory price control w.e.f. February 2, 1979. Depending upon the grade, the prices of fertiliser are fixed. For instance, urea ammonium phosphate in three different grades were priced as follows:

Table 2: Maximum Sales Prices of Fertilisers (Rs)

Date	*Grades*		
	@24-24-0	*28-28-0*	*14-35-14*
2. 2. 1979 *	1950	2340	2230
10.3.1979 **	1950	2200	2100
8. 6. 1980***	2600	3050	2900
11.7.1981	3050	3600	3400
29.7.1983	2800	3350	3150
31.1.1986	3050	3600	3400

Notes:

Prices are Exclusive of Central & State Sales Tax and Local Tax

* Inclusive of 15% exclusive duty + 5% Auxiliary duty + 5% special duty on excise duty w.e.f. March 1978.

** Inclusive of 7.5% excise duty + 5% Auxiliary duty + 5% special duty w.e.f. March 1, 1978.

*** Excise duty, Auxiliary duty and special duty on excise with on all fertilisers w.e.f. June 7, 1980 except ammonium sulphate and calcium ammonium nitrate in which case also it was withdrawn w.e.f. Feb. 1983.

The provision in Union Budget for the year 1990-91 states that :

33. In so far as fertiliser subsidies are concerned, with effect from this evening (i.e. July 24, 1991), low analysis fertilisers such as calcium ammonium nitrate, ammonium chloride, ammonium sulphate and sulphate of potass will be free from price and movement controls. There will be an increase of 40 per cent, on an average, in the price of all other fertilisers. In addition, in respect of single super phosphate, there shall also be a ceiling on the subsidy per tonne payable to producers so as to move towards total deregulation in the next few years; this should act as an incentive for all high cost units to reduce costs and improve efficiency. The necessary notifications in this regard are being issued separately, today, by the Ministry of Agriculture.

34. The economic rationale for an increase in the price of fertilisers is so obvious that it does not need to be stated. Nevertheless, I would like to draw the attention of the House to the fact that there has been no increase in fertiliser prices since July, 1981. In these ten years, there has been a continuous increase in the procurement prices of paddy and what, as also in the market prices of other crops, received by the agricultural sector. Farmers will be compensated for the proposed increase in the prices of fertilisers through suitable increase in procurement prices."

From the above text, it will be clear that subsidies on fertilisers were withdrawn and 40 per cent price increase. Perhaps, it was heavy dose on poor farmers. There was dual pricing concept on fertiliser. The international prices of fertiliser were too low as compared with domestically produced fertiliser. The international competitive prices through domestic production and withdrawal of subsidies were somehow stated to be related.

7.05 Dual Pricing of Fertilisers

That is, fertiliser sold at controlled prices plus availability of fertiliser in open market. In other words, most of the requirements of fertiliser be met through controlled market and rest of the requirement through open market. The three steps, as suggested by Yoginder K. Alagh (The Hindustan Times dated August 14, 1991) comprised of :

1. Small and marginal farmers in rainfed and dry districts should get nitrogenous fertilizers at subsidised rates up to say 40 kg./hectare of owned land and balance fertiliser should be marketed in the open market.
2. Instead of individual retention or control prices which encourage inefficiency and corruption, fertiliser companies should get group retention prices, i.e. normative efficiency price separately worked out for gas, FC, LSHS, Naptha and coal feedstock based companies, with the open market price regulated through imports to correspond to weighted average group realisation from the subsidised and open market price.
3. Once the transitional problems of individual factory level price control as at present are resolved and the world price falls as the "Middle East" effect wears off, to implement a tariff regulated price with say a 45 per cent protection to be tapered down".

The implication of such dual pricing would be, as envisaged by Dr Y.K. Alagh in his article Fertilizer Pricing (Hindustan Times dated August 14, 1991, pp. 11) are :

(i) At the farmer level, it is genuinely promotional rather than a giveaway. It is sensible to target the subsidy at less endowed farmers and through time, only at poor farmers in poor regions. The "administrative" problems are no more complex than a list of other credit, input and investment support schemes for small and marginal farmers. Some poor farmers will sell their quota, as in the case of urban consumers selling sugar, rations but will get an income return.

(ii) The group retention prices fertiliser companies will get powerful incentives to reduce material and energy costs. Output above their levy percentage will be sold in the open market at a higher price. This will be a powerful incentive to increase capacity use and reduce energy cost. Plant level research shows that a 10 per cent increase in capacity utilisation leads to a 3 per cent to 5 per cent fall in energy consumption per tonne of ammonia produced. This leads to a powerful cost reducing effect and the need for subsidy will fall in a few years.

(iii) The policy moderates the powerful output controlling effect of a single price regime. Kirit Parikh and Narayana have reported that a 30 per cent price rise by itself would reduce wheat and rice endangering by 13 per cent thus output would go down by 15 million tonnes endangering the nation's food supply. The dual pricing policy would benefit producers whose output response rates for fertilizers are the best. In fact, the shortfall in protected fertilizer demand should not be more than half a million tonne, or around 5 to 8 per cent. According to Bhalkla-Alag estimates based on experience of 280 districts across a decade, a 10 per cent decline in fertilizer application per hectare leads to a 2.5 per cent decline in agricultural yield for all crops. Thus, the output contracting effect of the present policy should at the outside be around 1.0 million tonnes of grain and much smaller amounts of other crops, which can be made by other measures.

(iv) The policy makes a beginning of the transition to a globally competitive fertilizer producing and distribution regime which should be our objective in the next three to five years. The Indian farmer is entitled to the best quality product at the cheapest possible price in the world ....

However, Central Government has announced the guidelines on August 14, 1991, exempting the small and marginal farmers from the price increase in fertilisers, over-ruling objections from the States on the dual pricing policy. According to guidelines dated August 14, 1991, the States have been given fixed amount for subsidising the fertilizers for the small and marginal farmers, but they would have some flexibility in developing systems of reimbursement to these farmers. The reimbursement, however, would be related to identification proof of purchase, area held, previous use and the quality of fertilisers available in a given area for subsidised supply.

The revised prices of fertilizers came into effect on August 14, 1991 and 30 per cent hike was agreed to (as against 40 per cent proposed in the Budget).

7.06 Sources of Subsidies

The form, elements and effects of subsidies are difficult to identify clearly as those are overlapping in both private and public or government. The support provided by government to sustain economic activities of private, either large, small or tiny enterprise in any form, kind, type, direct or indirect is source of subsidy. Similarly, government has onus to develop infrastructural facilities, services, education, health, etc. but the nominal charges or token fee or symbolic charges collected from public utilising them are far below the actual charges that could have been collected and are, therefore, treated as subsidised form. Though list could be exhaustive and difficult to prepare where subsidies exist, but following could be few types of subsidies :

Table 3 : Types of Subsidies and Their Purpose

Description	*Purpose for subsidies*
1. Payroll subsidies	Promote employment (e.g. employment to disabled, rehabilitation of mentally retarded, etc.)
2. Capital investment subsidies	Promote employment, entrepreneurship, investment in identified areas, industrialisation.
3. Tax subsidies	Promote manufacturing of particular goods or items
4. Excise duty exemption, turnover tax, exemption from value added tax	Protection against competition from large scale or multinational companies
5. Export subsidies and reduced import duty (i.e. border tax adjustment)	Promote export to earn foreign exchange.
6. Capital goods subsidies	Promote entrepreneurship, and employment
7. Interest rate subsidies	Promote financing, encourage entrepreneurship and regional development
8. Exemption from income tax, tax holidays, higher rate of depreciation	Promote saving, investment, purchase of bonds, shares, equity participation, etc.
9. Sales subsidies	Promote market development (of say, handicrafts, traditional items, janata cloth, etc.)
10. Export credits	Promote export
11. Reservation of items for purchase by government from small scale, traditional or tiny sector manufacturers	Promote small scale, tradition or tiny sector
12. Transport subsidies	Promote movement of finished goods, raw material, to sustain both manufacturing and trade.

7.07 'Injury only' School Relating Subsidies

The 'trade impact' in the context of disciplining subsidies can be viewed from "injury only" school of thought as well as "antidistortion" school of thought. While the former is "concerned with redressing the harm that comes from subsidized trade", the latter "focusses on the inefficient consequences of government intervention". While explaining above schools of thought, Gary Clyde Hufbauer and Joanna Shelton Erb (*Ref.* [13]) says that "Briefly, the injury-only school believes that a country should retaliate against foreign subsidies only when those subsidies exert a significant impact on trade, and further, the remedy should be designed to redress that impact. By contrast, the antidistortion school believes that subsidies are a fit subject for retaliation even if they exert only a slight impact on trade, and that retaliation should be precisely designed to offset the subsidy." The further explanation on injury-only school goes like this : The injury-only school takes the view that subsidies, and other froms of government intervention in private economic activity are a fact of modern life. Subsidies, according to this school, are often used to correct pre-existing market imperfections and are almost impossible to apportion over units of output. Exchange rate movements will offset gross differences in subsidization between countries, leaving only micro problems for specific trade remedies. This school holds that the principal discipline against subsidization must come from domestic political process, not international rules."

7.08 Antidistortion School on Subsidies

Antidistortion holds belief that subsidies are bad on account of three reasons (*Ref.* [14]) as follows:

— First, as used in practice (if not in economic theory), subsidies generally reduce world economic efficiency and thereby diminish the gain of international exchange to all nations.

— Second and worse, a subsidy programme may enable a country to gain an early lead in establishing a promising new industry (for example, fibre optics), or to avoid or delay painful adjustment in an old industry (for example, steel).

— Third and finally, because other countries only the early lead or adjustment avoided, subsidies may provoke emulation. Emulation will bring a spiral of wasteful distortion (as in shipbuilding) or over-investment in seemingly promising technologies (as in supersonic aircraft).

Some of the aspects relevant to tariff and non-tariff barriers are :

— import quotas
— approval and settlement system
— customs practice
— application of standards
— government procurement policies
— government monopolies and pricing policies
— explicit trade subsidies to specific industries
— export incentive measures
— voluntary export restraint imposed on trading partner.

The high ratio of imports to GDP indicates liberalization of economy as "it proxies the country's heavy dependence on trade and futility of protectionism. The high ratio of exports to GDP may indicate highly protected economy", but some argue "rising production and exports of manufactures by competitor countries need not imply hightened protectionist pressure." (*Ref.* [15]).

The measure of sectoral specialization is given as

$$\frac{[Xi - Mi]}{[Xi + Mi]}$$

Where Xi = export of sector i

Mi = import in sector i

In manufacturing industry, trade or balanced trade in each sector may result when numerator is zero i.e. when import in each sector equals export in it. The numerator equals denominator when trade follows one way path.

To show how the above measure is used, it may be found that "for the United States in 1980, a measure of sectoral specialization (ranging from zero for complete sectoral trade balance — or interindustry trade) trade 1 for complete one-way sectoral specialization — of inter-industry trade) showed higher inter-industry trade — in manufactures with Japan (0.71) and the developing countries (0.58) than Western Europe (0.35)" (*Ref.* [16]).

7.09 Subsidies in India

Subsidising has become the way of life in India. Subsidising the prices of everything like milk, bread, electricity tariff to both farmers and small scale industries, fertilisers, price protection for agricultural products, cloth, transport service in metropolitan cities, education, health care, communication, irrigation, etc. Infact, such subsidies neither help farmers not small scale industries as uneconomical inputs give rise to uneconomical output of both farmers and small scale industries. State Road Transport Corporations have an average rate of return of minus 12 per cent in the range of minus two to minus 83 per cent.

It is widely acknowledged that subsidies are introduced in the name of poor and providing them the services needed but in reality, it does not reach to poor, backwards and deserving targetted population. The middle people and elites are more beneficiaries than the targetted people. India has a network of about 4,00,000 nos. of fair price shops under the name of Public Distribution System. Government's commitment to strengthen the PDS at all costs for the benefits of the poorer sections of the people is obvious. Wheat, rice, sugar and edible oils are usually supplied through fair price shops. In fact, this is one kind of intervention mechanism to check the prices of essential items. But its effect is very peculiar, because shortage of sugar, wheat and rice in PDS leads to higher prices of these items in market. Dual pricing of sugar, wheat and rice is obviously putting pressure on the subsidies. Because subsidised prices are always kept low while market prices for same items are very high with the result subsidies are always going up every year. As a measure for setting right the prices, government has raised the prices for several items i.e. inflationary measure hike of price, on December 27, 1991.

Item	*Existing prices*	*Revised prices*
Rice		
a. Common variety	234	377
b. Fine variety	234	437
c. Superfine variety	—	458
Wheat	234	280
Sugarcane support price		

7.10 Subsidy in Agriculture

Indian agriculture is not exceptional to subsidising inputs. Indian economy in general and agriculture in particular is excessively protective. Both industry and trade are protective and governed by controls, licences and intervention. To certain extent, agriculture is discriminated in comparison with industry and trade, the decline in agriculture trade as compared trade of industrial manufactured item.

The commitment for intervention in market by the government to keep prices down has made it necessary to market output of agricultural commodities as well as excessive control over trade. This is attributed to enlargement of public distributive system, financial burden, maintaining administrative machinery, allocating public resources for less productive or unproductive activities of marketing and trade control causing disincentive to producers and exporters as well as breeding corruption in the economy. To be realistic, every control mechanism is a source of corruption. The food distributive mechanism is not properly devised to reach targetted needy poorest of poor in rural areas.

The estimated subsidies on food and agricultural inputs in 1989-90 was Rs 13,500 crores which accounted for 3.1 per cent of gross domestic product (GDP) of India. The sectoral public investment in the same year was Rs 11,000 crores whereas subsidies had been Rs 13,500 crores. According to the report on the Indian Agriculture, the World Bank prescribed treatment to overcome the deficiencies in agricultural incentive pattern:

1. Immediate reduction in subsidies by raising electricity tariffs and fertilisers prices in phases.
2. Controlling food subsidies through better targetting to the poor.
3. Reduction in high levels of protection for oilseeds sugarcane and increase in incentive for rice, cotton and wheat production, which would necessitate suitably reorienting the public procurement and pricing mechanism.
4. Reduction in both trade and domestic market controls.

The symptoms of declining capital formation in agriculture sector has been the consequences of declining at commensurate rate the real public investment and stagnating private capital investment as well as shortcomings in credit systems. Other problems identified are loan write offs on mass scale in some areas to benefit rich farmers, mandatory lending, inadequate interest rates and margins and unviable spread of bank branches. The prescription of the World Bank to rectify the situation arising out of above identified problems includes following four corrective steps:

(a) To review the composition of agricultural investments at the Central and the State levels.
(b) To stop small programmes to economise on scarce resources.
(c) To concentrate on such areas as research, irrigation, resource management, rural electrification, trading and education.
(d) To consolidate rural banking system.

About irrigation system, the World Bank suggested four point strategies :

(a) enunciate a coherent water policy;
(b) set investment priorities and control public expenditure;
(c) improve system productivity and assure sustainability; and
(d) strengthen both public and private institutional capacity and make institutions more accountable to the farmer.

For diversification of agricultural activities to produce more varieties of commodities, emphasis has to be placed on R&D to cover more commodities and issues like land management, farming system, agro-forestry, etc.

7.11 Non-plan Expenditure and Subsidies in India

Let us have a look on non-Plan expenditure of the Central Government. The Budget Estimate of 1990-91 indicates the non-Plan expenditure of Rs 68843 crores on the following heads :

Table 4: Non-plan Expenditure (Rs Crores)

Sl. No.	*Items*	*Budget 1990-91*	*Revised 1990-91*	*+ Increase —Decrease*
1.	Interest payment	20850	21850	1000
2.	Food subsidy	2200	2450	250
3.	Subsidy on indigenous fertiliser	3250	3650	400

4. Export promotion and Market development assistance	2316	2700	384
5. Scheme for debt relief to Farmer	1000	1500	500
6. Defence pension	1500	1670	170
7. Loans to States against :			
i) Small savings Collections	4500	6770	2270
ii) To cover with RBI deficits	0	521	521
8. Technical Credits to Foreign Govt.	350	1150	800
9. Non-plan Loans to public Enterpr.	969	1070	101
10. Police	1394	1581	187
11. Write-off loans to States	96	966	870
12. Badarpur Thermal Power Stations	288	348	60
13. Gulf Evacuation	0	300	300
14. Postal deficit	84	150	66
15. Punjab Action Plan	20	79	59
16. Conversion of loans to equity in respect of Shipping Corporation of India	0	191	191
17. Others	30026	29815	—211
Total	68843	76761	7918
Central Plan	17618	17594	—24
Central Assistance to States and U.T. Plans	12848	12362	—486
Grand Total	99309	106717	7408

Total subsidies were of the order of Rs 8,516 crores in 1990-91 (B.E.) which was raised to 9550 (1990-91 R.E.) as a part of non-Plan expenditure, which comprises :

Table 5 : Details of Subsidies

	Rs Crores	
	1990-91 BE	*1990-91 RE*
Major subsidies:	8,516	9550
A. Food subsidy	2,200	2450
B. Fertiliser subsidy	4,000	4400
a. Indigenous fertiliser	3,250	3650
b. Imported fertiliser	750	750
C. Export promotion	2,316	2700
Total (A+B+C) :	8,516	9550
Debt Relief to Farmers	1000	1500
Interest subsidies	391.29	378.65
Other subsidies	716.38	692.36
Total subsidies	10623.67	12121.01

Apart from Rs 8,516 crores (1990-91 BE) as subsidies, the provision for subsidies during the same year for railways and handloom were as follows :

A.	Railway	Rs 278.75 crores
B.	Mill made and handloom cloth	Rs 230.50 crores
C.	Interest on subsidies	Rs 391.29 crores
	Total :	Rs 900.54 crores

The details of interest subsidy are as follows:

Table 6 : Interest Subsidies in India (Rs crores)

Sl. No.	*Name of Public Enterprises etc.*	*Budget 1990-91*	*Revised 1990-91*	*Budget 1991-92*
1.	Garden Reach Ship Builders & Engineers	4.64	4.64	0.00
2.	Mazagaon Dock Ltd.	15.35	15.35	0.00
3.	Coal India Ltd.	58.08	58.08	58.08
4.	Industrial Reconstruction Bank of India	2.00	2.00	5.00
5.	Gaon Banks	0.10	0.10	0.10
6.	Denotified Sugar Undertakings	0.10	0.10	0.00
7.	Khadi and village Industries Commission	34.00	34.00	34.00
(a)	For Khadi Industries	23.00	23.00	23.00
(b)	For Other Village Industries	11.00	11.00	11.00
8.	Burn Standard & Co. Ltd.	5.70	5.70	5.70
9.	Tungabhadra Steel Products Ltd.	0.48	0.48	0.48
10.	Interest subsidy to Press Trust of India	0.05	0.03	0.03
11.	Bharat Refractories Ltd. (IFICO)	1.63	1.63	0.00
12.	Bharat Gold Mines Ltd.	14.00	0.00	0.00
13.	Hindustan Antibiotics Ltd.	5.15	5.15	0.00
14.	National Textile Corporation	230.00	229.68	210.00
15.	Binny & Co.	0.01	1.17	2.16
16.	Heavy Engineering Corporation	20.00	20.00	0.00
	Total — Interest Subsidies	391.29	378.11	315.55

7.12 Subsidies and Industrial Policy

Industrial Policy germinates the seeds of subsidies. Though policies of subsidies and industrial development are different in character, it is obvious that subsidies have origin in industrial policy. Developing countries derive inspiration from policies of developed countries. Whatever policies are practiced by developing countries are basically imitation of developed countries, justified stating those prevails in developed countries. The aims and objectives of industrial policies may differ primarily on the basis of level of industrial development but macro economic policies are within the identified realm. Say for example, Swedish industrial policy has been same as for its macro economic policy: full and efficient use of resources (the resource allocation objective); an acceptable distribution of welfare (the distribution objectives); and as small fluctuations as possible in the level of economic activity (the stabilisation objective" (*Ref.* 17). The influence of above objective could be in terms of both 'defensive' and 'offensive' measures. What precisely these measures are meant could be seen from the prevailing unemployment and promoting structural changes. According to Carl Hamilton, in above policy Statement 'Defensive measures include, among other things, paying subsidies to prevent an industry from reducing its labour force too fast from a political point of view'. Similarly 'offensive measures on other hand, are meant to increase industry's efficiency and to speed up structural changes' (*Ref.*18). Just to explain defensive and offensive measures generally stipulated in industrial policy let us recapitulate the paraphrase relevant to emuniciated goals in industrial policy of Sweden, identified by Carl Hamilton:

1. Industrial policy shall contribute towards a reduction in society's cost in connection with structural changes. An important component in this effort is for industrial policy towards structural changes taking place under socially acceptable condition.
2. Industrial policy shall contribute towards an efficient production in industry. The endeavour for efficient production implies considerable structural changes.

Defensive industrial policy refers to para 1 above and Offensive industrial policy refers to para 2 above. The effect of such defensive and offensive industrial policy measures as compared with macroeconomic measures such as changes in taxes or exchange rates, could be obviously identifiable. According to Carl Hamilton" by using defensive industrial policy measures, specifically subsidies, a private industry or firm remains profitable at the expense of the profitability of other private industries and times. Taxes are increased for all production units or there is an indirect 'tax' through an increase in the budget deficit, and the prices of the factors of production for non-subsidised production units"(*Ref.* 19). In contrast with defensive measure, "with macro-economic measures, it is hoped that employment can be maintained through a general reduction in the real wage. A lower real wage will tend to slow down structural changes, but will still force production units to adjust to changes in competitiveness. Subsidies, on the other hand, tend to 'freeze' the industrial structure at a higher wage level, and as a result the adjustment period is prolonged. The optimum duration of the adjustment period is a matter of political judgement" (*Ref.*20). Above statement needs to qualify from the facts that 'subsidies are financed in part by those employed in the subsidized production units'. Therefore, increased subsidies do not necessarily mean as wage drift.

The detailed analysis of Public subsidies to Industry was carried out by Carl Hamilton. The subsidies and loans for Swedish Industry for the period from 1970-71 to 1979-80 has been increasing despite the fact that Sweden is considered to be well developed country/and loan was treated as a part to improve competitiveness of the Swedish industry and its intended objective has been achieved but subsidies per employee have suddenly increased to $ 1245 in 1976-77 from $ 434 in 1975-76. This has been gradually rising upto $ 1432 per employee in 1979. Subsidies were about 20 times higher in 1979-80 as compared with 1970-71.

In contrast with total subsidies loan and credit guarantees granted to total Swedish Industry in general, the details of ship-building industry are very interesting (as shown in table-2) particularly the share of subsidies in value added, which exceeded 152 per cent in 1978-79 and 60 per cent in 1979-80. Also subsidies per employee have been highest in 1978-79 with the figure of $ 50,480 and $ 20,320 in 1979-80. Such high subsidies are in no way contributing to direct growth of industry.

The conclusion that could be derived from such an analysis is that "Stabilisation policy is of decisive importance if the objective of full employment is to be achieved. Government subsidies can maintain employment only marginally and temporarily. New or extended subsidies to industry cannot increase employment unless the Government and the agents in the labour market can also maintain the general competitiveness of the country's industry". (*Ref.* 21).

Objective of full employment can be achieved through industry and labour policies, but this must ensure competitiveness both in domestic and international market. The analysis of shipbuilding industry in Sweden could reveal that beneficiares are not the target group. Carl Hamilton writes" It is very conceivable that the increase in Government subsidies in Sweden did not go to those groups in society which had the greatest needs, but rather went to groups which had been the most effective in mobilising the mass media, members of parliament, influential trade union leaders, leading individuals within management, local councils, politicians, etc. for their cause". It is also debatable 'as to how one group's needs were balanced against another". The criteria for 'distributing public subsidies aimed at maintaining employment' should be decided taking into account the facts of "what is to be subsidized?". i.e. the place of work or the worker". In other words depending upon the objectives the criteria of subsidies may differ. As pointed out by Carl Hamilton, "If Government's objective is limited to maintaining the income level of those threatened by unemployment, the subsidy should go to these individuals, irrespective of whether the work place is kept or not. If the Government's objective is to maintain the income level and, in addition, to secure the workplace for individual, then the Government should give a subsidy per employee to the production units. Such a subsidy would stimulate firms to use relatively labour intensive methods of production and if it is regional, to encourage relatively labour intensive industries to remain or to establish themselves in the region. To subsidize capital (for example, investment), would to the contrary, stimulate firms to substitute relatively cheap capital for relatively expensive labour".

Finally the two criteria for a system of public subsidies are (1) Priority to the groups with the greatest needs and (2) A system that is transparent and pedagogical in nature. The first criteria implies robust and noninfluencing decision making, while second criteria implies promoting the cause of democracy and pedagogy to 'show citizens how they depend on each other in spite of living in different regions'.

Stabilizing policy has aim to maintain general competitiveness. Usually rising production costs, create uncertainty of competitiveness. Expansion of existing industry if not allowed; it creates situation where creation of further employment is restricted. That is movement of labour from subsidized industry also in restricted and further opportunity for unemployed to job entry in both subsidised and non-subsidised industries is restricted.

Subsidy in ideal situation should reach directly to those who deserve but this rarely happens. Subsidy in productive units should have criterion of amount per employee not exceeding certain level but this does not happen in reality. In almost every country there is tendency to form the forum by those in same business and influence the decision making.

If any industry tends to subcontract its manufacturing activities then subsidies should be equally distributed. Obviously more the number of subcontractors catering to major sector availing Government subsidies, more apportionment of benefits of subsidies would be. Obvious employment generated by such subcontractors industries would be at the cost of the subsidies. But this argument is partially valid because it tantamounts to say that subcontracting came into existence solely to survive on particular subsidised sector and capital goods or investment made in such sub-contracting firms is of fixed nature which does not permit change in product mix. Or subsidising is the only way to support both subcontracting enterprises and major sectors of the economy.

Role of Bureaucrats

Though not a universal truth, but there are reasons to believe that all the countries experience some or other or identical problems at one or other time. As no country can remain isolated from the impact of international economic trade, crisis due to prices of internationally traded commmodities. Also the countries with dominating role of bureaucrats may have identical way to solve the problems. The protectionism is outcome of latent urge for prominence between bureaucrats and politically elected Ministers. But as Ministers may come and go on expiry of terms, it is the role of bureaucrats and other permanent officials imitating like bureaucrats which favour continuance of some problems. The hidden non-tariff barriers or subsidies prevail in almost every country. That is why it could be generalised to say that 'the bureaus (or bureaucrats) have often resorted to complex subsidy programmes or hidden non-tariff barriers that are hard to measure, rather than to transparent protection measurers" (*Ref.*22).

Among various aspects of role played by bureaucrats the three arguments (*Ref.*23) very much concerned with trade are:

1. Bureaus role as 'partial dictator' with respect to the industry it supervises.
2. Inability of a bureaus to capture the profits that result from protection.
3. The cost to a bureau of information about the impact of protection.

None of the countries enunciated explicit subsidy policy. However, both industrial policy and trade policy have explicit or implicit reference to subsidy. As stated earlier, subsidies have definite role in promoting and sustaining at desirable level economic activities, commerce, trade, transport, infrastructure development, welfare functions etc. The basic objectives of macroeconomic policies viz. (1) full and efficient use of resources that is, aim to achieve resources allocation; (2) ensure optimum economic welfare, this is aim to achieve distributive justice cannot be easily achieved without pricing policies. Because the prices are likely to exert not only pressure on economy but create complete 'economic crisis'. In under-developed countries where industries, traditional industries, low size of market, low trade activities exist, if price stabilisation is left to market it is quite possible that economic situation will create deep rooted dichotomies of 'haves' and 'havenots' and prices will shoot up to unaffordable level whereby complete market may collapse by slackened demand. To induce some traditional activities subsidies are granted where the prices of output are higher than market price of such goods. The problems in such subsidies are twin in nature. Firstly if subsidies are granted it tantamounts to foster economically unviable activities. Secondly, if subsidies granted one are withdrawn later would tantamount to pass a death knell on the already sick thereby promoting unemployment as well as allowing demise of the traditional skill, art and crafts, but in order to avoid economic crisis (i.e price inflation, deficits to unmanageable level, negative trade balance etc.), some measures are necessary so that prices get stabilized. In the circumstances of rising cost of manufacturing due to hike in prices of inputs; raw material, wages of employees, transport tariff, taxes, duties etc. maintaining the competitiveness among the industries is difficult task, which in turn depends upon scale of economies, technological superiority and proximity of raw materials. Therefore, stabilizing policies must have aim to enhance competitiveness among the industries.

REFERENCES

[1] Gary Clyde Hafbauer and Joanna Shelton Erb: *Subsidies in International Trade;* Institute for International Economics, Washington D.C. MIT Press, Cambridge; 1984, pp. 2.

[2] *Ibid.*

[3] *Ibid*, pp. 9.

[4] *Ibid*, pp. 351.

[5] William R. Cline: *Trade Policy in the 1980s;* Institute for International Economics, Washington, 1983; pp. 26-29.

[6] Steven J.Warnecks (ed.) : *International Trade and Industrial Policies;* Holmes and Meir Publishers, Inc., 1978; pp. 92.

[7] Gerald M.Meir (ed.) *Pricing Policy for Development Management;* EDI of World Bank; John *Hopkin University Press;* 1989; pp. 137.

[8] *Ibid.*

[9] *Ibid*, pp. 221-222.

[10] Gary Clyde Hafbauer and Joanna Shelton Erb : *Subsidies in International Trade;* MIT Press Cambridge; pp. 10.

[11] *Ibid*, pp. 2.

[12] *Ibid.*

[13] Gary Clyde Hufbauer and Joanna Shelton Erb: *Subsidies in International Trade;* Institute for International Economics, Washington, D.C. 1984, pp. 19.

[14] *Ibid.*

[15] C. Fred Bergesten and William R. in William R. Cline (Edt.); *Trade Policies in 1980s;* Institute for International Economics; 1983, pp. 81.

[16] *Ibid.*

[17] Public subsidies to industry, the case of Sweden and its Shipbuilding industry: Carl Hamilton, World Bank Staff Working Papers; number 556; The World Bank, Washington DC, USA, pp. 1.

[18] *Ibid*, p.2.

[19] *Ibid*, p.2.

[20] Carl Hamilton Public Subsidies to Industry—the Case of Sweden and Its Shipbuilding Industry :

[21] Carl Hamilton (1983) pp. 20.

[22] Patrick A. Messertin: Bureaucracies and the political economy of protection —reflection of a continental European World Bank staff working paper no. 568 Note that terms bureaus and bureaucrats are used synonymously.

[23] *Ibid.*

8

Subsidies in Indian Economy

8.01 Introduction

The term subsidy connates meaning of "financial aid from government towards expenses of institutions etc. held to be public utility, or to producers of commodity etc. enabling goods or services to be provided at lower cost to consumer". There is not and unlikely to exist the agreed universal definition of subsidy. Both supply side and demand side of economics have their own justifications for subsidy. Both merits and demerits of subsidy are equally strong and pose really a question as to whether subsidy contributes to economic growth or not. Whether subsidy should be continued or withdrawn is a question, which requires in depth study.

There is no economic theory justifying or refuting the role of subsidies to be given to small scale industries. In India subsidies have been in existence and continued for one or other economic and political reasons. In fact the objectives behind subsidies will be to stimulate the domestic economy, continuance of activities, trade in remote areas and welfare of specific group. In a crude way subsidies refer to a kind of transfer of payments from advantageous group to the disadvantageous group. It involves transfer of real income from taxpayers to socially and economically weaker group or to consumers of the goods by ensuring sustaining of economic activities to produce goods and compensate the price difference of higher prices to the producers of designated commodities, if those commodities are supplied at designated prices to the consumers.

The Government by virtue of enactment impose certain taxes on a group of a society. Therefore, the subsidy tantamounts to negative tax and aimed to promote the identified activities. Similarly in the framework of national account statistics, the subsidy refers to payment, or compensation for production which is not currently in progress. A subsidy may be in various forms, kind, means and modes such as grant-in-aid, social security, subsidies on interest, subsidies on sale, subsidies on investment, deferred payment etc.

Theoretically subsidy tends to distort the prices in the economy. The concept of administered prices prevails in India which tantamounts to say that prices are fixed by the Government based on some criterion to control the inflation in the country. However, market mechanism has its own implications and prices of most of the commodities and goods available in the market are distinct from administered prices for some commodities including wheat, rice sugar etc. The administered prices are applicable to few categories and commodities supplied through well identified channel under the control of Government. Therefore, only fraction of the inflationary items are controlled leaving major items to be controlled by the market forces. This kind of intervention mechanism leads to compensate supply side by way of subsidy to ensure price stability. The trade theory has obvious reference to subsidy and injury. Only school, tariff and export subsidy etc. explains the effect of subsidy on domestic and international trade.

However, in this paper the subsidy as applicable for industrial production shall be dealt with. The subsidies form the part of government consumption expenditure and could be studied under the fiscal policies of the Government. The Total government expenditure is controlled through budget exercise of the Central Government as well as State Governments. Therefore, the first part of this paper will deal with the budgetary measures of the Central Government to explain the size and its implication.

The later part of the paper will deal with the subsidies at the State level.

8.02 Subsidies in the Central Government Budget

The centre's revenue received and revenue expenditure indicate the details of total current expenditure of Central Government. In principle the expenditure of the Government comprises various items such as interest payment, subsidies different expenditure grant to the States and UTs and other expenditure. Current

Table 1 : Centre's Revenue Receipts and Revenue Expenditure
(As per cent of GDP)

	1980-81	1981-82	1982-83	1983-84	1984-85	1985-86	1986-87	1987-88	1988-89	1989-90	1990-91*
1. Tax Revenue (Net of States' share)	6.9	7.3	7.3	7.5	7.6	8.1	8.3	8.4	8.6	8.7	8.6
2. Non-Tax Revenue	2.5	2.5	2.8	2.4	2.9	3.1	3.4	3.1	2.8	3.5	2.9
3. Total Current Revenue	9.4	9.8	10.1	9.9	10.5	11.2	11.7	11.5	11.4	12.2	11.5
4. Total Current Expenditure	10.0	9.8	10.9	11.0	12.0	13.3	14.4	14.3	14.1	14.9	14.9
(a) Interest Payment	2.0	2.0	2.2	2.3	2.6	2.9	3.2	3.4	3.6	4.0	4.3
(b) Subsidies 1	1.2	1.2	1.3	1.3	1.6	1.8	1.9	1.8	2.0	2.5	1.8
(c) Defence Expenditure 2	2.6	2.6	2.7	2.7	2.8	2.9	3.4	3.0	2.9	2.7	2.4
(d) Grants to the State & UTs	2.1	1.7	2.0	2.1	2.3	2.7	2.7	2.8	2.6	2.0	2.2
(e) Others	2.2	2.4	2.6	2.5	2.8	3.0	3.3	3.3	3.0	3.8	4.2
5. Revenue Accounts Surplus (+) Deficit (—) Col. (3-4)	—0.6	—0.1	—0.8	—1.1	—1.5	—2.1	—2.7	—2.8	—2.7	—2.7	—3.4

1. Excludes subsidies on imported fertilizer upto 185 -86
2. Includes defence pension.
*. R.E.

Notes :

(a) The ratio in this table from 1980-81 onwards are based on the new series on GDP released by the CSO and therefore these will differ from the figures given in the earlier issues of Economic Survey.

(b) Totals may not add up because of rounding.

Source :Economic Survey 1990-91; page 102, for the year 1981-82 Economic Survey 1987-88, page 55. Ref. cd poverty, file Revenue, range al. 0.28.

expenditure of the Government since 1990-91 has been gradually increasing from 10% of GDP to 14.9% of the GDP. The subsidies account for about 1.8% of the GDP in year 1990-91 (See Table - 1 on Centre's revenue received and revenue expenditure). The details of subsidies at the national level could be seen from any of the budget documents. For the sake of the convenience of the details about 1990-91 budget, 1990-91 revised estimates and the budget estimates of 1991-92 shall be dealt in order to give size of major subsidies prevailing in India. In India over Rs, 10,000 crores are apportioned as a subsidy out of total government expenditure. These items under explicit subsidies include the following as shown in table 2.

Table 2 : Items of Explicit Subsidies

A. Major Subsidies
   1. Food
   2. Indigenous Fertilisers
   3. Imported Fertilisers
   4. Export Promotion and Market Development

B. Other Subsidies
   5. Railways
   6. Mill-made Cloth
   7. Handloom Cloth
   8. Import/Export of Sugar, Edible Oils etc.
   9. Interest Subsidies
   10. Debt. Relief to Farmers
   11. Other Subsidies

It could be seen from Tables 3, 4, 5 and 6 that since 1989-90 the subsidies have crossed Rs 10,000 crores annually. As restructuring of the economy is under progress there is a need to reconcile the justification of subsidies and study in depth details about subsidies in India. The justification for such huge amount of subsidy needs sectoral study but for the sake of convenience only few items could be cited as an example.

8.03 Food Subsidies of Rs 260.00 crores in Non-Plan Expenditure 1991-92 Budget

The Food Corporation of India purchases foodgrains for the Central pool on procurement prices fixed by Government from time to time. These grains are issued to (a) public through public

Table 3 : Trends in Central Government Expenditure (In crores of Rupees)

Sl. No.	Description	Actuals 1984-85	Actuals 1985-86	Actuals 1986-87	Actuals 1987-88	Actuals 1988-89	Actuals 1989-90	Growth % p.a.	Actuals 1990-91	Revised 1991-92	Budget 1992-93
	A. Non-Plan Expenditure	27026	32811	39920	44052	52960	65388	19.33	76198	80070	84475
1.	Interest Payments	5974	7512	9246	11251	14278	17757	24.34	21471	27250	32000
2.	Defence Expenditure	7061	7988	10477	11968	13341	14416	15.34	15427	16350	17500
3.	Subsidies	4038	4796	5451	5980	7732	10474	21.00	12121	12290	10487
4.	Grants to States and UTs	1027	1786	1714	1789	2186	2143	15.85	3981	2660	2535
5.	Grants to Foreign Govt.	89	81	114	139	124	120	6.16	140	166	190
6.	Other Non-plan Revenue exp.	4250	5430	6491	7782	8386	10693	20.27	10477	11771	12749
7.	Non-Plan Capital Expend.	853	382	380	667	788	1091	5.04	1012	866	1131
8.	Loans and Advances to States & UT governments	3272	4206	3722	3134	4293	5793	12.10	7606	5479	5801
9.	Other Loans	141	217	1769	905	1107	2036	70.57	2875	2157	974
10.	Non-plan Exp. of UTs without Legislature	321	413	556	437	725	865	21.93	1088	1081	1108
	B. Plan Expenditure	16606	19854	22996	24209	26151	27520	10.63	29118	33032	34612
	Total Capital Expenditure	43632	52665	62916	68261	79111	92908	16.32	105316	113102	119087
	GDP of at Current Prices	207869	234159	260442	294408	348896	401569	14.08	472599		
	GDP at 1980-81 Prices	149966	157348	163924	170716	188481	199329	5.86	210477		

Table 4 : Percentage Share of Different Items of Expenditure

Sl. No.	Description	*Actuals 1984-85*	*Actuals 1985-86*	*Actuals 1986-87*	*Actuals 1987-88*	*Actuals 1988-89*	*Actuals 1989-90*	*Actuals 1990-91*	*Revised 1991-92*	*Budget 1992-93*
	A. Non-Plan Expenditure	61.94	62.30	63.45	64.53	66.94	70.38	72.35	70.79	70.94
1.	Interest Payment	13.69	14.26	14.70	16.48	18.05	19.11	20.39	24.09	26.87
2.	Defence Expenditure	16.18	15.17	16.65	17.53	16.86	15.52	14.65	14.46	14.70
3.	Subsidies	9.25	9.11	8.66	8.76	9.77	11.27	11.51	10.87	8.81
4.	Grants to States and UTs	2.35	3.39	2.72	2.62	2.76	2.31	3.78	2.35	2.13
5.	Grants to Foreign Govt.	0.20	0.15	0.18	0.20	0.16	0.13	0.13	0.15	0.16
6.	Other Non-plan Revenue Exp.	9.74	10.31	10.32	11.40	10.60	11.51	9.95	10.41	10.71
7.	Non-Plan Capital expend.	1.95	0.73	0.60	0.98	1.00	1.17	0.96	0.7	0.95
8.	Loans and Advances to States & UT Governments	7.50	7.99	5.92	4.59	5.43	6.24	7.22	4.84	4.87
9.	Other Loans	0.32	0.41	2.81	1.33	1.40	2.19	2.73	1.91	0.82
10.	Non-plan Exp. of UTs	0.00	0.00	0.00	0.00	0.00	0.00	0.00	0.00	0.00
	without Legislature	0.74	0.78	0.88	0.64	0.92	0.93	1.03	0.96	0.93
	B. Plan Expenditure	38.06	37.70	36.55	35.47	33.06	29.62	27.65	29.21	29.06
	Total Capital Expenditure	100.00	100.00	100.00	100.00	100.00	100.00	100.00	100.00	100.00
	Percentage of GDP at Current Prices									
	Non-plan Expenditure	13.00	14.01	15.33	14.96	15.18	16.28	16.12		
	Plan Expenditure	7.99	8.48	8.83	8.22	7.50	6.85	6.16		
	Total Expenditure	20.99	22.49	24.16	23.19	22.67	23.14	22.28		

Table 5: Details of Subsidies in India

(In crores of Rupees)

Sl. No.	Description	Actuals 1984-85	Actuals 1985-86	Actuals 1986-87	Actuals 1987-88	Actuals 1988-89	Actuals 1989-90	Growth % p.a.	Actuals 1990-91	Revised 1991-92	Budget 1992-93
A.	Major Subsidies	3547	4177	4683	5126	6787	9032	20.55	9550	9829	7980
1.	Food Subsidies	1101	1650	2000	2000	2200	2476	17.60	2450	2850	2500
2.	Indigeneous Fertilisers	1200	1600	1700	2050	3000	3771	25.73	3650	3500	3500
3.	Imported Subsidies	728	324	198	114	201	771	1.15	750	1300	1500
4.	Fertiliser Subsidy to Small and Marginal Farmer									405	
5.	Export Promotion and Market Development	518	603	785	962	1386	2014	31.20	2700	1774	480
									1500	1425	1500
B.	Debt Relief to Farmer										
C.	Other Subsidies	491	619	768	854	945	1442	24.04	1071	1036	1007
6.	Railway	100	128	144	174	207	233	18.43	276	313	339
7.	Mill Made Cloth	73	51	36	23	27	10	—32.81	10	15	15
8.	Handloom Cloth	73	86	123	124	146	181	19.91	188	187	205
9.	Import/Export of Sugar Edible Oils etc.	38	23	76	5	40					
10.	Interest Subsidies	135	271	229	393	406	881	45.52	379	316	325
11.	Other Subsidies	72	60	160	135	119	137	13.73	218	205	123
	Total Subsidies	4038	4796	5451	5980	7732	10474	21.00	12121	12290	10487

Table 6 : Percentage Share of each of the Items in Subsidies

Sl. No.	Description	*Actuals 1984-85*	*Actuals 1985-86*	*Actuals 1986-87*	*Actuals 1987-88*	*Actuals 1988-89*	*Growth 1989-90*	*Actuals 1990-91*	*Revised 1991-92*	*Budget 1992-93*
A.	Major Subsidies	87.84	87.09	85.91	85.72	87.78	86.23	78.79	79.98	76.09
1.	Food Subsidies	27.27	34.40	36.69	33.44	28.45	23.64	20.21	23.19	23.84
2.	Indigeneous Fertilisers	29.72	33.36	31.19	34.28	38.80	36.00	30.11	28.48	33.37
3.	Imported Fertilisers	18.03	6.76	3.63	1.91	2.60	7.36	6.19	10.58	14.30
4.	Fertiliser Subsidy to Small and Marginal Farmer								3.30	
5.	Export Promotion and Market Development	12.83	12.57	14.40	16.09	17.93	19.23	22.28	14.43	4.58
								12.38	11.59	14.30
B.	Debt Relief to Farmer									
C.	Other Subsidies	12.16	12.91	14.09	14.28	12.22	13.77	8.84	8.43	9.60
6.	Railway	2.48	2.67	2.64	2.91	2.68	2.22	2.28	2.55	3.23
7.	Mill Made Cloth	1.81	1.06	0.66	0.38	0.35	0.10	0.08	0.12	0.14
8.	Handloom Cloth	1.81	1.79	2.26	2.07	1.89	1.73	1.55	1.52	1.95
9.	Import/Export of Sugar Edible Oils etc.	0.94	0.48	1.39	0.08	0.52				
10.	Interest Subsidies	3.34	5.65	4.20	6.57	5.25	8.41	3.13	2.57	3.10
11.	Other Subsidies	1.78	1.25	2.96	2.26	1.54	1.31	1.80	1.67	1.17
	Total Subsidies	100.00	100.00	100.00	100.00	100.00	100.00	100.00	100.00	100.00

distribution (b) roller flour mills and (c) for rural employment programme and other relief schemes at issues prices fixed by Government. The difference between economic cost and the issue price is reimbursed to the corporation as consumer subsidy. The corporation also carries buffer stock on behalf of government and is reimbursed the carrying cost including handling, storage, interest and administrative charges. Important parameters on which the subsidy estimate has been framed are :—

	Quantity in Lakh tonnes	
	Wheat	*Rice*
Procurement	97.00	110.00
Offtake	85.00	85.00
Average buffer stock	61.98	71.98
	Rate per quintal in rupees	
Purchase cost and procurement incidental	269.05	383.43
Distribution cost (pooled)*	72.29	72.29
Total economic cost*	341.34	455.72
Sales realisation (average)	229.42	378.22
Consumer subsidy*	11.92	80.50
*Excludes storage at transit losses	72.29	69.51

Details	*Distribution Cost*	*Carrying Cost*
Freight	30.38	4.07
Handling	6.67	5.09
Storage	5.02	16.04
Interest	23.74	39.38
Administration Overheads	6.48	4.93

8.04 Subsidy on Indigenous Fertilisers (Rs 2900.00 crores in BE 1991-92)

A retention price scheme for indigenous fertiliser is in operation since 1977. This scheme is intended to make fertilisers available to the farmers at reasonable prices and give producers of fertiliser a reasonable return on their investment. The fertilisers are sold at issue price fixed from time to time.

The retention prices scheme allows a 12% return on net worth. The difference between the retention prices so fixed less distribution margin and the statutorily controlled consumer price is allowed as subsidy. The retention price is fixed for each plant over the pricing period. Necessary adjustments are, however, made during the pricing period on account of variation in the prices of major inputs. The quantum of subsidy, therefore, depends on the retention prices, the consumers' price and the level of production. In addition, the manufacturers are also allowed freight subsidy for movement of fertilizers from factory to delivery points.

8.05 Interest Subsidies Rs 315.55 Crores in 1990-91 Budget

Interest on loans sanctioned by the Government is normally payable at the rates prescribed from time to time. In specific cases where a concession is allowed in the rate of interest to a party or where the loan is exempted from payment of interest on the loans, subsidies are paid in lieu of interest. An amount equal to the subsidy is taken as interest receipt of the Government.

Subsidies interest rates are allowed on loans for Khadi and Village industries. Interest exemption has been allowed as a part of restructuring of capital base of certain public enterprises like Steel Authority of India, Delhi Transport Corporation and the Central Inland Water Transport Corporation.

8.06 Per Capita Subsidy

Subsidies in India have been estimated at Rs 104,87 crores. The earlier highest was of Rs 12,290 crores in 1991-92. By introduction of debt relief to farmers the amount of subsidies has increased to Rs 12,121 crores in 1990-91. This indicates the per capita subsidies of Rs 122.8 in 1992-93. As subsidies are treated as a part of government expenditure it will be better to compare rise in both per capita expenditure and per capita subsidies as follows :

Table 7 : Per Capita Expenditure and Subsidy

Year	*Per capita govt. Expenditure Rs*	*Per capita subsidies Rs*
1984-85	602.7	55.8
1985-86	712.7	64.9
1986-87	833.3	72.7
1988-89	1007.8	98.7
1989-90	1161.4	130.9
1990-91	1284.3	147.8
1991-92	1351.3	146.8
1992-93	1394.5	122.8

It will be obvious from the above that while per capita expenditure grew at a rate of 14.02% p.a., the subsidies grew at a rate of 18.60% p.a. during the period from 1984-85 to 1989-90. That is the elasticity of subsidies was 1.33 with respect to per capita expenditure. Both per capita subsidies and per capita expenditure has increased by 2.2 and 2.3 times respectively during the period from 1984-85 to 1992-93. In the year 1990-91 the per capita subsidies were found to be of highest order when these reached Rs 147.8. This was due to introduction of debt relief to farmers. The debt relief to farmers was of the order of Rs 1500 crores in 1990-91 onwards.

8.07 Trend in Government Expenditure

The non-plan and plan expenditure of the central government comprises numerous items. The subsidies are categorised as a part of non-plan expenditure besides interest payments, grants to states and UTs. During the period from 1984-85 to 1989-90 the non-plan expenditure of the Central Government has increased by 19.33 percent and Plan expenditure has increased by 10.63 per cent. The total capital expenditure has grown by 16.32 per cent per annum.

The trends in Central Government Expenditure (Ref. Table 3) indicates that there has been growth of 70.57 per cent per annum in other loans, items like interest payments, defence expenditure, loans etc. have grown at a rate exceeding 20 per cent. Based on actuals for the period from 1984-85 to 1989-90 subsidies have grown at a rate of 21.00% per annum (at current prices). In absolute terms subsidies have increased from Rs 4038 crores to Rs 10474 crores (by 2.6 times) from 1984-85 to 1989-90. For the year 1992-93 the estimated subsidies are Rs 10487 crores.

8.08 The Share of Subsidies in Govt. Expenditure

Based on the actual expenditure of different items of non-plan and plan expenditure it could be possible to reveal the share of subsidies in different years (See Table 2). Though in terms of total expenditure the share of subsidies has increased from 9.25% in 1984-85 to 11.27 per cent in 1989-90 and later decline to 8.81 in 1992-93, but in terms of its share in non-plan expenditure the subsidies would be as follows :

Table 8 : Share of Subsidies

Year	*Share in non-plan Expenditure*	*Share in total (Plan+Non Plan) Expenditure*
1984-85	14.94	9.25
1985-86	14.62	9.11
1986-87	13.65	8.66
1987-88	13.57	8.76
1988-89	14.60	9.77
1989-90	16.02	11.27
1990-91	15.90	11.51
1991-92	15.35	10.87
1992-93	12.41	8.81

That is, though share of subsidies in total of non-plan and plan expenditure is, say 10.87 in 1991-92, its share in non-plan expenditure is about 15.35 in the same year.

8.09 Per Capita Subsidy on Food and Fertiliser

The amount of subsidies has been highest in 1991-92 and gradual decline has been noticed in past two years, viz. 1991-92 and 1992-93. The highest amount of subsidies are apportioned as food subsidies and subsidies on fertiliser. The food subsidies and fertiliser in different years are shown below :—

Table 9 : Per Capita Subsidies (Rs)

Year	*Food Subsidies*	*Fertiliser Indigeneous*	*Fertiliser Imported*	*Total Rs*
1984-85	15.2	16.6	10.1	41.9
1985-86	22.3	21.7	4.4	48.4
1986-87	26.5	22.5	2.6	51.6
1987-88	26.0	26.6	1.5	54.1
1988-89	28.0	38.2	2.6	68.8
1989-90	31.0	47.1	9.6	87.7
1990-91	29.9	44.5	9.1	83.5
1991-92	34.1	41.8	15.5	91.4
1992-93	29.3	41.0	17.6	87.9

The subsidies in railways, handloom cloth, etc. has been of the order of Rs 11.8 per capita in the year 1992-93. In fact handloom sector which is widely dispersed and employs the largest manpower in rural areas has very low per capita subsidy. It is Rs 2.4 per capita subsidy in handloom sector. The interest subsidies are increasing from Rs 1.9 in 1984-85 to Rs 3.8 in 1992-93. However, these are used in various forms, and its amount is also less. The explicit subsidies on different items is shown in Table 5. It could be seen (from Table 6) that major subsidies (comprising of total subsidies and fertiliser subsidies) constitute above 76% in 1992-93 BE. The share of food subsidies in 1992-93 is 23.84% and fertiliser subsidies is 47.67. This obviously means that it is agriculture sector which is consuming more subsidies than any other sector. Particularly fertiliser sector consumes more subsidies than any other sector of the economy.

8.10 Growth in Subsidies

In the period from 1984-85 to 1989-90 the compound growth of total subsidies had been 21.00 per cent per annum. The growth in non-plan expenditure had been 19.33 per cent per annum and capital expenditure's growth had been 16.2 per cent during the same period. GDP at current prices of country has grown at a rate 14.08 per cent per annum for the period from 1984-85 to 1989-90. These growth rate gives the following elasticities ratios of relative growth.

1. Subsidies/GDP at current price = 21.00/14.08 = 1.49
2. Subsidies/non-plan expenditure = 21.00/19.33 = 1.086
3. Subsidies/capital expenditure = 21.00/16.32 = 1.286

In other words subsidies grew by 1.49 times the GDP at current prices and 1.086 times the non-plan expenditure and 1.286 times the capital expenditure of the Central Government of India.

The data for the period from 1982-83 to 1990-91 (i.e. nine years data) were subjected to double log regression analysis. The actual data, its analysis, and four models alongwith inference are shown in Table 10-A. From equation no.4 above, it will be obvious that subsidies have grown at a rate 1.92 times the growth rate of non-plan expenditure. Similarly equation 5 indicates that the growth of subsidies with respect to GDP had been 1.36 times the GDP at current prices. These equations could be used to estimate the size of subsidies at prevailing rate once the growth of GDP at current prices is known.

Table 10 : Expenditure of Indian Government

I. Expenditure of Government of India

Year	Expenditure Rs Cr.			Subsidies	GDP Current Pr.Rs Cr.
	Non-plan	Plan	Total		
1982-83	17774	11913	29687	2262	158851
1983-84	20017	14038	34055	2902	185991
1984-85	27026	16606	43632	4038	207869
1985-86	32811	19854	52665	4796	234159
1986-87	39920	22996	62916	5451	260442
1987-88	44052	24209	68261	5980	294408
1988-89	52960	26151	79111	7732	348896
1989-90	65388	27520	92908	10474	401569
1990-91	76198	29118	105316	12121	472599

II. Expenditure as percentage of GDP at Current Prices

Year	Expenditure Rs Cr.			Subsidies	GDP Current Pr.Rs Cr.
	Nonplan	Plan	Total		
1982-83	11.19	7.50	18.69	1.42	100.00
1983-84	10.76	7.55	18.31	1.56	100.00
1984-85	13.00	7.99	20.99	1.94	100.00
1985-86	14.01	8.48	22.49	2.05	100.00
1986-87	15.33	8.83	24.16	2.09	100.00
1987-88	14.96	8.22	23.19	2.03	100.00
1988-89	15.18	7.50	22.67	2.22	100.00
1989-90	16.28	6.85	23.14	2.61	100.00
1990-91	16.12	6.16	22.28	2.56	100.00

III. Share of Plan Non-plan Expenditure and Share of Subsidies

Year	Expenditure Rs Cr.			Subsidies
	Non-plan	Plan	Total	
1982-83	59.87	40.13	100.00	7.62
1983-84	58.78	41.22	100.00	8.52
1984-85	61.94	38.06	100.00	9.25
1985-86	62.30	37.70	100.00	9.11

Year	*Expenditure Rs. Cr.*			*Subsidies*
	Non-plan	*Plan*	*Total*	
1986-87	63.45	36.55	100.00	8.66
1987-88	64.53	35.47	100.00	8.76
1988-89	66.94	33.06	100.00	9.77
1989-90	70.38	29.62	100.00	11.27
1990-91	72.35	27.65	100.00	11.51

Model No.	Double log regression equation
Model 1 :	$\log Y = -2.91 + 1.38 \log X$; $R^2 = 0.98$ (—92.95) (19.65) where : Y = Non-plan expenditure in Rs Crores X = GDP at current prices Rs Crores
Model 2 :	$\text{Log } Y = -0.19 + 0.83 \log X$; $R^2 = 0.91$ (—4.52) (8.67) Y = Plan expenditure in Rs Crores X = GDP at current prices Rs Crores
Model 3 :	$\log Y = -1.69 + 1.19 \log X$; $R^2 = 0.97$ (—52.58) (16.48) where Y = Total of Non-plan + Plan expenditure in Rs Crores X = GDP at current prices Rs Crores
Model 4 :	$\log Y = -4.52 + 1.52 \log X$; $R^2 = 0.98$ (—141.19) (21.18) Y = Total explicit subsidy in expenditure in Rs Crore X = GDP at current prices Rs Crores

Notes:

A) Model 1 explains that India's non-plan expenditure is growing at a rate 1.38 times the growth of GDP at current prices.

B) Model 2 explains that India's plan expenditure is growing at a rate 0.83 times the growth of GDP at current prices

C) Model 3 explains that total (Plan+Non-plan) expenditure is growing at a rate 1.19 times GDP at current prices

D) Model 4 explains that subsidies in India grow at rate 1.52 time the growth rate of GDP at current price.

8.11 Statewise Subsidies

Though subsidies as calculated and shown in Central Government budget expenditure are explicit, there are various other schemes with subsidy content. The study conducted by S. Mundle and M. Govind Rao indicates that total subsidies in 1987-88 were of the order of Rs 42324 crores comprising Rs 16065 crores as Central subsidies and Rs 26259 crores as state subsidies and welfare programmes would be more. Though the budget expenditure for 1987-88 indicates Rs 5980 crores, the total of implicit subsidies and welfare programmes would be more. Taking the basis of the study of Mundle and Rao and Rs 42324 as total subsidy in India the subsidy on social services would be of the order of 39.60 per cent and Agriculture and Cooperation had 60.40 per cent. The share of Central and State governments in total subsidies in India was 37.96: 62.04 in 1987-88 (See Table 10).

The budgetary subsidies for different states are shown in Table 11. It will be obvious from Table 11 that Punjab has been the highest beneficiary of subsidies though it has only 2.6% of India's population.

The indicators of social development and per capita subsidies in social services for different states as worked out by Mundle and Rao indicates that the states with higher index of social and health facilities have availed higher per capita subsidies in social services namely Education, Medical and public health and water supply sanitation and housing (See Table 12).

The percentage share of subsidies in agricultural and allied services, irrigation for different states has been shown in Table 13. The per capita subsidy in economic services has been highest in Punjab with Rs 326 followed by Haryana with Rs 267. Gross irrigated area was highest in Uttar Pradesh and accounted for 14.2 per cent share in Agriculture and allied services and 13.4 per cent in Irrigation but per capita subsidies in economic service were only Rs 133.

Table 10A : Subsidies on Social and Economic Services in India

Sl.No.	Heads of Subsidy	Amount of Subsidy Rs Cr.	Share of State Govt. per cent	Subsidy as % of total
(1)	(2)	(3)	(4)	(5)
I.	Total Subsidies (A+B)	42324		100.00
(i)	Centre	16065		37.96
(ii)	State	26259		62.04
A.	Subsidy on Social Services	16760	86.3	39.60
1.	Education	9576	86.7	22.63
	of which Elementary Education	4116	42.9	9.72
2.	Health	2925	88.2	6.91
	of which Rural	575	98.4	1.36
3.	Water Supply, Sanitation	2363	87.2	5.58
	and Housing of which Rural	823	98.0	1.94
4.	Other Services	1895	79.9	4.48
	Total (item 1 to 4)	16759		39.60
	of which Rural Total :	5514		13.03
B.	Subsidy on Economic Services	25564	46.1	60.40
1.	Agriculture & Cooperation	6980	57.4	16.49
2.	Irrigation & Flood Control	4574	97.6	10.81
3.	Power & Energy	3221	44.5	7.61
4.	Industry	4879	2.4	11.53
5.	Transport	3122	53	7.38
6.	Communication	1043	0.9	2.46
7.	Other Economic Services	1745	4.9	4.12
	Total Economic Services	25564		60.40

Source : S. Mundle & M. Govind Rao; "Volume & Composition of Government Subsidies in India ; Economic and Political Weekly ; May 4, 1991; Table 1-4.
Dr R.V. Dadibhavi & S.M. Basavaraju : Subsidy : Has it served the Purpose? Yojana, January 15, 1992; vol.35 : no.24; pp. 12 to 15.

8.12 General Subsidies in Maharashtra

Govt. of Maharashtra has various schemes for granting the subsidies in different sectors of the economy. Table 14 indicates the classification of the sectors where the substantial subsidies are found. The actual expenditure on subsidies in different sectors for the year 1989-90 and 1990-91 is shown in the said Table. The

Table 11 : Budgetary Subsidies in Major States 1987-88

Sl. No.	State	Total Subsidy (Rs in Lakhs)	Share of States subsidy in all states subsidy	Share of States populn. in all states Populn.	Per Capita subsidy (Rs)	Share of social services in total state subsidy	Share of economic services in total state subsidy
1	2	3	4	5	6	7	8
1.	Punjab	114303	4.35	2.6	604	46.0	54.0
2.	Haryana	77572	2.95	2.1	507	47.4	52.6
3.	Maharashtra	279674	10.65	9.8	392	64.5	35.5
4.	Gujarat	200717	7.64	5.3	520	50.8	49.1
5.	West Bengal	198802	7.57	8.5	322	60.9	39.0
6.	Tamil Nadu	232996	8.87	7.4	434	48.8	51.0
7.	Karnataka	170473	6.49	5.8	402	56.5	43.5
8.	Kerala	116110	4.42	3.9	408	68.2	31.8
9.	Andhra Pradesh	228933	8.72	8.3	380	57.5	42.5
10.	Rajasthan	166740	6.35	5.6	411	49.0	51.0
11.	Uttar Pradesh	337948	12.87	17.4	267	50.2	49.8
12.	Madhya Pradesh	205765	7.84	8.2	344	54.6	45.4
13.	Orissa	104273	3.97	4.1	353	53.0	47.0
14.	Bihar	191604	7.30	11.0	240	59.1	40.9
	Total All States	2625910	99.99	100.0	361	55.1	44.9

Sources : *S. Mundle & Govinda Rao "Volume and Composition of Government Subsidies in India, Economic and Political Weekly, May 4, 1991, Table 1-4.*

Dr R.V. Dadibhavi & S.M. Basavaraju; Subsidy : Has It served the Purpose? Yojana, January, 15, 1992 vol. 35, no.24 pp. 14, Table - 2.

Table 12 : Statewise Budgetary Subsidy in Social Services and Indicators of Social Development in India 1987-88

Sl. No.	*States*	*Per Capita Subsidies in Social Services (Rs)*				*Indicators of Social Development*			
		Education	*Medical and Public Health*	*Water Supply Sanitation & Housing*	*Total (col.3-5)*	*Literacy per cent in 1981*	*Infant Mortality Rate*	*Poverty Ratio (1987-88)*	*Index of Education & Health Facilities (1985-86)*
1	2	3	4	5	6	7	8	9	10
1.	Punjab	176	56	30	278	41	68	20	10.637
2.	Haryana	144	41	37	241	36	85	22	6.204
3.	Maharashtra	147	45	45	253	47	63	47	9.858
4.	Gujarat	143	37	50	264	44	107	41	8.013
5.	West Bengal	116	38	27	196	41	71	50	6.597
6.	Tamil Nadu	122	37	33	212	46	90	47	7.21
7.	Karnataka	132	42	24	227	38	74	43	6.941
8.	Kerala	178	47	30	278	70	27	44	11.765
9.	Andhra Pradesh	112	40	27	218	30	82	34	5.969
10.	Rajasthan	116	37	40	201	24	107	42	4.49
11.	Uttar Pradesh	74	29	13	134	27	132	46	4.509
12.	Madhya Pradesh	89	32	37	188	28	118	49	4.113
13.	Orissa	98	32	27	187	34	123	63	5.542
14.	Bihar	97	22	14	142	26	101	65	4.277
Total All States		114	35	28	199	38	89	44	6.86

Table 12 (*Contd.*)

Composite index of education and health facilities is prepared for 10 variables relating to education and health aspects.

Source : *S. Mundle and M.G. Rao Op. Cit. Table 8.*
B.S. Minhas, L.R. Jain and S.D. Tendulkar : "Declining incidence of poverty in the 1980s ; Economic and Political Weekly, July 6-13, 1991 Tables.
R.V. Dadibhavi, "Disparities in social infrastructure development in India—1970-71 to 1985-86", The Asian Economic Review, vol, XXXIII(1), April 1991, 40-41.

Table 13 : Statewise Budgetary Subsidy in Economic Service in India 1987-88

Sl.No.	States	Per cent share of subsidies in (a) Agriculture and allied service	Per cent share of subsidies in (b) Irrigation	Per Capita subsidies in economic services Rs	Per cent share in (a) Rural population. (1981)	Per cent share in (b) Gross irrigated area (1984-85)	Index of economic infrastructure (1985-86)
1	2	3	4	5	6	7	8
1.	Punjab	2.9	3.9	326	2.5	12.4	10.921
2.	Haryana	3.0	4.0	267	2.1	7.0	7.231
3.	Maharashtra	9.8	8.5	139	8.3	4.7	6.797
4.	Gujarat	9.0	9.1	255	4.8	5.3	7.844
5.	West Bengal	7.8	4.1	126	8.2	3.6	4.866
6.	Tamil Nadu	10.7	2.2	223	6.6	6.2	5.690
7.	Karnataka	6.2	7.4	175	5.4	3.8	6.060
8.	Kerala	2.7	3.0	130	4.2	0.8	6.276
9.	Andhra Pradesh	13.2	7.9	161	8.4	8.3	5.343
10.	Rajasthan	5.7	7.8	209	5.5	7.4	4.090
11.	Uttar Pradesh	14.2	13.4	133	18.5	23.2	4.403
12.	Madhya Pradesh	2.6	10.6	156	8.5	5.9	4.290
13.	Orissa	3.2	5.7	166	4.6	4.1	3.974
14.	Bihar	9.0	12.2	98	12.4	7.3	3.549
	Total All States	100.0	99.8	162	100.0	100.0	5.809

Table 13 (*Contd.*)

Composite index of education and health facilities is prepared for 10 variables relating to irrigation, electricity consumption, transport, communication.

Sources : *S. Mundle and M.G. Rao, Op. Cit. Table 10.*

R.V. Dadibhavi, "Infrastructure Disparities in Development"; Economic Times, May 25, 1990.

R.V. Dadibhavi & S.M. Basavaraju; Subsidy : Has It Served The Purpose? Yojana, January 15, 1992; vol. 35, no. 24, pp. 16, Table 4.

sectoral distribution of general subsidy indicates that social and community services had the share of 70.65% of the total subsidies in Maharashtra, agricultural and allied services had 12.64% of the total subsidies in 1989-90. However, in the year 1990-91 the share of agricultural and allied services has come down to 11.12% and 57.95% in the social and community services. This decline in the subsidies is attributed to the fact that the subsidies in the sector of power department have increased to 12.49%. According to the classification of plan and non-plan subsidies in the budget estimates of 1989-90, 1990-91 of Govt. of Maharashtra there is substantial increase in non-plan subsidies. According to one of the reports published by Govt. of Maharashtra the classification of the said subsidies of Maharashtra is based upon the 3 concepts namely, explicit subsidies, grant in aid, hidden subsidies. The actual subsidies according to this classification is shown in table for the year 1989-90 and 1990-91. The non-plan subsidies have increased from Rs 989.53 crores in the year 1989-90 to Rs 1505.127 crores in the year 1990-91. The total subsidies in Maharashtra have been of the order of Rs 1819.421 crores. The total revenue expenditure of Maharashtra in the year 1989-1990 (BE) and 1990-91(BE) was Rs 7966.24 lakhs and Rs 834043.99 lakhs respectively. This represents the subsidy of 13.19% of the total revenue expenditure in the year 1989-90 (BE). The details of explicit subsidies and grant in aid for the referred year is shown in table.

It will be difficult to deal with every sector of the economy but to give an ideal about the schemes in existence in Govt. of Maharashtra, industry and mining sector shall be dealt below. The central government assistance to the state government of Maharashtra is given under the two categories namely :—

Central assistance received directly by department of Mantralaya from Ministry of Central government.

2. Central assistance received directly by department of Mantralaya from corporations or agencies of central government. The pattern of sharing of expenditure varies from 100% to 33% between state and central government. For the sake of brevity, the schemes operating under different categories are shown in Annexures.

To give an idea about the purpose of the subsidies given suffice it to say that it takes different form. In handloom sector the subsidy is given under different schemes. The following are few :—

1. Special Rebate on handloom cloth
2. Subsidy on Janta cloth
3. Centrally sponsored schemes in handloom
4. Other handloom schemes
5. Assistance to central Handloom Development Corporation

The details about these subsidies are given below :—

8.13 Special Rebate in Handloom Cloth

According to the available information this scheme is operating since long time back. The Market Development Assistance Scheme has been formulated and being implemented from 1.4.89 as an alternative to rebate scheme assistance is provided to handloom sector launched with performance of the organisation. The assistance is on the basis of 8% of the average turnover of the handloom fabrics made-ups and garments for the past 3 years or on the basis of the average rebate assistance received/receivable by the organisation and shared equally by state government and central government.

8.14 Subsidy on Janata Cloth

Subsidy on janata cloth scheme is implemented in 19 states and one union territory. Approximately 3 lakh looms are at present engaged in the Janata Cloth Scheme in the country. Since the inception of scheme up to 31.3.91 around 4789 million sq. metres of janta cloth was produced in the handloom sector. The janata cloth production for 1991-92 as well as 1992-93 has been fixed at 450 million sq.mts. The rate of subsidy payable on the production of woollen janata cloth is Rs 13.60 per sq. metres. During 1990-91 over 500 million sp.mts were produced. The logic of this scheme was commitment under the government policy of making available cloth at affordable prices to the masses and a subsidy of Rs 3.40 per sq. mts was paid on the quantum of handloom janata cloth produced and delivered by the handloom sector.

8.15 Other Subsidies

The subsidy under this category includes provision for payment to North Eastern Handloom and Handicrafts Development Corporation, Central Handloom Development Corporation/Rehabilitation Industries Corporation towards rebate of Handloom

Cloth, Special Rebate/MDA; Rebate on Handloom Cloth on the Industrial Cooperatives.

8.16 Centrally Sponsored Schemes in Handloom

Under this category the production covers for handloom weavers for purchase/renovation/modernisation to looms. The other schemes are as under:—

1. Grants for weavers-cum-housing scheme for handloom weavers.
2. The grants to set up enforcement
3. Organisational Development Package assistance to handloom weavers.

8.17 Other Handloom Schemes

Under this category provision covers administration expenditure of the office of Development Commissioner, Research and Development, assistance for setting up of marketing complex, yarn procurement, administration of weavers services, Institution of Handloom Technology, rebate on Handloom Cloth, Welfare package Scheme for weavers, Scheme for quality production and marketing of Handloom products of isolated and Heal assistance schemes for Handloom exports and grant on Margin Money to Destitute Weavers. Grant in aid to Union Territory government for construction of Weavers Services and Indian Institute of Handloom Technology.

8.18 National Handloom Development Corporation

This organisation has been entrusted with the task of supplying yarn and dyes and other inputs to Handloom weavers by supplying the weavers State Handloom assistance augmenting marketing efforts and other agencies. The recommendation of workshop on Development Strategy for Handicraft Cooperation, National Institute of Cooperative Management (Ganeshkhind Road, Puna)

1. Ensuring a guaranteed minimum income to 1.9 million artisans in the country.
2. Providing employment opportunity to an additional one million households specially to those which belong to SC/ST and BC and those which are located in backward regions and

3. Increasing exports of Handicrafts to Rs 1500 cr. by 1984. Subsidy: The workshop was of the view that subsidy by the state to artisans could be justified on the following ground for different categories of Handicraft.

Cat 1: Crafts which are essential to provide employment until such time as the other sector of the economy can absorb the surplus labour. Here the development of Handicrafts has to be seen as a holding operation. Such craft cannot be compared with other sectors of the economy which have higher productivity. Assistance to such craft is to be given as a part of the social welfare, like food for work programme.

Cat II: Crafts which are seen as cultural heritage and which need to be presented and protected. State assistance to such craft is necessary for mailing cultural links and preserving our rich tradition and heritage.

Cat III: Craft which can help increase export and foreign exchange earnings. These crafts are entitled for state assistance on the same grant on which export subsidy is provided in the other sectors of the economy.

— Promotion of economic independence, social status and individual dignity of the craft person.

Handicraft cooperative has objective to provide the artisan an institutional structure, which is sensitive to their needs, participation in character, non-exploitation and dependable, so as to ensure that he can invest in earning capacity, improve his status and dignity.

8.19 Rate of Interest

The rate of interest which was initially the Bank Rate was lowered in August 1977 (effective from Ist July 1977) to 7.5% below bank rate in order to boost up industrial finance. This rate was further reduced to 2.5% below the bank from Ist March 1978. In the case of advances to rural artisans through PACS/LAMS; the rate of interest which was 2% below the bank rate was made 3% below the bank rate from Ist March 1978. In both the cases the Reserve Bank suggested margin of interest to be retained at various levels in order that the interest burden in the ultimate borrowers should not be unduly high. The margin suggested was as follows :—

Categ. of Bank	*Margin to be retained*	*Rate of Int. to be charged*
1. State Co.Op Banks lending to		
a) Central Co-Op Bank	.5%	7.5%
b) Urban Co-Op Bank	1%	7.5%
2) Central Cooperation Bank lending to		
a) Industrial Co-Op. Society	1%	8%
b) Urban Co-op Banks	1%	8%
3) Urban Co-op. Banks to individual unit engaged in cottage and small scale industrial activities	2%	10% borrowed from SCB district 10% if bound through CCB.

1. State Directorate of Industries
2. State Small Industries Corporation
3. State Financial Corporation.

State Dir: Registrars of SSI essentially certificate for the import of raw materials, distributions of raw material, giving loans under the State Aid to Industries Act and also development of industrial Estates and areas in states. In some cases exporting small industry products like Maharashtra.

8.20 State Small Industrial Corporation

To advise the state govt. on the organisation and development of small industries to individual examine and supervise scheme for development of SSI—marketing, testing and quality marketing.

8.21 State Financial Corporation

To advance medium and long term loans to these industries. The loans are mostly acquiring capital assets in the form of land, building, plant and machinery on moderate rate of interest. The repayment has to be completed normally in 10-12 years. Corporation is empowered to subscribe to the debenture of industries concerned, guarantee loans raised by industrial concern, under write the issues of stock, bonds or debentures by industrial corporation. Corporation can raise share capital by issuing bonds and accepting deposits from the public to enhance their funds.

All India Handloom Board
All India Handicraft Board
All India Silk Board
All India Coir Board

8.22 Industrial Corporations

Industrial Investment Corporation: Financing/Small, medium and large units upto certain investment ceiling with direct participation share capital as well as underwriting of new issues of shares besides assisting entrepreneurs with feasibility studies project reports, and helping in securing licences and all available concern;

1. Reserve bank of India
2. Industrial Bank of India (IDBI)
3. Industry Finance Corporation of India (IFCI)
4. Industrial Credit and Investment Corporation of India (ICIC)
5. Industrial Reconstruction Corporation of India (IRCI)
6. (SFC) State Financial Corporation
7. Commercial Banks (Nationalised and Non-Nationalised)
8. Rural banks

(Ref.: Swapna Mukhopadhyay and Chee Peng Lime (Ed) —The Rural Non Farm Sector in Asia.

Asian Pacific Development Centre, Kuala Lumpur, Malaysia, 1985

Village Industries	*No. of Units*	*Average Investment Per unit in Rs*	
		Own	*Private bank*
1. Carpentry	8	3000	
2. Blacksmithy	9	1800	
3. Goldsmithy	6	1700	1000
4. Bricks & Tittles	10	6800	
5. Mat Weaving	5	5220	
6. Coir Products	9	11000	
7. Leather Products	4	6000	
8. Cottage Match	2	3000	
9. Lime Products	2	2500	
10. Palm Leave Products	2	5050	
11. Beekeeping	2	3050	
12. Handloom	2	50,000	
	61		

Table 14 : Maharashtra State

Head of Development : Industry and Mining : Rs lakhs

Name of the Scheme	Pattern of Sharing Exp.50:50 and 100%	Seventh Plan 1985-90 Actual Expenditure	Annual Plan 1990-91 Actual Expenditure	Annual Plan (1991-92) Approved Outlay	Physical Target
1	2	3	4	5	6
Industry, Energy and Labour Department Category I.					
Central Assistance received directly by Departments of Mantralaya from Ministry of Central Government					
1. 10/15% outright grant or subsidy to industrials units in the selected backward areas	100%	315.86			
2. Engineer's Entrepreneurs' Training Programme (Interest Subsidy)	100%	44.88	—	1.00	437
3. Establishment of District Industries Centres	50%	678.59	116.00 Staff 23.96 Loan	116.00 30.14	
4. Census cum Sample Survey of SSI, nucleus Cell	100%	49.73	14.72	25.00	
5. Schemes for preparation of opportunity profile in respect of Nanded Distt. for S & T persons	100%	11.76	4.75	9.70	
6. Infrastructure development for no industry district (Gadchinli).	33-1/3	52.00	—	26.00	

Table 14 (Contd.)

	Name of the Scheme	Pattern of Sharing Exp.50:50 and 100%	Seventh Plan 1985-90 Actual Expenditure	Annual Plan 1990-91 Actual Expenditure	Annual Plan (1991-92) Approved Outlay	Annual Plan (1991-92) Physical Target
	1	2	3	4	5	6
7.	Margin money assistance for rehabilitation of sick SSI units	50%	3.02	—	—	
8.	Central Footwear Training Centre	—	70.50	36.25	60.00	
9.	Centre for Electronic Design Tech. (CEDT)	—	55.00	—	—	
10.	Industrial Tool Room & Training Centre	80%	30%	—	133.00	
11.	Demonstration of Oil Palm cultivate in Konkan Region	33%	112.43	—	63.61	
12.	Subsidy for production of Janta Cloth (CSP)	100%	5653.18	10,53.49	1,650.00	3 Socys
13.	(a) 20% special rebate for liquidation of accumulated st	50%	3,97.75	—	19.17	101
	(b) Market Development Assistance Scheme (CSP)	50%	30.00	—	173.00	527 SO
14.	Strengthening of share capital base of Apex/Regional primary weavers	50%	32.83	33.16	—	—
15.	Cooperation Societies (CSP) Partial Handloom Census	100%	—	—	—	—
16.	Loans to HLM Weavers or construction of showrooms (CSP)	75%	2.92	0.75	3.00	5 Socys
17.	Group Insurance Schemes (Handloom Weavers)	50%	—	—	1.00	—
18.	Share capital for construction of Workshed by Apex/Regional/Primary Wev. Co. Society	Share Cap. 15% Loan 50%	14.41	1.20 9.50	8.16	4

Table 14 (Contd.)

Name of the Scheme	Pattern of Sharing Exp.50:50 and 100%	Seventh Plan 1985-90 Actual Expenditure	Annual Plan 1990-91 Actual Expenditure	Annual Plan (1991-92) Approved Outlay	Annual Plan (1991-92) Physical Target
1	2	3	4	5	6
19. Share capital to Maharashtra State Handloom Cor. Partially CSP	50%	60.00	—	—	—
20. National Handloom Expo	50%	—	—	—	—
21. Managerial subsidy to Primary Weavers Co.op Society (CSP)	50%	1.80	—	—	—
22. Creation of processing facilities by Apex/Regional Weavers Co. of SOC (Loan)	100%	—	—	200.00	
23. Financial assistance for purchase/modernisation of loans/subsidy	50%	3.98		10.00	2000 looms
24. Financial Assistance for construction of worksheds by Apex/Regional handloom weavers Co.Op. Society (Loan)	50%	6.56	—	—	
25. Grants of Interest subsidy to S.C. Weavers	66%	—	—	—	
26. Interest subsidy to CFAS	33%	—	—	—	
27. Draught Relief Schemes for Handloom weavers	100%	—	—	—	
28. Share Capital contribution to Primary weavers Co-op. Society (1:3)	50%				
29. Loans for purchase of share of weavers Co-op. Society (1:3)	50%	—	—	—	

Table 14 (Contd.)

Name of the Scheme	Pattern of Sharing Exp.50:50 and 100%	Seventh Plan 1985-90 Actual Expenditure	Annual Plan 1990-91 Actual Expenditure	Annual Plan (1991-92)	
				Approved Outlay	Physical Target
1	2	3	4	5	6
30. Assistance for purchase, modernisation, renovation of 100% loans of ministry					
1. Loan		6.67	1.00	2.00	100 persons
2. Share Capital		5.00	—	—	—
3. Subsidy		3.33	1.00	1.00	100 persons
31. Scheme for House-cum-workshed for weavers	50%	6.75	—	2.00	80
32. Contribution to Thrift Fund	1:5	5.44	0.28	16.12	1000
Total Textile and Co-operation Department Schemes Category I	—	62,09.62	10,91.22	18,94.45	—
Total Category I	—	7638.39	1286.90	2359.40	

Table 14 (Contd.)

Name of the Scheme	Pattern of Sharing Exp.50:50 and 100%	Seventh Plan 1985-90 Actual Expenditure	Annual Plan 1990-91 Actual Expenditure	Annual Plan (1991-92)	
				Approved Outlay	Physical Target
1	2	3	4	5	6
Category II					
Central Assistance received directly by Deptt. of Mantralaya from Corporations or Agencies of Cent.Govt.					
33. Share capital Contribution to Cooperative spinning mills (NCDC)	50%	932.13	1105.90	1809.00	8 mills
34. Share capital contribution to Handloom weavers Co-op. Society (NCDC)					
35. Loans to Apex Co-op Marketing Federation through State Govt. for oil complexes (85% NCDC) Khamgaon	65%	139.39	—	—	—
36. Financial assistance for modernisation of infrastructure facilities cold storage	100%	—	—	—	—
37. Loans for agro processing societies	65%	—	—	—	—
38. Assistance for preparation of project to Agro processing industry	100%				
39. Assistance for cold storage of agro processing industry	100%				
40. Development of Agro processing units	20%				
Co-op. and textile Department of Total II	—	1078.02	11,08.82	1818.00	
Grand Total — Industry and Mining	—	8716.41	2395.72	4172.40	

9

Implication of GATT with S & T

9.01 Introduction

By seeing the multi-directional pressure from developed countries through organisation like IMF and GATT rounds, one can hardly say that poor countries are running their government out of their own wit, intellect and prudence. The external pressure is so strong that the destiny of poor countries has to be mortgaged or forefeited with developed countries. It was not too late for Indian thinkers to realise the external pressure, while country was implementing IMF's prescription for structural adjustment since mid 1991. The press report indicates that on January 10, 1992, about 40 top political leaders and other eminent personalities issued a joint appeal to the President and Prime Minister of India to ensure that India did not "mortgage its economic sovereignty" in any way while dealing with the IMF or at the Uruguay Round of trade negotiation. What these people said goes somewhat like this : India should

(i) Not bend before external pressure.

(ii) Not yield to Western pressure to change the Indian Patent Act, 1970 at the Uruguay Round negotiations.

(iii) Not accept implicitly or explicitly any conditionalities of the IMF and other international financial institutions that could jeopardise the country's economic sovereignty.

(iv) Uphold the Independence of India, the socio-economic values of the constitution, the imperatives of self-reliance, industrial progress and prosperous agriculture.

About the liberalisation of economy, the view held was that these may seem to be very attractive but in its deeper implications run counter to our legacy from Gandhiji and Panditji and to the whole history of Independence, of sustainable development with justice" or "Distributive justice in regard to basic needs is being subverted and any further subordination of Indian interests to Western or Japanese interests may spell horrowing conditions for the millions and eventually lead to an avalanche of unrest."

9.02 Scientific Institutions in India

It is really irony of the situation as none of the scientific institutions in India was able to invent the means of production meant for poorest of poor, or devise a technology which will ensure the adequate return to poorest of poor. None of scientists of India came forward with the technology which can be afforded, controlled or owned by poorest of poor. While people in every part of the country are starving, the scientists of India are sitting in airconditioned Technology Bhavan in New Delhi. It is strange that despite their training, education and assured employment still they want protection ignoring the fact that it is western inventions which gave them every scientific concept, equipment, accessories, etc. found in Indian laboratories . Either individually or collectively except few, scientists in India are almost identical to any government employees or white collar employees.

The scientific manpower of India is luxuriously paid creatures which eats luxury facilities and encroach upon the resources needed for starving people in Kalahandi, District of Orissa, tribals of Tripura, weavers of Andhra Pradesh, tribals in Chandrapur or Gadchiroli Districts of Maharashtra, tribals of Rajasthan and so on. If they cannot compete with the world's scientists, why government expects poor weavers to compete with powerloom's cloth.

Those scientists who could not contribute even a single patent throughout their career and had long service, are they really going to bring any kind of innovation? Indians in general, and in tune with such generality, scientists in particular, are outward looking in nature and every concept, basic ideas and innovative inspiration is derived from western scientists. Still, they prefer to call their endeavour as scientific, original and unique. It is really irony. No doubt, India has highest number of research laboratories where instruments, equipment and accessories are imported which are likely to be declared soon as obsolete or need for modernising is likely to be acceded than return if any, it had paid since their purchase or under utilisation. In fact, as Einstein said "Science is built on facts as house is of stones and bricks but holding stock of stones and bricks is not house" so is Indian stock of scientific manpower and scientific laboratory do not ensure scientific research in India.

9.03 Foreigner's Patents

It is absurd to say that by allowing foreigners' patents to work in India would suppress or ruin scientific progress in India. Because India's science is in the state of perpetual imitation, holding the third largest stock of the world does not ensure the basic or applied research leading to new patents or inventions because had it been so India would have achieved scientific excellence long back. Compared with world's inventions, India's contribution is far behind the international standard. Firstly, India's research is confined to government laboratories and it is basically addition, modification or replacement in nature and not aimed at achieving scientific breakthroughs or achieve scientific and technological revolution in the country. Secondly, there is neither capability to convert patented scientific incentives to commercially or economically viable technology affordable by ordinary Indian nor there are resources to find such endeavours to exploit commercialisation of patented scientific facts. Patents are not capital goods or skill or tangible assets but to convert patents into technological embodied capital goods, it needs not only money and other resources but it needs time and expertise to make its success. Indian science is of ornamental or ritual use and scientists are creatures of excess expenditure than their return or utility of society.

9.04 Protection to Indian Patent System

It is really shameful that Indian scientists need protection to their talent, invention, patents or inventive activity. But the same people plead to take away such protectionism measures, subsidies, incentives of poor and expect free competition. Infant industry arguments and protectionism has been denounced and poor people are usually blamed for inefficiency or policies are blamed for fostering inefficient and economical unviable but why scientists of India want protection for their activities. Are they not trying to cheat India by claiming unique and novel inventions which exist somewhere else? Are they not trying to reinvent the invention which exists in the state of the art. Let people be not cheated by such misguided propaganda and blocking the flow of technological information, technologies and scientific novel.

It would be in the interest of not only India but also in the interest of those who are afraid of foreign inventions' applicability in India, to accept the change in patent laws in India. It will be commensurate with the needs of industrialisation.

Extending the term of patent from existing 7 years for processes and 14 years for other invention reality to products to 20 years should cause concern to Indian, unless they have intention to infringe the patent and products of multinational. Or treatment to foreign national at par with own nationals or reciprocity should always by useful if 100 per cent equity irrespective of area of investment or use of domestic resource brings new era of development. Because by preventing such new investment for last 40 years, we have remained under-developed and would like to remain under-developed by not accepting the terms of GATT.

9.05 Flaws in Indian Patent System

From point of view of United States, the deficiencies in India's intellectual property laws, policies and practices include :

(i) Failure to provide product protection for wide range of products including pharmaceuticals and products resulting from chemical process—thereby Indian Patent Act, 1970 needs to be changed as drugs and medicines are not governed by patent law.

(ii) Lack of protection for service marks and restrictions on use of foreign trademarks thereby change in Trade and Merchandise Act.

(iii) Copyright compulsory licensing provision thereby revoking the clause of compulsory licensing if the patent invented is not licensed to meet reasonable requirements of the public.

The fear in India is that if patents of drugs and medicines are made applicable or chemical formulae are patented then the prices of medicines would go up. Similarly, manufacturing in India of those medicines would be banned which have patents outside India.

In fact, this is mere fear, if medicines of best companies are made available in India, why its population be deprived of them simply to protect the spurious drug manufacturers and Indian scientists who are engaged in sporadic experiments for the years. Poor are simply ignored even in today's scientific endeavours of Indian scientists. None of the scientists in India ever visited snail eating tribals to give them any productive means or to invent medicine to fight hunger or hunger related deaths. None of the scientists ever thought of any measures to get rid of scavengers headload of human nightsoil. Then what kind of science they want to protect by not agreeing to the terms of GATT or USA. In fact, Indian scientists are in dire danger of loosing their monopoly on expenditure, lavish living, luxury, salary and perks which they enjoy irrespective or any scientific activity, they are using the shield of medicine or pharmaceuticals for poor at cheaper prices.

Indian scientists are surely afraid of competitiveness in scientific research activities as they lack real science, real novelty and capability to convert science into commercial viable technology. Basically given them the concept or shown them the working of newly designed medicine, Indian scientists think they can easily initiate it in shortest possible time. Had this not been so, there would not have been so many foreign technological collaboration, import of technology, import of capital goods, scientific instruments, etc.

9.06 TRIMS and TRIP

Two new concepts have been evolved prior to Uruguay Round of General Agreement of Tariff and Trade (GATT). They are : Trade-Related Intellectual Property Rights (TRIPR) and Trade-Related Investment Measures (TRIMS). With acceptance of these, India may face problems in services, agriculture and textiles. In letter and spirit of the new draft initiated by Mr Arthur Dunkel, Director General of GATT, the aim is to increase the monopoly control that the developed countries generally and their multinational corporations in particular, have been exercising over the global economy".

9.07 Expenditure on S & T

It is false propaganda of Indian scientists that India might find it difficult to preserve their growth of economic pace. Despite enormous expenditure made on science and technology, see Table I for outlays on S & T despite extensive network of science laboratories, centres of excellence like IITs and Universities, Indian

Table 1 : Outlay on Science and Technology

	Plan Period	*Outlays Rs Cr.*
I.	Sixth Plan Outlay	865.2
	(i) Annual Plan 1980-81	97.4
	(ii) Annual Plan 1981-82	148.4
	(iii) Annual Plan 1982-83	208.1
	(iv) Annual Plan 1983-84	228.5
	(v) Annual Plan 1984-85	338.1
	Total Actual Expenditure	1020.5
II.	Seventh Plan (1985-90) outlay	2463.1
	(i) Annual Plan 1985-86	404.8
	(ii) Annual Plan 1986-87	512.4
	(iii) Annual Plan 1987-88	585.4
	(iv) Annual Plan 1988-89	751.4
	(v) Annual Plan 1989-90	695.5
	Total Actual Expenditure @	2949.5
	Annual Plan 1990-91 Outlay	892.9

@ includes Rs 2.85 cr. for national Test Houses
(*Source* : Economic Survey 1990-91 pp. S44, S46)

Table 1 (*Contd.*)

The Details of outlays for research are as follows :

	Head of Development	B.E. *1989-90*	R.E. *1989-90*	B.E. *1990-91*
I.	Science and Technology & Environment	752.50	653.59	845.37
1.	Atomic Energy Research	95.00	96.81	112.00
2.	Space Research	298.00	210.00	323.00
3.	Oceanographic Research	24.00	23.59	35.00
4.	Other Scientific Research	237.82	230.27	268.40
5.	Ecology & Environment	97.68	92.34	106.97
	Total (1 to 5)	752.50	653.59	845.37
II.	Agricultural Research and Education	110.00	11.69	154.20
	Total	862.50	665.28	999.57

The budget provision for each of the major department is as follows:

	Department	*Budget 1989-90*	*Revised 1990-91*	*Budget 1990-91*
1.	Department of Science & Technology	116.00	102.00	127.00
2.	Depart. of Scientific and Industrial Research	93.00	96.26	104.00
3.	Department of Biotechnology	55.00	52.25	62.50
	Total Ministry of S & T	264.90	250.83	293.50

scientists are scared of the competition on the scientific front. It is totally wrong to attribute entirely present economic growth after scientific work of Indian scientists. Irony of the situation is that every scientific work in India is outward looking. Every instrument, computer, software basic concepts, etc. have originated in Western world. To replicate the scientific process or initiate the products or try to reinvent the scientific facts already existed elsewhere tantamounts primarily to infringement and secondarily to wastage of scarce resources as well as cheating the people in dire need of food and shelter, etc. The scientific activities in India are sustaining at the cost of depriving poorest of poor of almost everything.

The output of scientific research in India is very pathetic. It will see output in general of scientific research and its relevance to solve Indian industries' problems, one can conclude that it is basically aimed at small or petty achievements. Its relevance to the poverty in India is negligible. When we know that weavers in Andhra Pradesh handloom sector are starving and committing suicides as they cannot get even Rs 400 per month despite efforts of all the members of family or when tribals in Tripura State are unable to get even a day's meal and are forced to survive by eating raw snails, roots of plants in forests, can such expenditure on science and technology be justified whose beneficiaries would certainly not be tribals and weavers who are starving or scavengers who have to carry human night soil on head?

These same scientists who have not contributed a single patent despite enormous expenditure on their education upto doctorate level, training on imported equipment, and they enjoy every best facility available in India, highest salary, highest promotion prospects, retirement benefits and even post retirement employment, status of professor of emeritus etc. suddenly became prudent about implication of TRIPR and TRIMS and also became spokesmen of Indian community. Such a preferential treatment continues to exist concomitant with widespread poverty, squalor, hunger, beggary, slavery and all kinds of exploitations of poors.

In India, there is a tendency to justify higher expenditure on science and technology on the ground that the expenditure on S & T activities in developed countries like USA, Germany, France, Japan, etc. is over 2 per cent of GNP whereas in India, it is very less or say about 1.2 per cent of GNP and, therefore, there is a need to enhance the expenditure. There cannot be potentially more dangerous than such absurd arguments because all these developed countries have per capita income about 20 times higher than India and they spend only 2 per cent of GNP by maintaining highest possible standard of living in the world and affluence in the whole society, whereas in India, per capita income is very less that is one-twentieth of developed nations' standard and also it has more than 35 per cent of her population below the poverty line comprising destitutes, beggars, ragpickers, tribals compelled to eat raw snails with symptoms like sale of babies for want of food, sale of girls to gulf countries, Arabs, etc. Therefore, the spending of 2 per cent of GNP by USA and 1.2 per cent of GNP by India is not comparable, because this would tantamount to say that poverty in India is equivalent to affluence in USA and hence, identical expenditure on science and technology is justifiable. That is without comparable socio-economic factors, the expenditure in developed countries on S & T is not at all to be compared or taken as reference for expenditure on S & T and R & D in developing countries. Apart from this, USA is capitalist country with industrial base developed over a century. Therefore, it is absurd to increase S & T expenditure. Moreover, all the developed nations have global interest, urge to expand their imperialism or fascist tendency and India is yet to conquer hunger and other basic problems like untouchability, discrimination, inequality, exploitation, deprivation, feudal and hierarchial society, corrupt administrative, undeveloped political system, etc.

India is absolute imitator in every field, be it a constitutional framework, socialist concepts, parliamentary democracy, public sector enterprises concept, nationalisation concept, code of civil procedure or criminal laws, etc. Either individually or collectively majority of Indian science graduates lack basic ability to understand theories and its relevance to the real situation, leave aside the contribution. When the cost of manufacturing steel, aluminium or commodities is high in comparison with world market, it is pleaded for import rather than manufacturing; so when Indian scientific research is unable to provide higher living standard why to depend on it any more. Why not cut its expenditure?

India has been adapting the strategy of achieving self sufficiency in almost every field, forgetting the fact that endeavours of self sufficiency have resulted much more hazardous than it were initially envisaged. The hazards were due to the fact that it caused nation to pump money in different forms like subsidies, exemption from excise duties, exemption from custom duties, supply of raw material at lowest cost than market prices, low interest rates on the loans availed, tax holidays, etc. This kind of protectionism under infant industry arguments has neither helped achieving self sufficiency nor capability to withstand international competitiveness. Despite crores of rupees pumped in economy in the name of industrial development, science and technology, scientific research, etc. import of technology was inevitable in every field. Self sufficiency true but at what cost and in what context? Science is progressing at tremendous rate and technologies are emerging at a commensurate rate of scientific growth in western world. Obviously, self sufficiency means self destructive acts, dependence of nation on import of technologies, technical know how, etc.

9.08 Drugs and Medicines

The probable pressure for change in Indian Patent Act, 1970 in Uruguay Round of GATT is viewed with the suspicion that it would mean to destroy Indian science and its progress particularly drugs and medicine.

There are eight public sector enterprises in India engaged in manufacturing of chemicals, pharmaceuticals and petrochemicals, comprising :

1. Hindustan Organic Chemicals Ltd., Rasayani (Maharashtra)
2. Hindustan Insecticides Ltd., New Delhi
3. Indian Drug and Pharmaceuticals Ltd., Dundahera, Gurgaon (Haryana)
4. Hindustan Antibiotics Ltd., Pimpri, Pune (Maharashtra)
5. Smith Stanistreet Pharmaceuticals Ltd., Calcutta (West Bengal)
6. Bengal Chemicals & Pharmaceuticals Ltd.
7. Bengal Immunity Limited, Calcutta (West Bengal)
8. Indian Petrochemicals Corporation Ltd., Vadodara (Gujarat)

There are numerous private companies and even small scale units engaged in manufacturing in varying scale the chemical and pharmaceutical products. The production of drugs and pharmaceuticals from public sector enterprises for the period from 1985-86 to 1990-91 is as follows :

Year	*Bulk drugs Rs Crores*	*Formulations Rs Crores*
1985-86	416	1945
1986-87	458	2140
1987-88	480	2350
1988-89	550	3150
1989-90	640	3420
1990-91 (Est.)	700	3600

The imports of following drugs have been brought down due to indigenous production.

1.	Antibiotics	Chloramphenical powder
2.	Sulpha drugs	a. Sulphacetamide/sodium
		b. Sulphadimidine
		c. Sulphamethizole
		d. Phthalyl sulphathiazole
		e. Sulphaguanidine
		f. Sulphanilamide
3.	Vitamins	Vitamin C
		Nicotinic Acid
		Nicotinamide
		Vitamin B
		Vitamin E
		Vitamin K
4.	Analgesics,	Oxyphenyl Butazone
	Antipyretics ETC	Aspirin
5.	Anti T.B. Drugs	PAs and its salts
6.	Anti-malarials	Amodiaguin
7.	Anti-Diabetics	Chloropropamide
		Tolbutamide
		Insulin
8.	Anti-Histamines	Diaphenhydramine
9.	Tranquilizers and sedatives	Diazepem
10.	Anti-Helmentics	Clofazimine
11.	Immunological Agents	Triple vaccine
		Dipheria Anti Toxin

Though these products are not sufficient to meet entire demands of the countries' population but there was export from India which was possible due to public sector enterprises. The export earnings from drugs and pharmaceuticals for 1982-83 to 1990-91 is as follows:

Year	*Export earnings Rs crores*	*Year*	*Export earnings Rs crores*
1982-83	111.00	1987-88	289.69
1983-84	162.00	1988-89	467.50
1984-85	217.00	1989-90	843.70
1985-86	194.00	1990-91	1230.00
1986-87	222.96		

Also see Table Nos. 2, 3 and 4 indicating production of some drugs, chemicals, and Petro chemicals.

Some people in India termed liberalisation drive as "barter away sovereignty" of India in 1991 to IMF or other developed countries. The anti-liberalisation of economy drive pleads that "distributive justice in regard to basic needs is being subverted and any further subordination of Indian interests to Western or Japanese interests may spell harrowing conditions for the millions and eventually lead to an avalanche of unrest." It is strange how these people have suddenly become trustees of poor, millions deprived of basic needs and generations that have born and brought out in destitute conditions, rag picking, scavenging, tribals, etc. It is one kind of a lobby who were grappling the funds meants for poor or getting diverted for scientific activities or industrial substandard production, etc.

Strange enough, these people use the name of Gandhiji and Nehru to oppose the liberalisation drive in India and say these policies may seem to be very attractive but in their deeper implications run counter to our legacy from Gandhiji and Panditji and to the whole history of Independence, of sustainable development with justice. It is totally unreasonable to say that the condition arising out of economic liberalisation was worst than that was prior to resorting to IMF loan, pledging of gold, etc. Even with Gandhian principles, no justice was done as those were meant to restrain elected members of people to maintain immaculate char-

Table 2 : Drugs and Pharmaceuticals (Monitored Bulk Drugs)
Production Target and Achievement (Organised Sector)

Name of the Drug	A/c Unit	PRODUCTION			
		1988-89	1989-90		1990-91
		Actuals	Targets	Actuals	Targets
1	2	3	4	5	6
I. Antibiotics					
1. Penicillin	MMU	330.47	330.00	324.93	330.00
2. Streptomycin	T	243.79	180.00	134.15	180.00
3. Chloramphenicol Powder	T	92.84	200.00	100.26	200.00
4. Chloramphenicol Palmitate	T	14.50		19.04	
5. Tetracycline	T	184.33	241.00	305.38	254.00
6. Oxytetracycline	T	162.52	157.00	192.84	165.00
7. Ampicillin	T	332.56	345.00	285.32	397.00
8. Erythromycin	T	37.44	70.00	76.74	76.00
9. Amoxicillin	T	80.95	115.00	89.19	132.00
10. Doxycycline	T	9.25	10.00	8.53	11.00
11. Gentamycin	Kg.	883.00	5500.00	1468.00	6050.00
12. Framycetin	T	4.40	3.00	N.A	4.00
13. Rifampicin	T	73.66	155.00	39.07	179.00
14. Ampicillin Sodium	T	—	69.00	—	79.00

Table 2 (*Contd.*)

Name of the Drug	*A/c Unit*	*PRODUCTION*			
		1988-89	*1989-90*		*1990-91*
		Actuals	*Targets*	*Actuals*	*Targets*
1	2	3	4	5	6
15. Cloxacillin	T	33.78	44.00	28.18	48.00
16. Cephalexin	T	45.84	69.00	68.81	79.00
17. Phenoxymethyl Penicillin	MMU	—	N.A.	36.90	N.A.
18. Griseofulvin	T	—	44.00	—	48.00
19. Prosaine Benzyl Penicillin	MMU	15.02	N.A.	19.46	N.A.
20. Cyproheptadine	T	—	N.A.	—	N.A
II. Sulpha Drugs					
1. Sulphamethoxazole	T	1445.56	550.00	1854.70	605.00
2. Sulphadimidine	T	465.72	250.00	340.01	250.00
3. Sulphacetamide/Sod	T	48.09	52.00	42.43	55.00
4. Phthalyl Sulphathiazole	t	13.57	21.00	1.30	22.00
5. Sulphadiazine	T	10.05	79.00	9.72	83.00
6. Sulphamoxole	T	92.90	63.00	63.46	66.00
7. Sulphaphenazole	T	2.49	50.00	3.73	50.00
8. Sulphaguanidine	T	219.56	180.00	96.50	180.00

Table 2 (*Contd.*)

Name of the Drug	*A/c Unit*	*PRODUCTION*			
		1988-89	*1989-90*		*1990-91*
		Actuals	*Targets*	*Actuals*	*Targets*
1	2	3	4	5	6
9. Sulphasomidine	T	45.74	60.00	14.71	60.00
10. Sulphanilamide	T	12.57	N.A.	0.44	N.A.
11. Sulphamethizole	T	—	N.A.	—	N.A.
12. Sulphadoxine	T	—	N.A.	—	N.A.
III. Vitamins					
1. Vitamin A	MMU	74.23	100.00	94.31	105.00
2. Vitamin B1	T	75.25	102.00	76.57	109.00
3. Vitamin B2	T	25.74	43.00	25.48	46.00
4. Vitamin B12	Kg.	101.63	235.00	300.18	252.00
5. Vitamin C	T	868.76	892.00	1034.74	937.00
6. Vitamin D3	Kg	249.00	446.00	355.00	469.00
7. Vitamin E	T	101.59	20.00	132.02	21.00
8. Vitamin K	T	—	N.A	—	N.A.
9. Vitamin P	T	1.83	5.00	—	5.00
10. Folic Acid	T	9.26	8.00	8.93	9.00
11. Nicotinic Acid	T	8.74	252.00	0.62	265.00
12. Nicotinamide	T	115.95	—	67.20	
13. Vitamin B6	T	31.08	58.00	23.51	61.00
14. Calcium Pantothenate	T	—	94.00	—	99.00

Table 2 (Contd.)

Name of the Drug	*A/c Unit*	*PRODUCTION*			
		1988-89	*1989-90*		*1990-91*
		Actuals	*Targets*	*Actuals*	*Targets*
1	2	3	4	5	6
IV. Analgesics & Antipyretics Etc.					
1. Analgin	T	271.80	1575.00	235.20	1654.00
2. Aspirin	T	1532.70	1680.00	1551.28	1764.00
3. Oxyphenbutazone	T	10.19	60.00	13.54	60.00
4. Phenyl Butazone	T	30.04	90.00	41.75	90.00
5. Paracetamol	T	1.19	2200.00	6.50	2420.000
6. Pethidine	Kg	515.00	630.00	615.00	661.00
7. Ibuprofen	T	124.55	138.00	207.75	159.00
8. Probenecid	T	6.80	N.A.	12.75	N.A.
9. Baralgan Ketone	T	2.82	N.A.	4.14	N.A.
10. Dextropropoxyphene Hel.	T	—	17.00	—	18.00
11. Methyl Salicylate	T	410.51	N.A.	454.23	N.A.
12. Piroxicam	T	—	1.10	0.65	1.21
V. Cortico Steroids					
1. Dexamethasone	Kg.	343.00	630.00	472.00	661.00
2. Betamethasone	Kg.	932.00	1260.00	1031.00	1323.00
3. Prednisolone	Kg	1923.00	4725.00	2128.00	4961.00
4. Hydrocortisone	Kg	11.00	997.00	14.00	1047.00

Table 2 (Contd.)

Name of the Drug	A/c Unit	PRODUCTION			
		1988-89	1989-90		1990-91
		Actuals	*Targets*	*Actuals*	*Targets*
1	2	3	4	5	6
VI. Anti T.B. Drugs					
1. Pas & its Salts	T	91.06	60.00	40.66	60.00
2. INH	T	140.29	275.00	161.15	302.00
3. Thiacetezone	T	24.69	73.00	21.48	77.00
4. Ethambutol	T	407.99	330.00	490.63	363.00
5. Pyrazinamide	T	3.86	60.00	2.76	67.00
VII. Anti Malarials					
1. Chloroquin	T	130.08	200.00	271.34	200.00
2. Amodiaquin	T	20.17	20.00	25.72	20.00
3. Pyrimethamine	T	—	2.62	0.13	2.76
VIII. Anti Dysentery Drugs					
1. Metronidazole	T	436.28	440.00	269.88	484.00
2. Tinidazole	T	44.20	44.00	76.40	48.00
3. Diloxanide Furoate	T	15.05	77.00	3.73	85.00
4. Iodochlorohydroxy quinoline	T	204.87	N.A	181.65	N.A

Table 2 (*Contd.*)

Name of the Drug	A/c Unit	PRODUCTION			
		1988-89	1989-90		1990-91
		Actuals	Targets	Actuals	Targets
1	2	3	4	5	6
5. Di-iodochlorohydroxy quinoline	T	6.08	N.A	7.16	N.A
6. Furazolidone	T	—	247.00	—	27.00
7. Leperamide	Kg.	—	385.00	—	423.0
IX. Anti Diabetics					
1. Chlorpropamide	T	50.09	42.00	109.50	44.00
2. Tolbutemide	T	132.88	25.00	36.76	25.00
3. Glybenclamide	T	1.43	2.00	2.80	2.00
4. Insulin	MU	2846.00	3850.00	2633.00	4235.00
X. CNS Stimulants					
1. Caffeine	T	26.47	142.00	47.29	149.00
2. Nikethamide	T	0.04	3.00	0.05	3.00
XI. Diuretics					
1. Frusemide	T	10.31	8.00	3.38	9.00
2. Acetazolamide	T	1.79	3.00	-	3.00

Table 2 (Contd.)

Name of the Drug	A/c Unit	PRODUCTION			
		1988-89	1989-90		1990-91
		Actuals	Targets	Actuals	Targets
1	2	3	4	5	6
3. Hydrochlorothiazide	T	22.16	3.00	25.15	4.00
4. Spiron Elactone	T	0.48	1.57	0.54	1.65
5. Amiloride	Kg	—	157.00	—	165.00
6. Triamterene	Kg	—	275.00	—	302.00
XII. Anti Asthamatics					
1. Ephedrine	T	35.50	52.00	33.27	55.00
2. Salbutamol	Kg.	2736.00	3150.00	4635.00	3307.00
3. Terbutaline	Kg	335.00	472.00	387.00	496.00
4. Theophylline	T	135.99	262.00	140.77	276.00
5. Aminophylline	T	2.89		1.32	
XIII. Cardiovascular Drugs					
1. Propranolol	T	3.15	13.00	3.64	13.00
2. Xanthinol Nicotinate	T	15.84	16.00	14.01	17.00
3. Digoxin	Kg	6.97	37.00	15.30	39.00
4. Methyl Dopa	T	60.48	52.00	45.18	55.00
5. Dihydralazine	T	15.20	N.A.	17.09	N.A.

Table 2 (*Contd.*)

Name of the Drug	A/c Unit	PRODUCTION			
		1988-89	1989-90		1990-91
		Actuals	Targets	Actuals	Targets
1	2	3	4	5	6
6. Glyceryl Trinitrate	T	—	N.A.	—	N.A.
7. Isosorbide Dinitrate	Kg	—	7350.00	—	7717.00
8. Isoprenaline	Kg	—	210.00	—	220.00
9. Quinidine	T	7.91	N.A.	9.74	N.A
10. Reserpine	T	—	N.A.	—	N.A
11. Verapamil	T	—	6.00	—	7.00
12. Dipyridamole	T	—	13.00	—	15.00
XIV. Anaesthetics					
1. Lignocaine/Xylocaine	T	7.45	22.00	9.02	24.0
2. Procaine	T	54.35	66.00	40.39	73.00
XV. Anti Histamins					
1. Pheneramine Maleate	T	24.48	26.00	26.81	28.00
2. Chlorpheneramine Maleate	T	—	5.00	—	6.00
3. Diphenhydramine	T	7.90	19.00	6.28	20.00
4. Mebhydroline	T	19.15	N.A.	16.09	N.A

Table 2 (*Contd.*)

Name of the Drug	A/c Unit	PRODUCTION 1988-89 Actuals	1989-90 Targets	1989-90 Actuals	1990-91 Targets
1	2	3	4	5	6
XVI. Anti Helmentics					
1. Piperazine & Salts	T	11.10	50.00	9.90	50.00
2. Mebandazole	T	18.11	52.00	9.41	60.00
3. Bephenium Hydroxy Naphthoate	T	—	8.00	—	8.00
4. Tetramisole	T	12.74]	22.00	15.57]	24.00
5. Levamisole	T	—	—	—	—
6. Pyrantel Palmoate	T	31.33	17.00	39.49	18.00
XVII. Tranquilizers & Sedatives					
1. Phenobarbitone/Sod.	T	5.12	20.00	2.58	20.00
2. Diazepam	T	5.22	21.00	3.90	23.00
3. Trifluperazine	T	1.13	2.50	0.24	2.50
4. Imnipramine	T	2.07	5.00	0.97	6.00
5. Lorazepan	Kg	—	214.00	—	229.00
6. Nitrazepan	Kg	90.00	428.00	11.00	458.00
7. Prochlorperazine	T	0.28	1.57	—	1.65

Table 2 (Contd.)

Name of the Drug	A/c Unit	PRODUCTION			
		1988-89	1989-90		1990-91
		Actuals	*Targets*	*Actuals*	*Targets*
1	2	3	4	5	6
XVIII. Anti Filarials					
1. Diethyl Carbamazine (D.E.C. Citrate)	T	17.17	45.00	12.83	45.00
XIX. Anti Leprotics					
1. Dapsone	T	23.54	52.00	3.49	55.00
2. Clofazamine	T	1.45	2.62	0.74	2.76
XX. Immunological Agents					
1. Triple Vaccine	KL	11.55	33.3	24.95	34.2
2. Tetanus Anti Toxin	MU	7700.00	13000.00	9659.00	13000.00
3. Diptheria Anti Toxin	MU	219.00	800.00	150.00	800.00
4. Heptatis B Vaccine	MU	—	N.A.	—	N.A
XXI. Other Anti Bacterial					
1. Trimethoprim	T	99.57	110.00	133.73	121.00
2. Nalidixic Acid	T	20.40	38.00	22.53	42.00
3. Nitrofurantoin	T	3.25	N.A.	1.36	N.A

Table 2 (Contd.)

Name of the Drug		A/c Unit	PRODUCTION			
			1988-89	1989-90		1990-91
			Actuals	Targets	Actuals	Targets
1		2	3	4	5	6
XXII.	**Anti Convulsant**					
1.	Carbamazine	T	0.24	N.A.	—	N.A
2.	Phenytoin	T	—	N.A.	—	N.A
3.	Valproic Acid	T	—	N.A.	—	N.A
XXIII.	**Gastro Intestinals**					
1.	Ranitidine	T	24.95	N.A.	30.26	N.A
2.	Aluminium Hydroxide	T	1378.80	N.A.	1142.33	N.A
XXIV.	**Other Drugs**					
1.	Hydralazine	Kg	224	N.A	159.00	N.A
2.	Heparin	MU	7439.00	15750.00	11955.00	16537.00
3.	Chlorpromazine	T	2.66	10.00	3.22	11.00
4.	Atropine	T	1.72	N.A.	—	N.A
5.	Iron Doxtran	KL	29.16	N.A.	25.45	N.A
6.	Menthol	T	17.62	N.A.	20.66	N.A
7.	Silver Nitrate	T	—	N.A.	—	N.A
8.	Warfarin	T	—	N.A.	—	N.A
9.	Oxytocin	MU	—	3150.00	—	3307.00
10.	Metoclopramide	T	1.36	2.10	1.98	2.20
11.	Cetrimide	.T	83.03	N.A.	52.57	N.A
12.	Parachlorometaxylenol	T	92.36	N.A.	100.69	N.A

N.A. : Not Available
— : Nill

Table 3 : Capacity and Production of Major Chemical Industries

QTY '000 Tonnes

Industry/Item	1989-90		1990-91	
	Inst. Cap.	Prodn.	Inst. Cap.	Prodn. (Estd)
Inorganic Chemicals				
1. Calcium Carbide	215.4	92.1	215.4	92.5
2. Potassium Chlorate	29.2	10.0	29.2	12.0
3. Soda Ash	1460.0	1377.0	1460.0	1400.0
4. Caustic Soda	1127.0	925.0	1127.0	960.0
Organic Chemicals				
5. Acetone	59.6	40.0	59.6	40.0
6. Phenol	65.6	47.5	65.6	50.0
7. Acetic Acid	105.0	80.0	130.0	80.0
8. Acetic Anhydride	36.1	23.3	36.1	25.0
9. Methanol	164.0	122.0	244.0	150.0
Pesticides (Tech)				
10. BHC	45.2	28.4	45.2	30.0
11. DDT	9.1	7.50	9.1	6.5
12. Malathion	12.3	3.4	12.3	3.4

Table 4 : Major Petrochemicals Target and Achievements

Product	1989-90		1990-91				1991-92	
	Actuals		Target		Anticipated		Target	
	C	P	C	P	C	P	C	P
1. LDPE	115.36	85.33	115.36	93	115.36	105	192.00	145
2. HDPE	50.00	34.39	50.00	37	50.00	33	205.00	110
3. PP	55.00	44.63	55.00	50	55.00	47	115.00	80
4. PVC	158.50	136.90	158.50	150	158.50	140	258.00	170
5. PS	28.00	23.53	28.00	25	28.00	23	28.00	25
6. SBR	36.75	37.45	36.75	40	36.75	40	36.75	40
7. PBR	20.00	15.12	20.00	16	20.00	14	20.00	15
8. PSF	210.06	127.41	210.06	140	210.06	142	268.00	150
9. PFY	85.43+a	155.83	85.43+a	170	85.43+a	180	85.43+a	200
10. NFY	24.84+b	38.75	24.84+b	42	24.84+b	40	24.84+b	45
11. NIY/TC	26.96+c	34.98	26.96+c	40	26.96+c	38	26.96+c	45
12. AF	48.00	31.58	63.00	35	63.00	43	63.00	50
13. DMT/PTA	235.00	248.51	235.00	270	235.00	290	335.00	300
14. ACN	30.00	25.20	30.00	27	30.00	26	30.00	27
15. LAB	153.50	125.57	153.50	140	153.50	180	153.50	180
16. Caprolactam	20.00	20.64	70.00	22	70.00	27	70.00	50

C = Capacity
P = Production
a+b+c+ = 65.25 thousand MT Capacity of six units for manufacture of NIY/TC/NFY and PFY under broad banding
* Based on actual data available upto December 1990
a: denotes installed capacity of 6 units to manufacture PFY, NFY and NIY/TC under broad banding.

acter, moral and public image. During the post independence era, the poverty has increased, inequality has increased, deprivation of basic needs was there, then why such cry. Those who now oppose economic liberalisation or support economic liberalisation, had enjoyed the official appointments, status, privileges and authority to make decisions, they were implicitly or explicitly party to mismanagement of economy and now they have suddenly become wise to find fault with IMF's prescription. Similarly, Panditji's policies of his time ought to be changed as he was more a product of his time. Every economic subject is influenced greatly by contemporary events. There cannot be great events in the world's economic and political history like unification of West and East Germany, jointly carried out destruction war on Iraq, disintegration of USSR, death of communism in Eastern Europe, formation of EC market. India's low per capita income, dependence on import of technology, luxurious or ornamental science and pursuit of goals diverted from its own poor people during past four decades cannot be made herself a target of joint economic cold war. As we have witnessed the pernicious effects of widely called as "Cold War" which was initiated by USA and Western European countries against Eastern Europe. Where economic interests are involved developed countries would certainly join or form the blocks under various names like EEC, EC, Eurocurrency, Eurodollar, big-7, etc. and they would adapt common strategy to demolish India's every move.

Gone are the days of military aggression or expansion of imperialism through military or use of force by capturing geographic territory to colonise the countries. Now economic blockade, trade, export of technology, technical knowhow, movement of resources, flow of foreign funds or investment, foreign collaboration etc. are the means of governing the poor countries' fate. Scientists, economists, politicians, academicians, intellectuals, etc. in developing countries continue to depend on developing countries for not only loans, funds, resources, technologies, tangible and intangible intellectual properties, capital goods, etc. but also depend heavily on theories, basic concepts, ideas, ideals, inspirations for literature, strategies to tackle the menace or crisis that emerges from one time to another and still, they claim ironically that they have determination of indigenisation assimilation, absorption, invent new and original, etc. It is nothing but hypocracy of highest order or cheating the country, countrymen and poor. Arthur Dunkel in the capacity of Director General of the "General Agreement of Tariffs and Trade (GATT)" has to safeguard the real interest of those countries where science is accelerating at much faster rate and the technologists are exported all over the world, and not of those countries like India which initiates or infringes implicitly the scientific endeavours of other countries. He proposed a draft on December 20, 1991 for GATT's Uruguay Round and asked 108 sovereign countries to respond within three weeks. There are apprehensions in India that Dunkel's draft has completely subordinated the interests of developing countries in favour of those powerful developed countries. But those who oppose any move from developed world, if offered a higher position with lucrative perks, would be the first to join there and justify the developed countries, IMF's or Dunkel's draft and plead India to accept it. There is change in philosophy of GATT from earlier philosophy of "free trade" to "market opening" which *ipso facto* would be available only to developed countries and it is alleged that the interest of all developing countries have been bartered away in the proposed agreement.

9.09 India's Apprehension

The fear of scientists in India is that agreeing to Dunkel's draft provisions, particularly Trade-Related Intellectual Property Rights (TRIPS) and Trade-Related Investment Measure, services and agriculture would lead to the winding up of several national research projects. More than 40 per cent of CSIR's own projects in the area of chemicals would have to be closed down. Similarly, its implication for agricultural sector is obvious, particularly advent of multinationals in diverse areas like oil seeds, pulses, seeds and so on in respect of control of scale of production which has been traditionally handled by Indian farmers with great efficacy.

The closure of CSIR's own 40 per cent of projects in the area of chemical means that those projects were either infringed or initiation which exist or patented somewhere else. Instead of imparting technology or scientific know how these projects have been taken up in India. The justification of these processes or projects is questionable. Usually, the justification in India goes like this : importing technology, technical know how or capital goods is very costly but we can find solution given us an opportunity. But such opportunity to experiment itself is much more costly than importing technology or technical know how and equipments, instruments, other accessories, etc. and despite the expenditure incurred, there is no guarantee that this innovative idea would give return to investment at the same rate had it been imported as technology or technical know how. The fact admitted is that about 40 per cent of CSIR's own projects have to be closed down tantamounts to say that it is working on the projects which are elsewhere patented or exist; that is reinventing the technology, process or product which is already existing, working and proven somewhere. Is not this an infringement of idea, process or patent? Is this not a wasteful expenditure on the items which can easily, honourably or diplomatically imported, used and divert funds for poorest of poor. This also by implication tantamounts to prove that Indian scientists are not only initiating but taking credit in their endeavours which is lagging behind several years because the patents abroad are result of several years' scientific struggle. Under Dunkel's proposal the term of patent would be extended for 20 years for product and next 20 years for process. That is patent for both product and process would be granted on reciprocity basis. The fear that India has to depend on developed countries for all new products, is meaningless because even today, every idea, product, process of giant industrial activities are imported and Indian science is imitating them once such idea, product, process or technology is exposed to them. If for last 40 years, they cannot give to this nation something original, new and novel, when are they going to provide it. Despite huge amount and funds spent on education, training, institutional build up of science and technology if they cannot give nation a confidence of facing international challenge or competitiveness in scientific activities how can these same people say small scale industries manufacturing items of giant private industries within nation to face competitiveness. Competitiveness in science is to be concomitant with trade, manufacturing, services, etc., why scientists in India are afraid of competition with developed countries' scientists is that they have been enjoying full honours, luxurious living, travelling in planes, attending conferences at the expense of poor tribals eating snails, selling babies, suffering from malnutrition, diseases like leprosy, tuberculosis, etc.

10

Bio-Technology—Challenge to Patent System

10.01 Introduction

Bio-technology has emerged as new area of scientific and technological research. At the time of evolving patent system there was no branch of biotechnology and commercialisation of its products were also not envisaged. But the last decade of twentieth century has seen the debate of inclusion of biotechnological products, into patent system as the social and economic gains are obvious.

In India, Department of Biotechnology (DBT) has successfully introduced Oil Palm in the States of Kerala, Karnataka, Andhra Pradesh, Tamil Nadu and Maharashtra which ensures the yield of four to five tons per hectare of oil as compared with 0.8 tons per hectare of groundnut, 0.7 tons per hectare of sunflower, 0.6 tons per hectare of soyabean. The yield of oil palm in terms of value in 1992 it was estimated as Rs 20,000 to 80,000 per year. Such return would be possible for 25 years through cultivation of oil palm.

Obviously this area of scientific and technological research is worth pursuing. Let us go into some of its aspects :

10.02 Definitions of Biotechnology

Of the numerous definitions following are the few (found in Appendix I of Alan T. Bulletan, which are rearranged here) :

1. Biotechnology is concerned with the use of biological activities in the context of technical processes and industrial production. It involves the application of microbiology and biochemistry in conjunction with technical chemistry and process engineering.

2. Application of biological organism, system or processes to manufacturing and service industries. (Report of Joint working party, UK. 1980).
3. The utilisation of a biological process, be it microbial, plant or animal cells, or their constituents, to provide goods and services. (Biotechnology: A development Plan for Canada 1981).
4. The Science of applied biological process...... The Science of the production process based on the action of microorganism and their active components, and of production processes involving the use of cells and tissues from higher organism (narrower definition). Medical technology, agriculture and traditional crop breeding are not generally regarded as biotechnology. (Biotechnology: A Dutch Perspective, 1981).
5. The application of biological organisms, systems, or processes to manufacturing or services industries. Biotechnology in Canada: Promises and Concerns, 1980.
6. The devising optimising and scaling up of biochemical and cellular processes for the industrial production of useful compounds and related applications. This definition envisages biotechnology as embracing all aspects of processes of which the Central and most characteristic feature is the involvement of biological catalysts. Plant agronomy falls outside this definition, but plants provide the raw material for most biotechnological processes, so research in plant breeding and productivity is of direct importance. Biotechnology for Australia, 1981.
7. The collection of industrial processes that involve the use of biological systems (in glossary). The use of living organisms of their components in industrial processes: OTA Report — Impact of Applied Genetics, 1981.
8. Sub-Programme Bio-society—research activities:

   The industrial processing of materials by micro organisms and other biological agents to provide desirable goods and ser-vices.—Forecasting and Assessment for Science and Technology.
9. The integrated use of biochemistry, microbiology and engineering sciences in order to achieve technological (industrial) application of the capabilities of micro organisms, cultured

tissue cells, and parts thereof. European Federation of Bio-technology, 1981.

10. The application of biochemistry, biology, microbiology and chemical engineering to industrial processes and products (including here the products in health care, energy and agriculture) and on environment. International Union of Pure and Applied Chemistry (IUPAC, 1981).
11. The application of scientific and engineering principles to the processing of materials by biological agents to provide goods and services. Biotechnology—International Trends and Perspectives - 1982.
12. Biotechnology is said to be for genetic manipulation. Accordingly a biotechnology is one which uses micro-organism, their functional ability, extracts or products as the basis for industrial mass production. This definition includes generic manipulation, but does not include improvement of agricultural crops by genetic manipulation, nor isolation and simulation of photosynthesis system in vitro.

Biotechnologies thus defined covered refers to the fermentation industries, brewing, distilling, antibiotics and production of fine chemicals; as well as involving extraction and use of enzymes and newer ones still in the early stages of development involving improvement of relevant organisms by generic manipulation.

10.03 Techniques and Application of Biotechnology

Techniques which are stimulating the development of biotechnology are

Recombinant DNA manipulation

Tissue culture

Protoplast fusion

Monoclonal antibody preparation

Protein structural modification (protein engineering)

Immobilized enzymes and cell catalysis

Sensing with the aid of biological molecules

Computer linkages of reactors and processes

New biocatalytic reactor design

1. *Application of Biotechnology to the Chemical Industry :*
   - i) Raw materials e.g. oil seeds, cellulose, lignins, fermentation, ethanol.
   - ii) Biocatalysis : e.g. enzymes working in organic solvents.
   - iii) Replacement for chemicals, e.g. polyhydroxybutyrate, lactide polymers.

   The list of chemicals and allied products :
   - i) Pharmaceuticals
   - ii) Organics.
   - iii) Miscellaneous special industrial and agricultural.
   - iv) Synthesis resins and plastics materials.
   - v) Inorganics.
   - vi) Perfumicis, cosmetics, toilet preparations.
   - vii) Paints, varnish, fillings.
   - viii) Soaps, synthetic detergents.
   - ix) Fertilizers.
   - x) Dyestuffs, pigments.
   - xi) Photographic materials & chemicals
   - xii) Formulated pesticides.
   - xiii) Formulated adhesives.
   - xiv) Miscellaneous household and office chemicals.
   - xv) Synthetic rubbers.
   - xvi) Essential oils, flavourings.
   - xvii) Printing inks.
   - xviii) Treatment of oils and fats.
   - xix) Adhesive film, cloth and foil.

2. *Food Industry :* Application of biotechnology to the food industry.
   - i) Provision of food ingredients, e.g. microbial polysauharides, sweaters, colouvants, single cell protein.
   - ii) Development of new form of biocatalysts, e.g. immobilized enzymes for ghiose isomerization.
   - iii) Improved physical processing and preservations, e.g. ultrafiltration, use of flexible restorable pouches.

   Food, drinks and tobacco products:

1. Milk and milk products.
2. Milk and cream.
3. Miscellaneous products.
4. Cheese.

5. Butter.
6. Miscellaneous food and beverages.
7. Tea, coffee and substitudes.
8. Malt extracts, infant and dietectic food etc.
9. Breakfast cereals.
10. Cornflour, cake mixture, desserts etc.
11. Soups, sanees.
12. Other food and beverages.
13. Meat processing, including bacon curing.
14. Bread and flour confectionary.
15. Compound animal feeds.
16. Cocoa, chocolate, sugar confectionary.
17. Brewing and malting.
18. Tobacco products.
19. Spirits.
20. Grain milling.
21. Soft drinks.
22. Sugar and by-products.
23. Fruit and veg processing, excluding juices.
24. Poultry slaughtering and processing.
25. Biscuit, crisp bread.
26. Processing, organic oils, and fats.
27. Pet foods and animal feeds not specified elsewhere.
28. Fish processing.
29. Animal by-products including crude fats.
30. Margarine, cooking fats.
31. Starch.
32. Ice Cream.
33. Wine, cider and perry.

3. *Agriculture :*

Application of biotechnology to agriculture :

1. Desirable agricultural traits in plants e.g. better disease resistance, salt tolerance.

2. Plant with increased levels or modification of storage compounds, e.g. high lysine soya, high polyunsaturated oils.
3. Pest control, e.g. microbial insecticides, fungicides.
4. Plant growth regulators, e.g. gibberllins.
5. Hydroponics.
6. Desirable traits in animals e.g. better disease resistance, better feed conversion.
7. Animal feed and growth promotion, e.g. single cell protein, amino acids.
8. Vaccines, e.g. foot and mouth, pig scours.

4. *Waste Treatment :*

Application of biotechnology to waste treatment are :

1. Improvement of existing systems by the application of more basic bioscience and more biochemical process engineering, e.g. knowledge of mixed culture, anaerobic fermentation, microbial flock characteristics.
2. New sensor and automation, e.g. for heavy metals, toxic trace organics.
3. Use of mutant strains and genetically engineered organisms. e.g. re-inoculation/correction of poorly performing plant, treatment of particular toxic wastes.
4. New catalysts and novel reactor designs, e.g. cell immobilized on sand, fluidized bed reactors.
5. Recovery of useful products from wastes, e.g. proteins, methane, metals.

5. *Energy supply or saving :*

Possible contributions of biotechnology to energy supply or saving:

1. Energy from biomass, e.g. wood, methane from anaerobic digestion, ethanol.
2. Surfactauts for enhanced oil recovery.
3. Energy saving, e.g. enzyme catalysis, separation by ultrafiltration, computer optimization of processes.

Service Sector :

Except for biomass the practical application of biotechnology is yet to gain wide acceptance. But potential for use of biotechnology in other areas is very high. The growth prospects of service sector is very high. The mention of services utilizing biotechnology is not uncommon at least to following areas:

1. Consultancy services, e.g. waste treatment process plant design and contract supervision.
2. Technical services, e.g. diagnostic testing, toxicity testing, prevention of biodeterioration, provision of microbial inocula.
3. Marketing of products, e.g. wholesaling and retailing.

Health Care :

Application of biotechnology to health care :

1. Pharmaceuticals : Small molecule products, e.g. antibiotics, macro molecules e.g. interferon, vaccines, drug directing agents, e.g. monoclonal antibodies, magnetic microspheres, purification reagents, e.g. immobilized monoclonal antibodies, new biocatalyst forms, e.g. immobilized enzymes and cells, diagnostic reagents, e.g. enzymes, monoclonal antibodies.
2. Biomedical engineering products : biomaterials, e.g. artificial skin, biomedical equipment, e.g. artificial kidney machines.

There are numerous applications of biotechnology in this area. Glaxo company of UK has been applying biotechnology to medicines, particularly using fermentation methods, ever since it introduced large scale manufacturing of penicillin to the UK in 1946. In 1957, Beecham research laboratories first isolated the most basic form of penicillin from fermentation broths. From this basic form was developed a wide range of so-called semi-synthetic penicillins of great value in medicine. The Welcome foundation has been working since 1974 on manufacturing interferon by a process based on human cells in culture. Welcome has established a plant which is producing material very much purer than other clinically used interferons. This is believed to be the first industrial scale plant of its type in the world. (Ref.: Report on Biotechnology, presented to Parliament by the Secretary of State for Industry by command of her Majesty March 1981, pp.3). There are various such success stories of biotechnologies. Recombinant DNA techniques is being used by ICI to modify the microorganism which it produces for animal feed so that the production process is more efficient.

The biotechnology process applications used on ease or scale of operation demanded and product price are shown below:

Table A : Example of Graded Objectives for Biotechnology

Technique	*Short term goal*	*Longer term goal*
1. Monoclonal antibody preparation	Clinical analysis	Product purification
2. Enzyme immobilization	Analysis and higher value products	Large tonnage industrial catalysis
3. Plant tissue culture	Plant propagation	Product synthesis
4. Polysaccharide fermentation	Food additives	Enhanced oil recovery

(Ref. : Peter Dunnil and Martin Rudd: *Biotechnology & British Industry: A report to the Biotechnology*, Directorate of Science and Engineering Research Council, UK, pp.83).

10.04 Genetics Application

Some examples of application of Genetic Manipulation in biotechnology:

A. *Humane Health*

1. Monoclonal antibodies (for purification techniques, assays, tissue typing, in vivo tumour location, clinical diagnosis, therapy including targetting of chemotherapeutic agents).
2. Inter-feron (possible use for cancer treatment, antiviral therapy, inflammatory diseases).
3. Vaccines (against e.g. hepatitis B, influenza, malaria, encephalitis, cholera, herpes, adenovirus).
4. Hormones (e.g. growth hormones, insulin, prolactin, relaxin, gastrin, erythropoietin, thromobopoietin, chrionic, gonadotropin, menopausal gonadotropin, steroids).
5. Enzymes (e.g. urokinase, heparinase, alcohol dehydrogenase).
6. Other proteins (e.g. specific antigens, blood factor, albumin, antithrombin, fibronectin).

7. Improved and new antibiotics, drugs, vitamins.
8. Gene therapy for generic diseases.

B. *Food, Agriculture and Horticulture*

1. Enzymes (e.g. amylases, rennin, B-galactosidase, invertase, glucose, isomerase, pectinases).
2. Food additives (e.g. sweeteners, aromas, flavours, colouring matter, thickeners and stabilizers, vitamins, amino acids, anti-oxidants, preservatives, surfactants.)
3. Additions for animal feed (e.g. new antibiotics).
4. Improved and new plant varieties (including enhanced yields crops specifically designed for particular land use, genes for proteins such as casein introduced into carbohydrate pre-dominant crops).
5. Pesticides and herbicides with increased specificity (e.g. use of bacillus thuringensis products, verticillium, baculoviruses, parastic nematodes, nematocides, protozoan pathogens, piper-dine derivatives).
6. Vaccines (against e.g. diarrhoeal colibacillosis, foot and mouth).
7. Plant growth hormones (e.g. cytokinnins).
8. Fertilizers, microbial nitrogen fixation and manipulation of symbionts.
9. Diagnostic reagents for plant and animal diseases.

C. *Energy, raw materials, chemicals and environmental management*

1. Biomass from chemical, wastes, residues and fuel crops (including production of ethanol, methanol, methane and SCP.)
2. Enhanced oil recovery (e.g. Xanthangum, surfactants).
3. Improved algal cultures for use in photobioreactors (production of e.g. carbohydrate, protein, lipids, hydrocarbons).
4. Hydrogen and carbon dioxide production.
5. Chemicals and solvents (acetic acids, adipic acid, butanol, iso-propanol, acetone, furtural, glycerol, waxes, polymers, alk-ene, oxides, and glycols, lubricants).
6. Metal extraction e.g. copper, uranium, nickel, zinc, lead from low grade minerals and recovery of valuable metals (e.g. mercury, cobalt).

7. Decomposition and detoxification of chemicals (e.g. oil spills, palapon, pentachlorophenol).
8. Improved microbial systems for environmental control of air, water and soil.

10.05 Birth of Oncogene

Biotechnology is also known as genetic manipulation. Gene is basic unit of heredity, a gene encodes a specific trait that can be passed on from one generation to the next. In molecular terms, a gene is a segment of nucleic acid, usually deosyribonucleic acid, that specifies the structure of a single protein chain. Both gene cloning and gene therapy have made significant progress in genetic engineering. While application of recombinant DNA methods to confer new traits on organisms by introducing new genes into their cells, is known as genetic engineering: gene therapy is concerned with treatment of human genetic disease by introducing a new gene into the patient to take over the function of the defective gene that is responsible for genetic disease or causing the disease. Genetic disease is caused by a defective gene and can be transmitted from one generation to the next. Gene cloning is accomplished through use of recombinant DNA technology to isolate and produce large quantities of an individual gene. The whole genetic engineering and biotechnology is based on manipulation of Deoxyribonucleic acid (DNA) which is one of the two types of nucleic acid and the material of which genes are composed. A strand of DNA is formed by linking together many individual building blocks called nucleotides in a large molecule. The linear sequence of the nucleotides specifies the linear sequence of amino acids in the protein of a product gene. A Recombinant DNA molecule is formed by joining DNA segments from two or more sources. Once gene had been the topic of very intensive research, which refers to a gene that can cause cells to undergo cancerous transformation. Oncogene are aberrant forms of normal cellular genes that are needed for growth and differentiation. Based on bioengineering techniques various research projects were initiated since 1981. According to literature available "in 1981 a rabbit globin gene became the first bioengineered gene to be inserted into animal embryo—in this case a mouse—and reproduce in all the cells of the mature animal. Since then a number of other genes, including oncogenes and genes coding for metallothionein, elastase and immunoglobulin, have been inserted, expressed and passed on to offspring in laboratory animals. A land mark experiment was the introduction into mice of a gene for growth hormone fused to the regulating DNA from metallothionein gene that caused growth hormone to be expressed whenever the mice were exposed to certain heavy metal. The mice transformed by the growth hormone gene grew to more than twice the size of their normal siblings" (*Ref.* Steven Olson: Biotechnology—An industry comes of Age: National Academy Press; Washington, D.C. 1984, pp.40). Its usage is expected to be in generically engineering farm animals as it would be more productive and disease resistant. Similarly prospects of application of growth hormone technique is very bright. Injected growth hormones in animals shows that animals producing elevated levels of their own growth hormone might grow faster, larger, leaner and with less consumption of feed. This obviously indicates swine farms and milk production of dairy cows may increase.

10.06 Onco Mouse and Patent System

Genetically engineered both plants and animals have generated worldwide debate, primarily in Europe and secondarily in Third world. Straightward question is asked whether "life patents" be granted or not, keeping in view contemporary ethics of moral, legal, social and scientific research. The pioneering work of Philip Leader of Harvard Medical School who introduced the onco-mouse has triggered a host of questions. Indian Patent Act 1970 in its section 3 states that following are not inventions within the meaning of this Act :

a) an invention which is frivolous or which claims obvious contrary to well established natural laws.

b) an invention the primary or intended use of which would be contrary to law or morality or injurious to public health.

c) the mere discovery of a scientific principle or the formulation of an abstract theory.

d) a method of agriculture or horticulture.

e) any process for the medicinal, surgical, curative, prophylactic or other treatment of human beings or any process for a similar treatment of animals or plants to render them free of disease or to increase their economic value or that of their products. These sections of Indian Patent Act 1970 do not support the claims of biotechnology as patentable inventions. Firstly, those are contrary to morality to patent biologically produced plants and animals no matter those are for onco gene mouse or cows for milk productions or plants for medicinal purpose. Even humans could be produced with test tube experiments to have predetermined traints and characteristics, should then such biologically produced human be patented.

Accordingly the Week, 19th October, 1991 European Patent Office (EPO) in Munich has decided in favour of cancer research, and the onco-mouse could be patented. But at the same time it ruled against a French creature—a mouse given various genes for hair and wool making if a model system for research into hair growth. This creature's raison d'etre was judged to be too trivial to be morally justifiable (New Scientist 4 January, 1992). In fact biotechnology is new area of scientific research and its potential for commercial technologies is too bright provided sufficient safeguards are available for patents, trade secrets, and international technology transfer.

10.07 Application of RDNA Techniques

Application of recombinant DNA has wide implication. The impact of genetic engineering on fermentation industry is likely to be greater than any other including animals or plants. The "bioindustry" is likely to emerge stronger and stronger as more research findings take place all over the world. To present concise view of the application of recombinant DNA are the following :

1. Pharmaceuticals: e.g. polypeptide drugs and vaccines, Monocolonal antibodies for diagnosis and therapy, new and cheaper antibiotics.
2. Food: e.g. modified yeasts for alcoholic beverages, elevation of levels of microbial enzymes.
3. Waste: e.g. genetically modified inocula, transfer of degradative enzymes to a single organism.
4. Agriculture: e.g. plant and animal breeding, biological pesticides, incorporation of nitrogen fixing ability.
5. Chemicals: e.g. new enzymes catalysts and elevated levels of existing ones are leading with genetically modified inocula.

6. Energy: e.g. thermophillic organisms for ethanol production, transfer of key genes to faster growing and more easily grown organisms, tailor-made organisms for enhanced oil recovery.

The world market for different biotechnological products is very high. The countries with strong base for biotechnological research, which have capability to convert inventions into commercial technologies and which have capital to invest on such projects would certainly try to safeguard her interest. The countries like India have been rather obstacle for universal growth of science and technologies as neither she has capability (scientific, managerial, technological, innovative etc.) nor she allows others to cater to her needs. The possible biotechnology products and services are :

1. Effective vaccines for common cold.
2. A competitive safer tobacco substitute.
3. A "Single Cell" collagen for steak.
4. Cheap premier wines.
5. Reliable self-diagnosis kits for common medical conditions.
6. Novel flowering plants.
7. Analytical models which will more reliably assess human response to new drugs and foods.
8. Site-specific 'targeted' drugs.

Patent system has existed since immemorial time in one or other form of granting honours, monopoly and exclusive rights. Its present form could be traced back to 1476 and 1910, when biotechnology did not exist. In 1989 EPO rejected a European patent for Philip Leader's "onco-mouse" on the ground that it was an animal "variety". This mouse which has cancer causing gene or onco-gene inserted into it, develops tumours within a few months of birth. This makes the creature a boon to medical researchers, and it has already been patented in the US (New Scientist 4 January, 1991. pp.9).

Granting the patents for humans and animals is a matter of concern. Similarly plant patents that are expected to have the most immediate impact. Plant patents have already been sanctioned by EPO "but have only been used extensively for three years in Europe and the US". (New Scientist, 4 January, 1992). While stating the implication of plant patent Debora Mackenzie (*Ref.*

Europe Debates the Ownership of Life; New Scientist, 4 January, 1992 pp.9), says, ordinary patents applying to a product are "exhausted" once it has been sold. The manufacturer will have negotiated a license to use the patent and will have agreed to pay royalties for the privilege. The product can then be resold without attracting further royalty payments. But under the proposed directive, living things would continue to be covered by patents after their sale. Their offspring would also be patented. Britain's Bioindustry Association points out that these were not so, competitors could make patented microorganisms patent free by simply leaving them in culture dish for a generation". About farmers problems using patented seeds, one can easily understand that "Farmers having to pay royalties on seed they save from patented crops. At present, no such duties must be paid. Storing seed saves farmers $80 million a year in Britain, and more in other community countries. American farmers save $500 million per year by setting aside seed from wheat, soyabean and cotton alone". Obviously such savings would hurt small farmers.

10.08 Biotechnology for Maize Crop

In Indonesia a project was initiated using biotechnology for maize crop. Its results were interesting for average farm size of 0.5 ha. farm sample for the four consecutive years from 1984-85 to 1987-88. (*Ref.* Biotechnology and Developing Country Agriculture: Maize in Indonesia, by Hidjat Nataamadjaetal; OECD Development Centre, Technical Paper No.34; OCDE/GD (91) 1990; pp. 21-22).

The release of 24 improved open pollinated variety has resulted decrease of maturity time, increase in average yield per hectare. The yield potential has increased by 96 per cent in between 1964-80. Similarly thought development of a gene pool, combining landraces and introduced materials, between 1980-85, yield potential further increased by 24 per cent. About other area of biotechnology, it has been reported that between 1964-85, animal increase in yield potential with open pollinated varieties was 2.9 per cent. If maturity is considered, this changes to 3.1 per cent (ibid pp. 39). An experimental level yield of new open pollinated varieties ranges from around four tons/ha. to more than five, depending on maturity, compared with six for hybrids. Yields are generally less at field level, depending on the land, season, facilities and management. In general 70-100 per cent of yield potential at experimental level could be realised by farmers for open pollinated varieties, but only 60-80 per cent for hybrids (ibid pp. 43). Indonesian experience shows that "Technology must be related to income generation, because technological know-how is an investment, an asset we have to buy, in terms of hard cash or shadow prices. We must be selective and cost and benefit conscious. We already have a lot of idle technological resources, expensive assets we have bought without being able to use profitably or transfer to the ultimate users. One of the most precious and expensive assets is trained research professionals". The report says "at this stage, domestic generation of technology means the ability of developing countries to explore and adapt the full potential of technology from abroad. International transfer and domestic generation of technology is not an alternative, but complementary. Japan is a unique example of success in importing, adopting, mastering and generating technology. (*Ref. ibid*. pp. 56).

This shows the importance of biotechnology in agriculture. As far as animals are concerned the story is different. There are reasons to believe that "to the non-scientist, the term genetic engineering probably conjures up visions of a modern Dr Frankenstein creating monstrous new creatures in his laboratory. Ironically, the genetic manipulation of animal genomes seem unlikely to make as much progress over the next few years as that of other organisms.... genetic manipulation involves selection of those cells whose genomes have been correctly altered from those which are either unaltered or incorrectly modified, followed by proliferation of the selected cells ('cloning'). This is the end of the story when we are dealing with unicellular organisms, such as bacteria or yeast or with animal or plant cell cultures; but for the production of generically engineered animals or plants whole organisms must then be regenerated from cloned cells... Added to this knowledge that characterists such as growth rate, milk yield, disease resistance and shape are determined by interaction between many different genes and it becomes evident that we still have a long way to go before quality of livestock can be improved by genetic engineering (*Ref*. S.A. Boffen et al: Biotechnology—The Biological Principles : Taylor & Francis, 1987; pp. 115-116).

While explanning the aims of genetic engineering it is said genetic engineering is defined as the changing of genes using in vitro processes, in contrast with conventional breeding process, in which genes are transferred by sexual or conjugative means. Since such gene transfer is a relatively random process, the breeder must select for desirable characteristics, and must rely on mutation to generate 'new genes' (*ibid*. pp. 117).

10.09 Patents for Seeds

In fact the patent for seeds is not a new term or concept. Coming back to Indonesia's drive for maize production through biotechnological experiments, OECD Technical paper No.34 indicates that there is a need for policies and attitudes towards intellectual property Rights and Patent Protection. Seeds are generally classified as breeder, foundation, stock or extension seeds. Extension seed is the seed sold to farmers. Stock seed is given to extension seed growers by certified seed firm. Breeder seed is only produced by breeders in research institutions. Production of foundation seed from breeder seed is tightly controlled. Various institutions have been set up in Indonesia and also national seed system came into being. The growth engine of scientific and industrial engine is capital investment. The country like India where capital is scarce cannot take risk in basic research. It is very costly affair. Using the Government laboratories and government recruited educated elites no science or public utility can be generated and proliferated. No Indian scientist can produce an invention, discovery or technology which will pass every test of international standard. There may be exception to such statement but the way in past four decades, the science in India has grown indicates that some science educated people are bent upon earning crores of rupees under the name of generating indigeneous capability for scientific research knowing the fact that millions of tribals, scavengers and poor die every year in destitute conditions without getting money to buy medicines for ailing kith and kin. Patients do not get admissions in hospitals set up at a cost of crores of rupees and doctors go on strike for pay hike. No scientist ever visits the poors' locality but claims to be spokesman of poor. In conclusion, there is no reason why India should not accept Arthur Dunkel's proposals of GATT including TRIPS and TRIMS. Even in present system, the poor farmers in India are deprived of the quality seed at the subsidized price nor fertilizer or other inputs are available to poor farmers in remote villages as compared with rich farmers of Haryana, Punjab or Himachal Pradesh. It is scientific community which is more worried than poor farmers or poor consumers of product. A common man is least interested in the source of production, manner of production or ownership of technology or type of technology. Irrespective of biotechnology or conventional technology, the cancer drugs, TB drugs, vaccines, medicines agricultural products like rice, wheat, maize etc. would be consumed by the people. As far as prices are concerned, no scientist can claim that prices would be controlled by his invention. The commercialisation, distribution policies, transport cost, demand supply gap, etc. cost of inputs, economies of scale etc. determine the prices of the goods and commodities.

Indian scientists have suddenly become the spokesmen and trustees of poor due to GATT's new proposals. It is their interest which is at stake than the poor's health or their poverty. These Indian scientists who could not contribute a single patentable invention have suddenly become prudent to join the opposition to Dunkel's draft without knowing its bright side. Anything that comes from USA Government is not bad and this must be told to scientists who try their best to get published their work in US journals, imitate the research findings, infringe the US's intellectuals propriety. There is a need to reconcile the approach to Dunkel's proposal of TRIPS and TRIMS. This will reduce technological gap and dependence on Indian scientists whose pace of scientific progress would neither remove hunger, poverty, squalor nor could establish India as developed economy in the world.

REFERENCES

1. Jean L. Marx (Edt.) *A Revolution in Biotechnology*, Cambridge University Press, 1989.
2. S. Natesh, V.L. Chopra, S. Ramachandran (Edt.) *Biotechnology in Agriculture:* Oxford & IBH Publishing Co. Pvt. Ltd. 1987.
3. Hidjat Nataamadja et al: *Biotechnology and Developing Country Agriculture: Maize in Indonesia*, OECD Development Centre, Technical Paper No.34, January, 1991.
4. *Engineering Education and Practice in the United States* - Foundations of our Techno-Economic Future, National Academy Press, Washington, D.C. 1985.
5. *Science Indicators*: The 1985 report; National Science Board; United States.
6. Stevon Olson: Biotechnology - *An Industry comes of Age*; National Academy Press Washington DC 1986.

7. L.F. Phelps and P.H. Clarke (Edt.) *Biotechnology: The Biochemical Society*, 7, Warwick Court, London 1983.

8. M.D. Trevan, S. Bottey, K.H. Goulding, P. Stanbury, *Biotechnology: The Biological Principles*; Open University Press, 12, Cotteridge Close, Stony Stratford Milton Keynes, MK 11 1 by England, 1987.

9. K. Lindsey MGK Jones, *Plant Biotechnology in Agriculture*; Open University Press, Milton Keynes, England, 1989.

10. Alan T. Bull, Geoffery Holt, Malcom D. Lilly. *Biotechnology: International Trends and Perspectives*; Oxford & IBH Publishing Co., New Delhi, India, 1982.

11. *Biotechnology - A Report presented to Parliament by the Secretary of State for Industry*, March 1981, London. Her Majesty's Stationary Office.

12. Peter Dunnil and Martin Rudd: *Biotechnology and British Industry: A report to the Biotechnology Directors of the Science and Engineering Research Council*, Poloris House, North Star Avenue, Swindon SN2 IET.

13. *Nature*: Vol.353, No. 6340, 12th September, 1991.

14. *Nature*: Vol.340, No. 6230, 20th July, 1989.

15. A. Crafts-Lightly: *Information Sources in Biotechnology*: Macmillan Publishers Ltd. 1986.

16. Bernard Atkinson and Ferda Mavituna: *Biochemical Engineering and Biotechnology Handbook*; Macmillan, The Nature Press, N.Y. 1983.

17. *Biotechnology: Report of a Joint Working Party*: March 1980, London Her Majesty's Stationary Office.

18. Pauline K. Marstrand: *Science Policy Research Unit: Patterns of Changing Biotechnology*, University of Sussex, UK, 1981.

INDEX